ROYAL CITY™

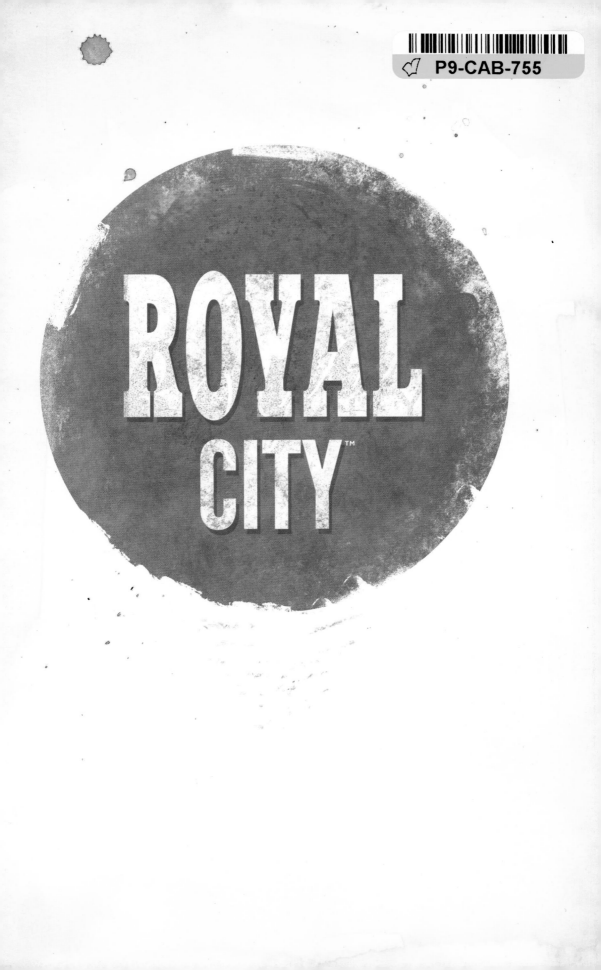

Created, Written, and Illustrated by
JEFF LEMIRE

Lettered by STEVE WANDS

Book Design by
VINCENT KUKUA

Special Thanks to
ERIN BURKE,
LARISSA GIROUX,
ROSEMARY DUNSMORE

ROYAL CITY, VOL. 1: NEXT OF KIN. First printing. September 2017. Published by Image Comics, Inc. Office of publication: 2701 NW Vaughn St., Suite 780, Portland, OR 97210. Copyright © 2017 171 Studios, Inc. All rights reserved. Contains material originally published in single magazine form as ROYAL CITY #1-5. "Royal City," its logos, and the likenesses of all characters herein are trademarks of 171 Studios, Inc., unless otherwise noted. "Image" and the Image Comics logos are registered trademarks of Image Comics, Inc. No part of this publication may be reproduced or transmitted, in any form or by any means (except for short excerpts for journalistic or review purposes), without the express written permission of 171 Studios, Inc. or Image Comics, Inc. All names, characters, events, and locales in this publication are entirely fictional. Any resemblance to actual persons (living or dead), events, or places, without satiric intent, is coincidental. Printed in the USA. For information regarding the CPSIA on this printed material call: 203-595-3636 and provide reference #RICH-762719. For international rights, contact: foreignlicensing@imagecomics.com. ISBN: 978-1-5343-0262-4.

IMAGE COMICS, INC. / Robert Kirkman–Chief Operating Officer / Erik Larsen–Chief Financial Officer / Todd McFarlane–President / Marc Silvestri–Chief Executive Officer / Jim Valentino–Vice President / Eric Stephenson–Publisher / Corey Murphy–Director of Sales / Jeff Boison–Director of Publishing Planning & Book Trade Sales / Chris Ross–Director of Digital Sales / Jeff Stang–Director of Specialty Sales / Kat Salazar–Director of PR & Marketing / Branwyn Bigglestone–Controller / Kali Dugan–Senior Accounting Manager / Sue Korpela–Accounting & HR Manager / Drew Gill–Art Director / Heather Doornink–Production Director / Leigh Thomas–Print Manager / Tricia Ramos–Traffic Manager / Briah Skelly–Publicist / Aly Hoffman–Events & Conventions Coordinator / Sasha Head–Sales & Marketing Production Designer / David Brothers–Branding Manager / Melissa Gifford–Content Manager / Drew Fitzgerald–Publicity Assistant / Vincent Kukua–Production Artist / Erika Schnatz–Production Artist / Ryan Brewer–Production Artist / Shanna Matuszak–Production Artist / Carey Hall–Production Artist / Esther Kim–Direct Market Sales Representative / Emilio Bautista–Digital Sales Representative / Leanna Caunter–Accounting Analyst / Chloe Ramos-Peterson–Library Market Sales Representative / Marla Eizik–Administrative Assistant / IMAGECOMICS.COM

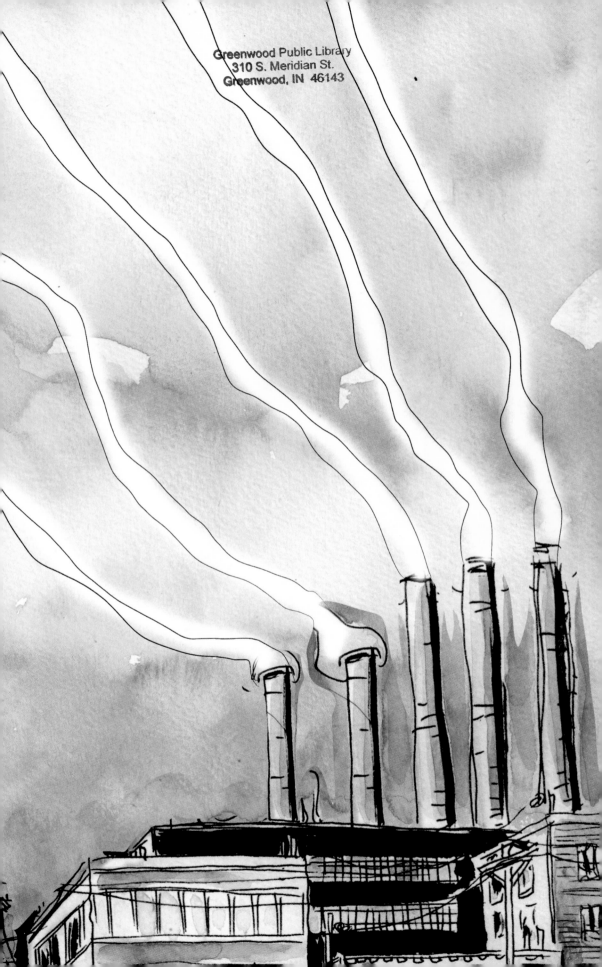

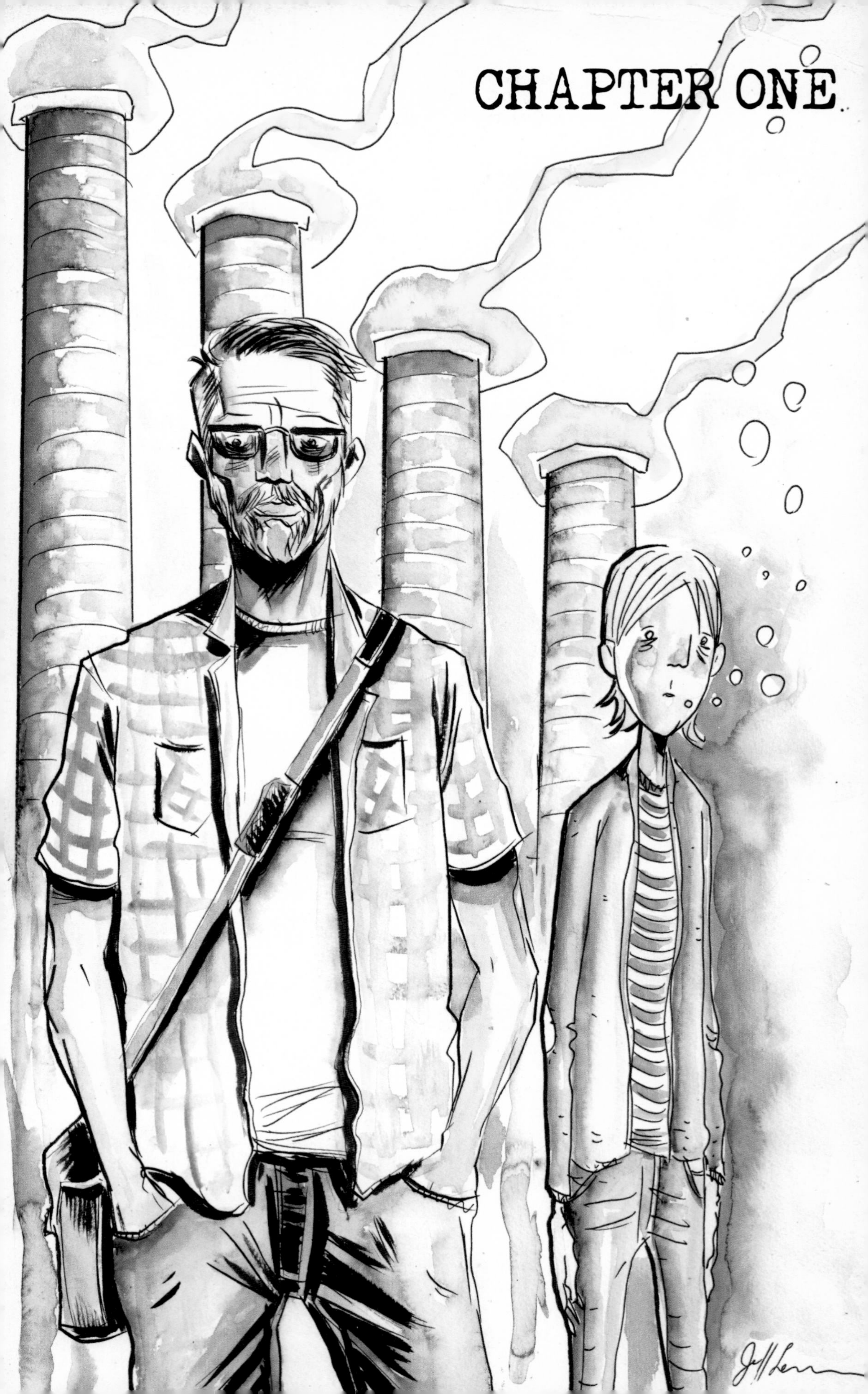
CHAPTER ONE

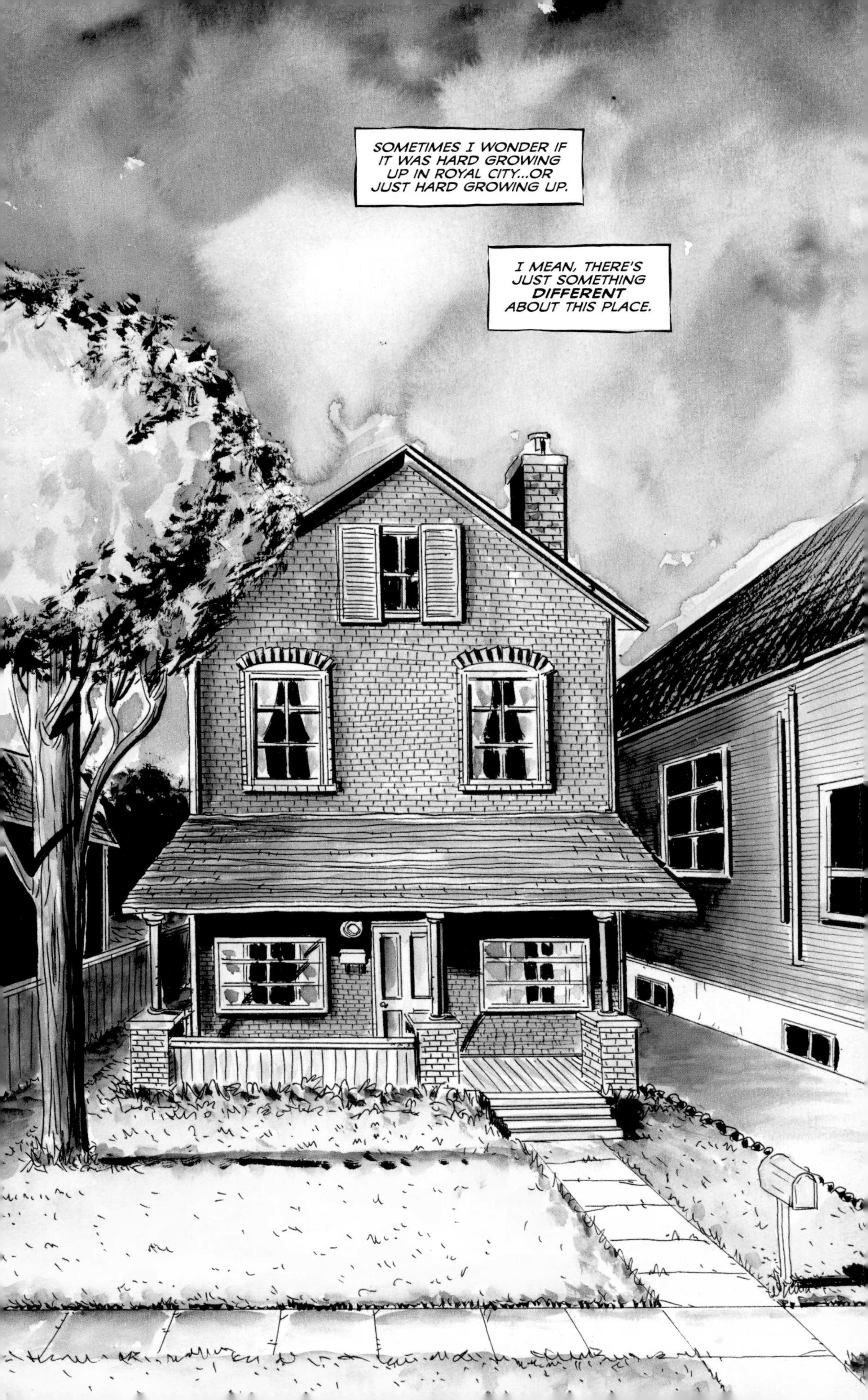
SOMETIMES I WONDER IF IT WAS HARD GROWING UP IN ROYAL CITY...OR JUST HARD GROWING UP.
I MEAN, THERE'S JUST SOMETHING **DIFFERENT** ABOUT THIS PLACE.

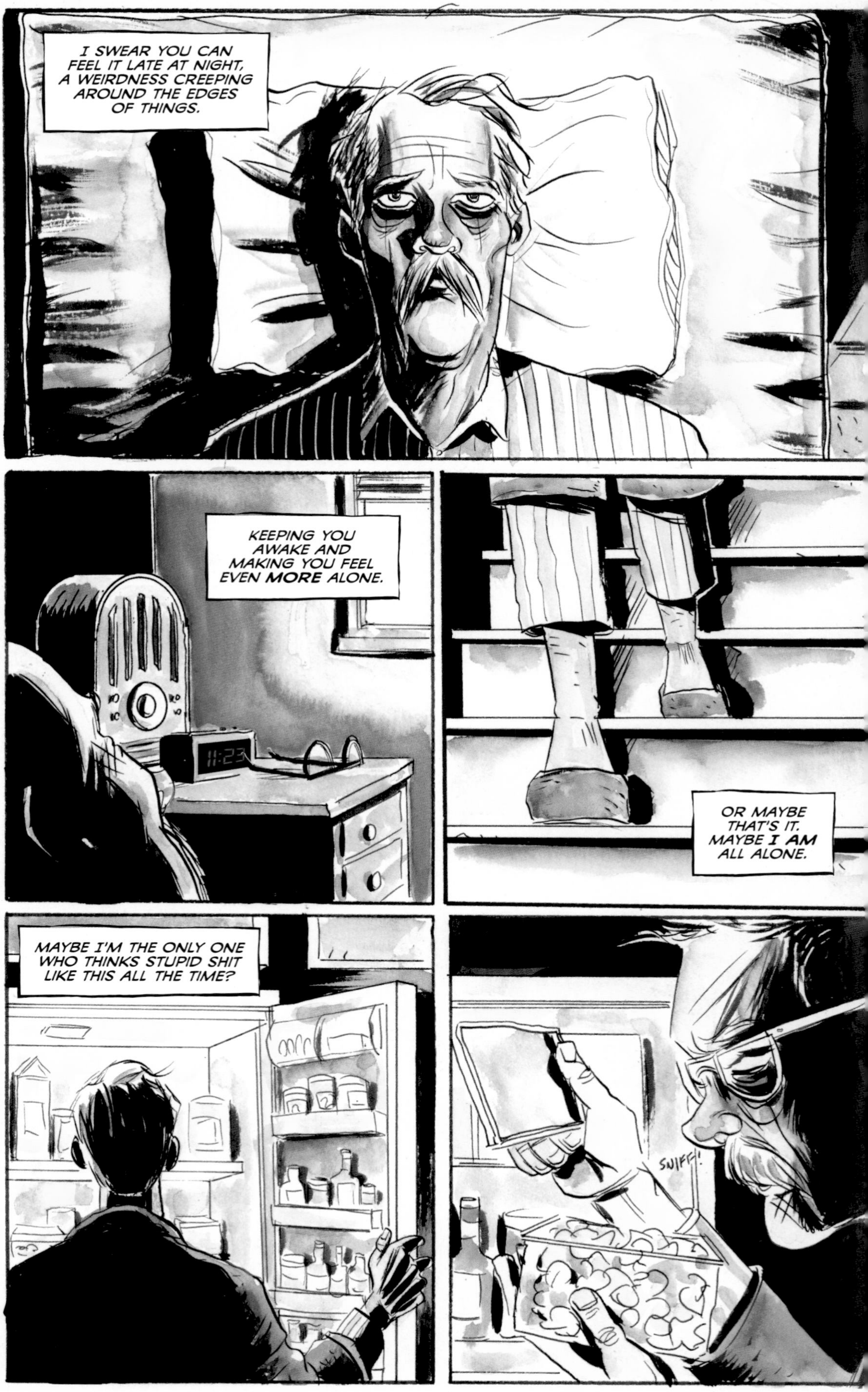
I SWEAR YOU CAN FEEL IT LATE AT NIGHT, A WEIRDNESS CREEPING AROUND THE EDGES OF THINGS.
KEEPING YOU AWAKE AND MAKING YOU FEEL EVEN MORE ALONE.
11:23
OR MAYBE THAT'S IT. MAYBE I AM ALL ALONE.
MAYBE I'M THE ONLY ONE WHO THINKS STUPID SHIT LIKE THIS ALL THE TIME?
SNIFF!

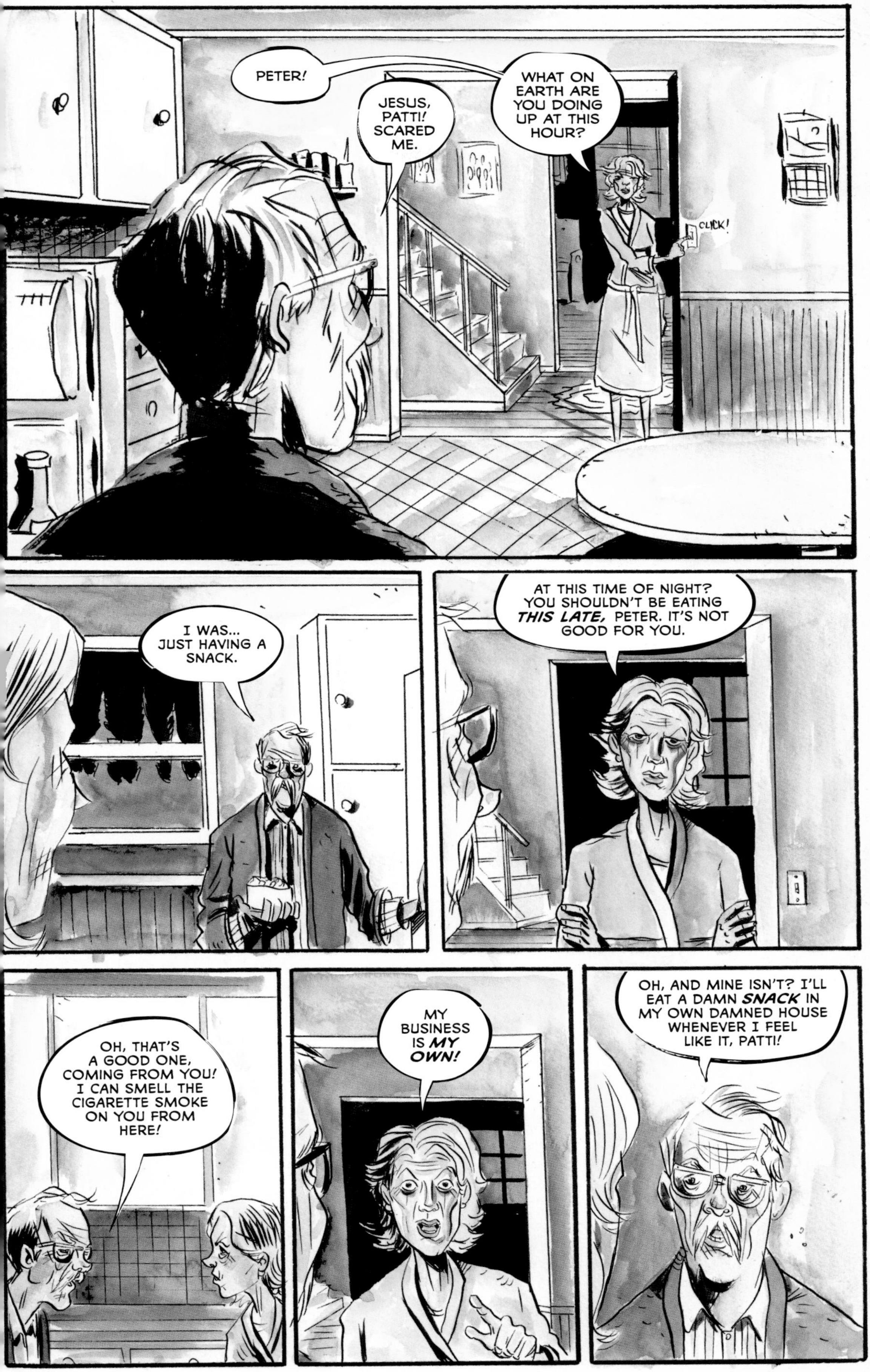
PETER!
WHAT ON EARTH ARE YOU DOING UP AT THIS HOUR?
JESUS, PATTI! SCARED ME.
CLICK!
I WAS... JUST HAVING A SNACK.
AT THIS TIME OF NIGHT? YOU SHOULDN'T BE EATING THIS LATE, PETER. IT'S NOT GOOD FOR YOU.
OH, THAT'S A GOOD ONE, COMING FROM YOU! I CAN SMELL THE CIGARETTE SMOKE ON YOU FROM HERE!
MY BUSINESS IS MY OWN!
OH, AND MINE ISN'T? I'LL EAT A DAMN SNACK IN MY OWN DAMNED HOUSE WHENEVER I FEEL LIKE IT, PATTI!

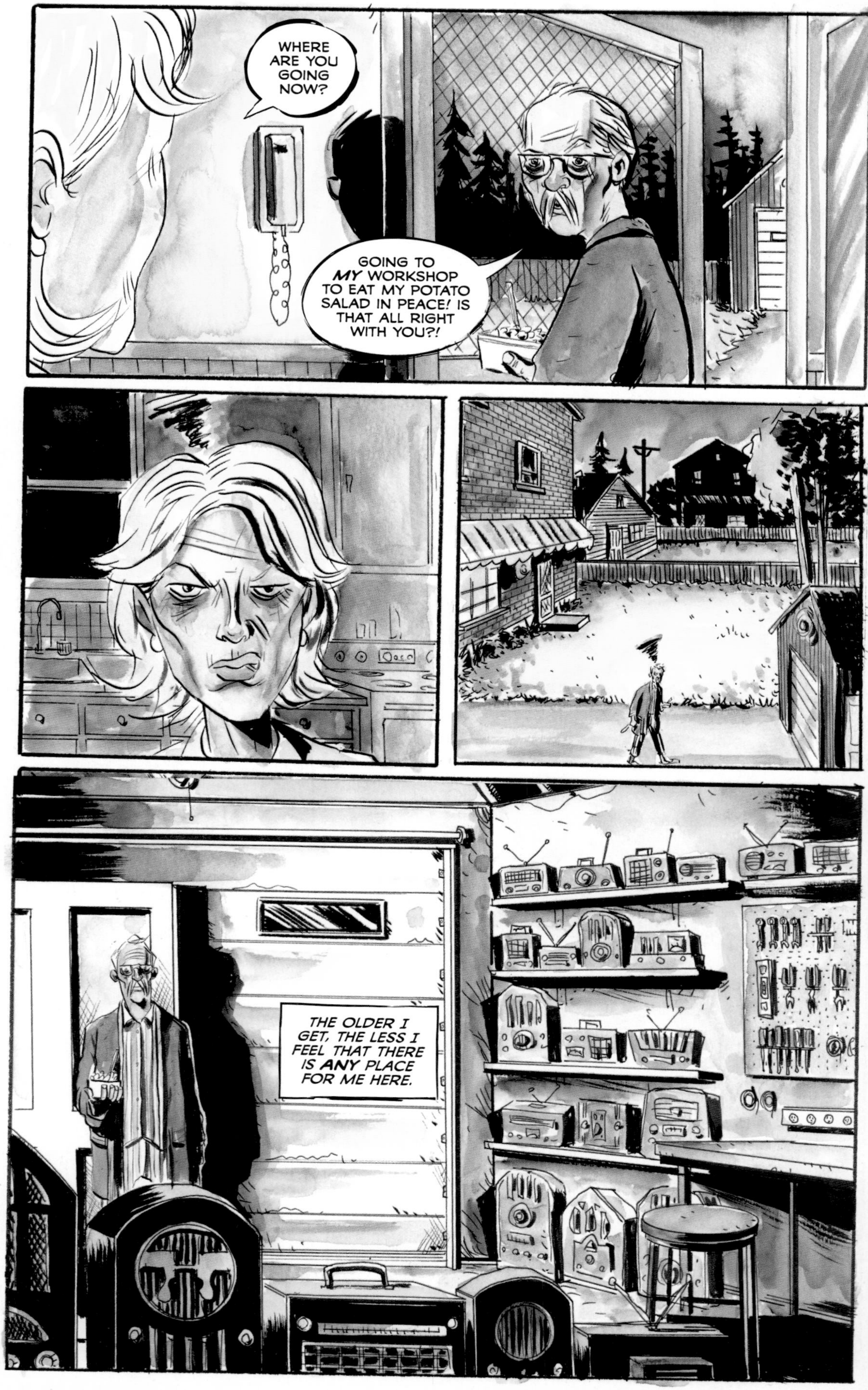
WHERE ARE YOU GOING NOW?
GOING TO *MY* WORKSHOP TO EAT MY POTATO SALAD IN PEACE! IS THAT ALL RIGHT WITH YOU?!
THE OLDER I GET, THE LESS I FEEL THAT THERE IS **ANY** PLACE FOR ME HERE.

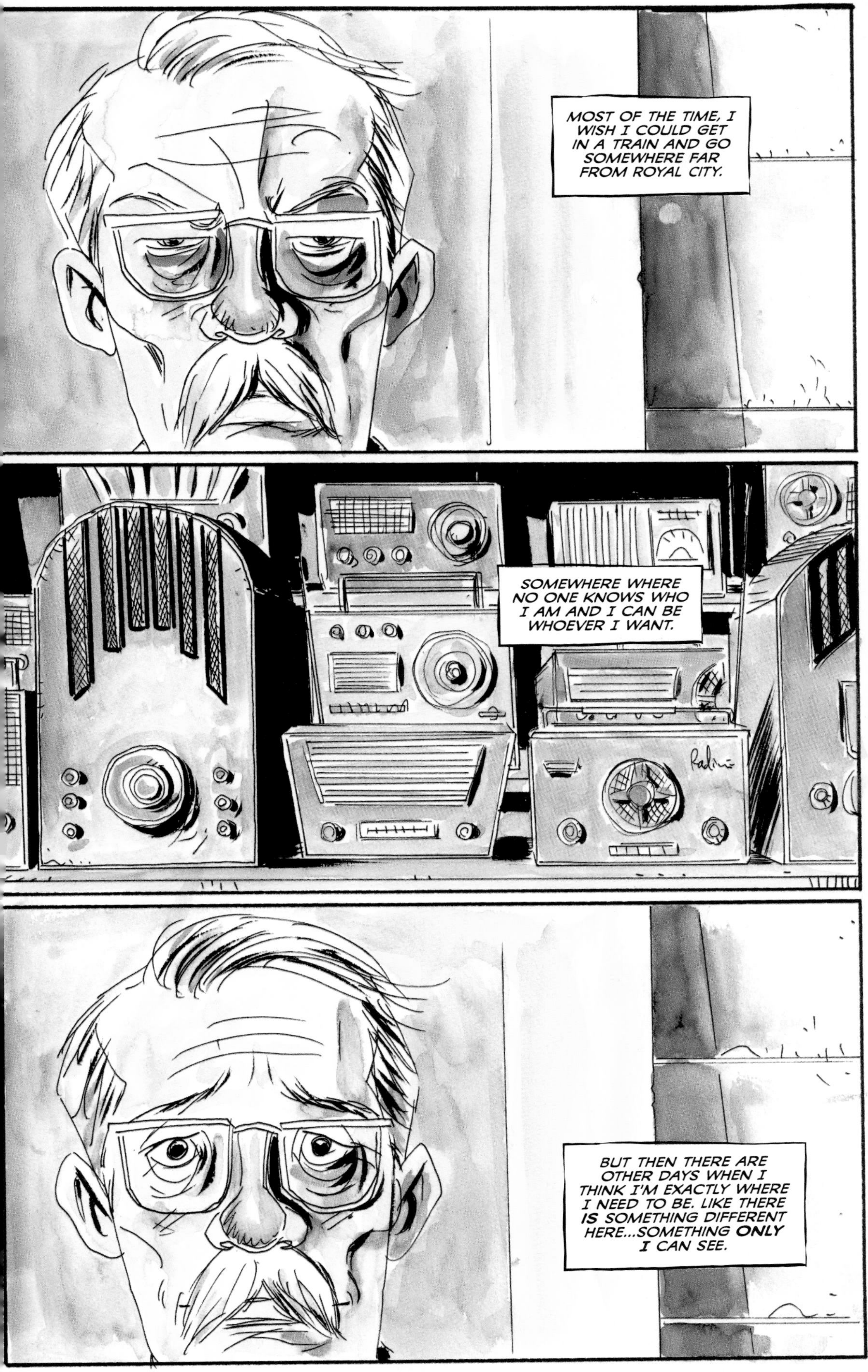
MOST OF THE TIME, I WISH I COULD GET IN A TRAIN AND GO SOMEWHERE FAR FROM ROYAL CITY.
SOMEWHERE WHERE NO ONE KNOWS WHO I AM AND I CAN BE WHOEVER I WANT.
BUT THEN THERE ARE OTHER DAYS WHEN I THINK I'M EXACTLY WHERE I NEED TO BE. LIKE THERE **IS** SOMETHING DIFFERENT HERE...SOMETHING **ONLY** I CAN SEE.

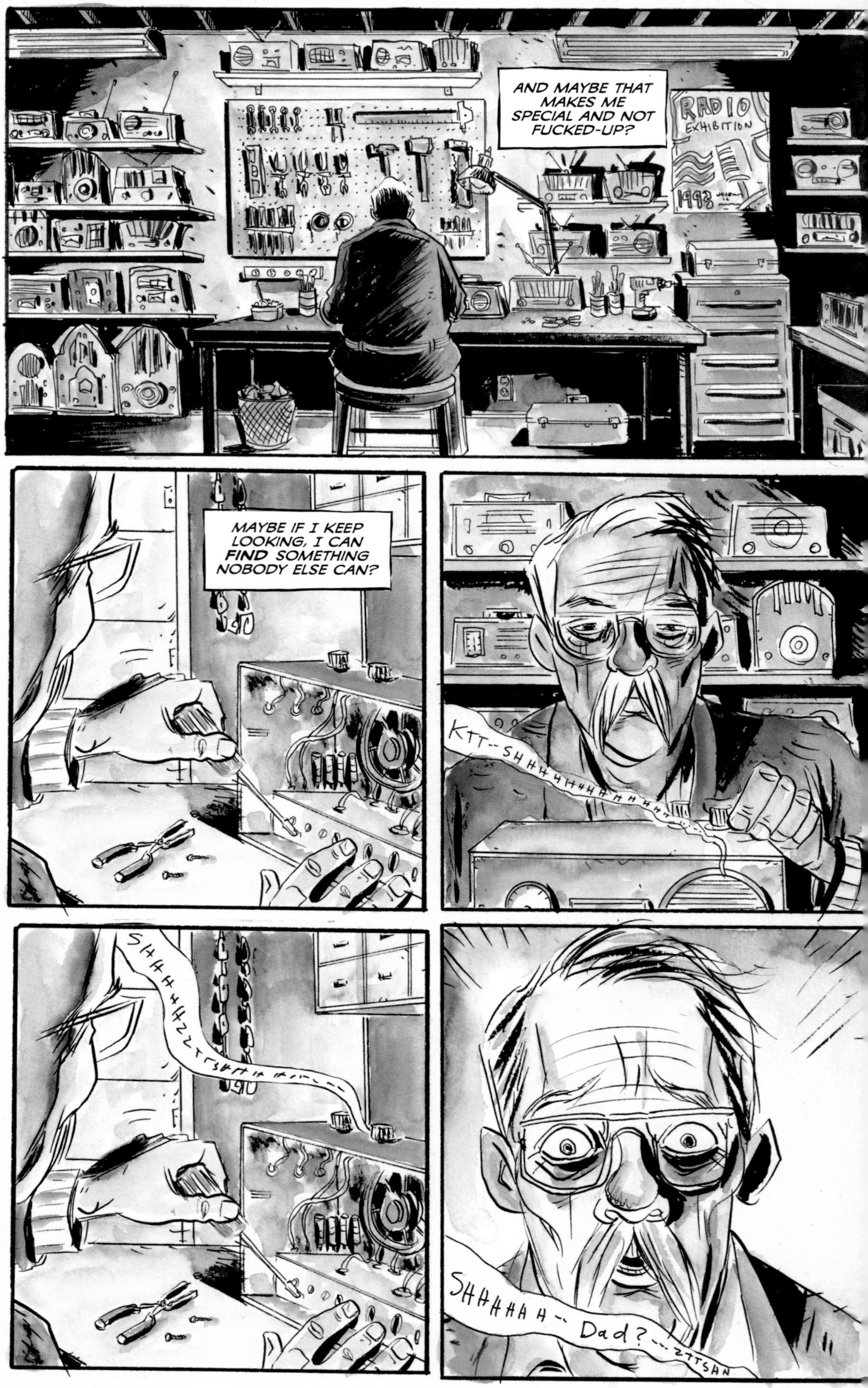
AND MAYBE THAT MAKES ME SPECIAL AND NOT FUCKED-UP?
RADIO EXHIBITION 1993
MAYBE IF I KEEP LOOKING, I CAN **FIND** SOMETHING NOBODY ELSE CAN?
KTT--SHHHHHHHHHHHHHH
SHHHHHHZZTTSHHHH
SHHHHHH-- Dad?...ZTTSHH

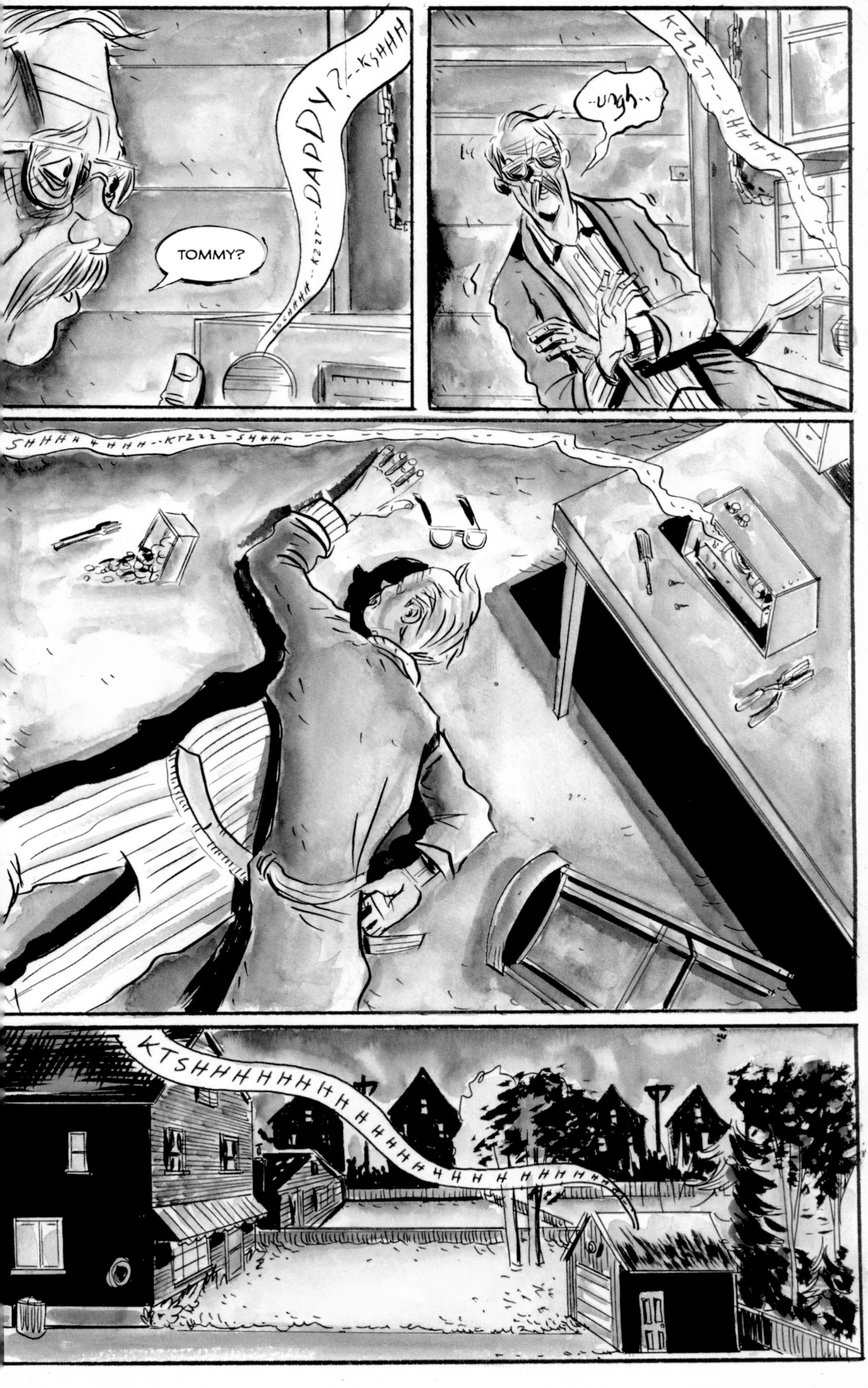
TOMMY?
SSCHHHH--KZZT--DADDY?!--KSHHH
--ungh--
KZZZT--SHHHHHH
SHHHHHHHH--KTZZZ--SHHH
KTSHHHHHHHHHHHHHHHHHHHHHHHH

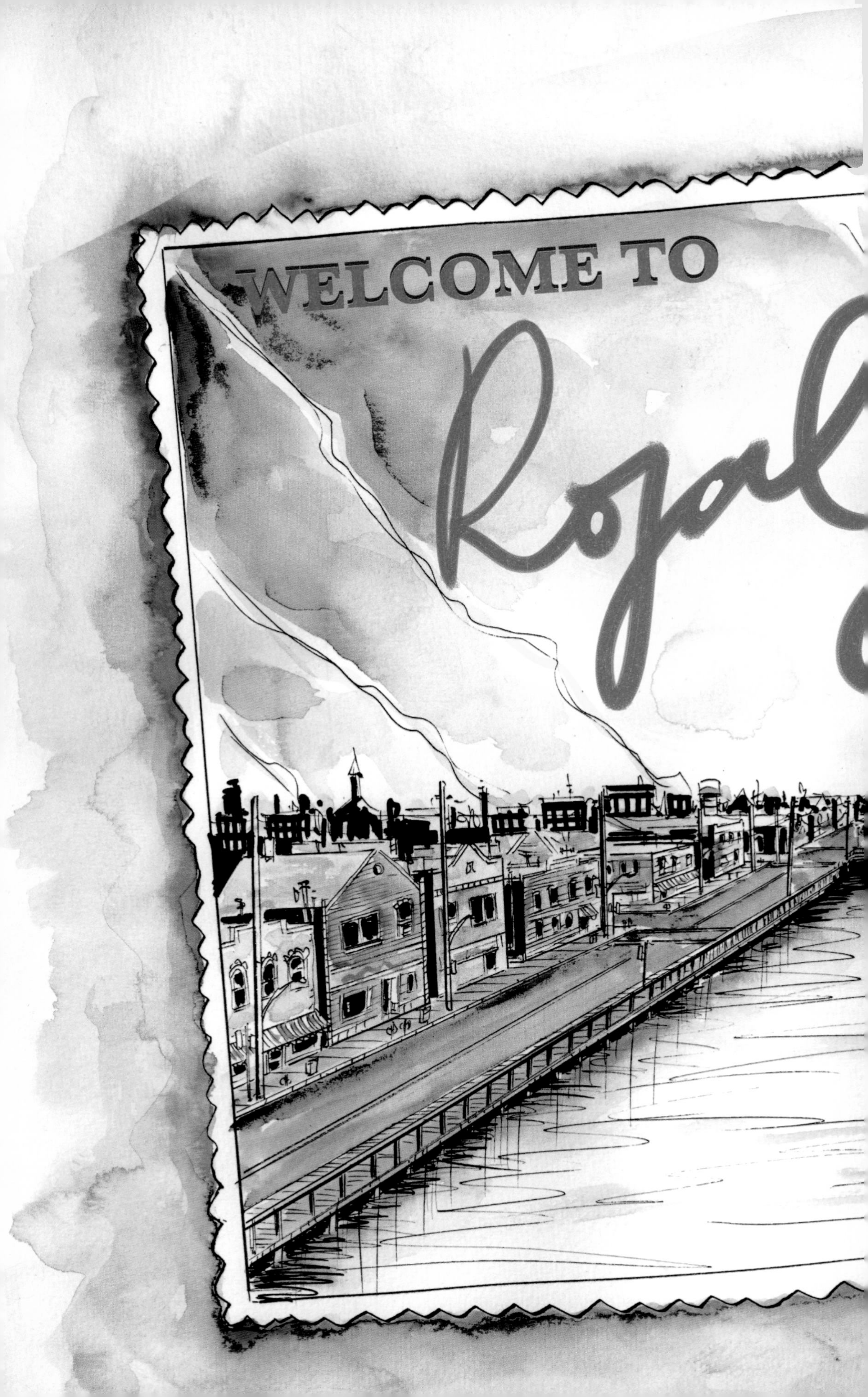
WELCOME TO

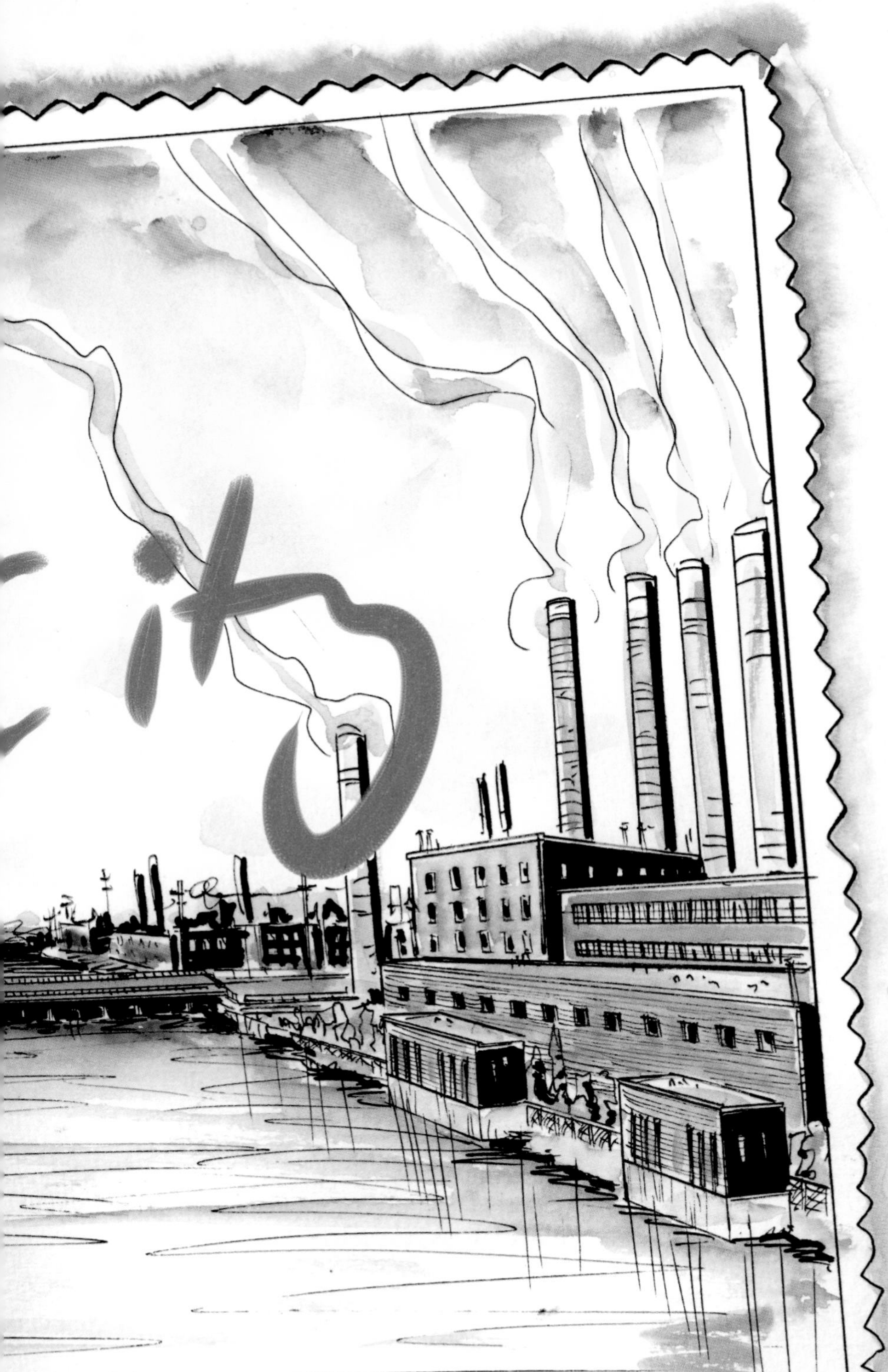

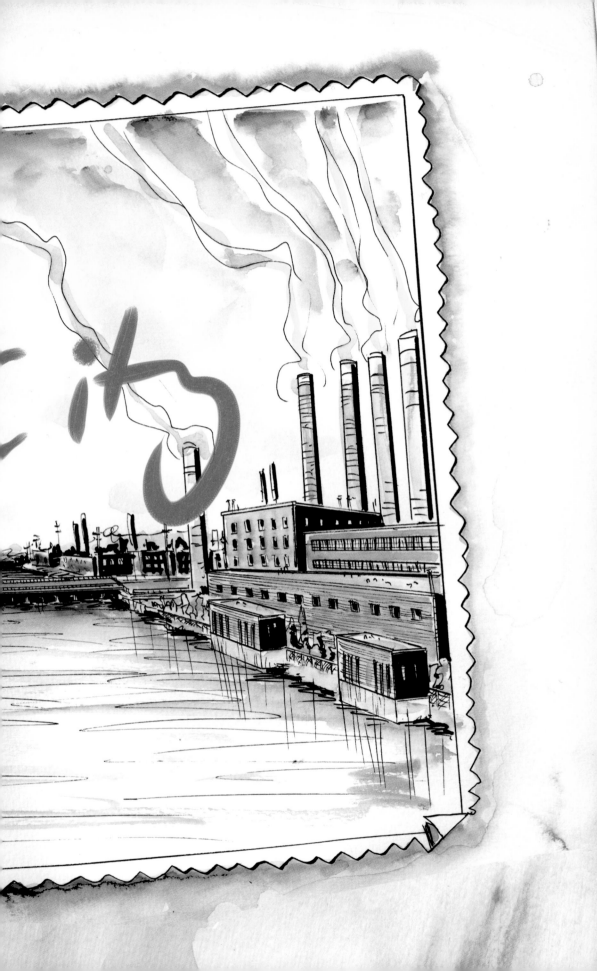

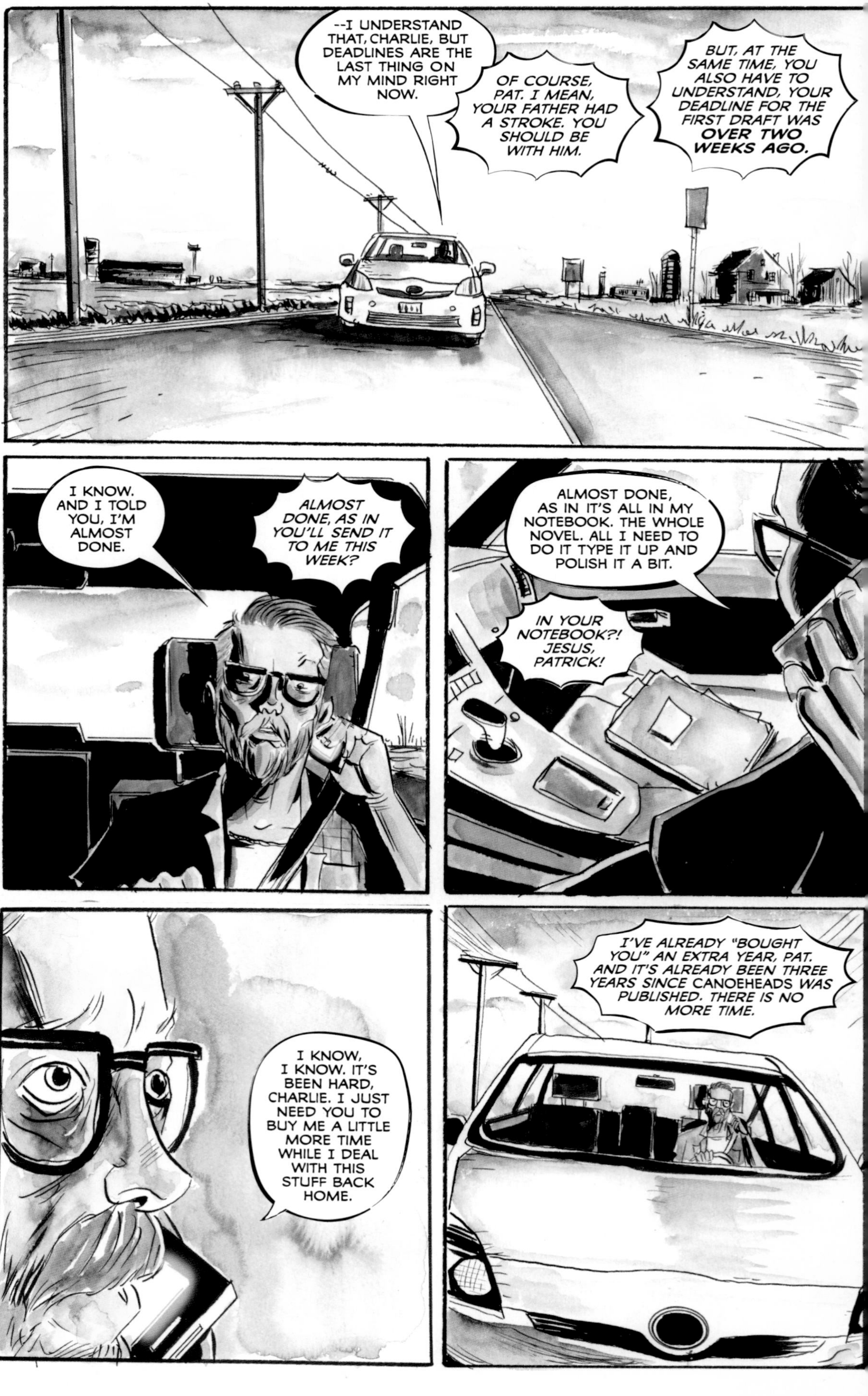
--I UNDERSTAND THAT, CHARLIE, BUT DEADLINES ARE THE LAST THING ON MY MIND RIGHT NOW.
OF COURSE, PAT. I MEAN, YOUR FATHER HAD A STROKE. YOU SHOULD BE WITH HIM.
BUT, AT THE SAME TIME, YOU ALSO HAVE TO UNDERSTAND, YOUR DEADLINE FOR THE FIRST DRAFT WAS OVER TWO WEEKS AGO.
I KNOW. AND I TOLD YOU, I'M ALMOST DONE.
ALMOST DONE, AS IN YOU'LL SEND IT TO ME THIS WEEK?
ALMOST DONE, AS IN IT'S ALL IN MY NOTEBOOK. THE WHOLE NOVEL. ALL I NEED TO DO IT TYPE IT UP AND POLISH IT A BIT.
IN YOUR NOTEBOOK?! JESUS, PATRICK!
I KNOW, I KNOW. IT'S BEEN HARD, CHARLIE. I JUST NEED YOU TO BUY ME A LITTLE MORE TIME WHILE I DEAL WITH THIS STUFF BACK HOME.
I'VE ALREADY "BOUGHT YOU" AN EXTRA YEAR, PAT. AND IT'S ALREADY BEEN THREE YEARS SINCE CANOEHEADS WAS PUBLISHED. THERE IS NO MORE TIME.

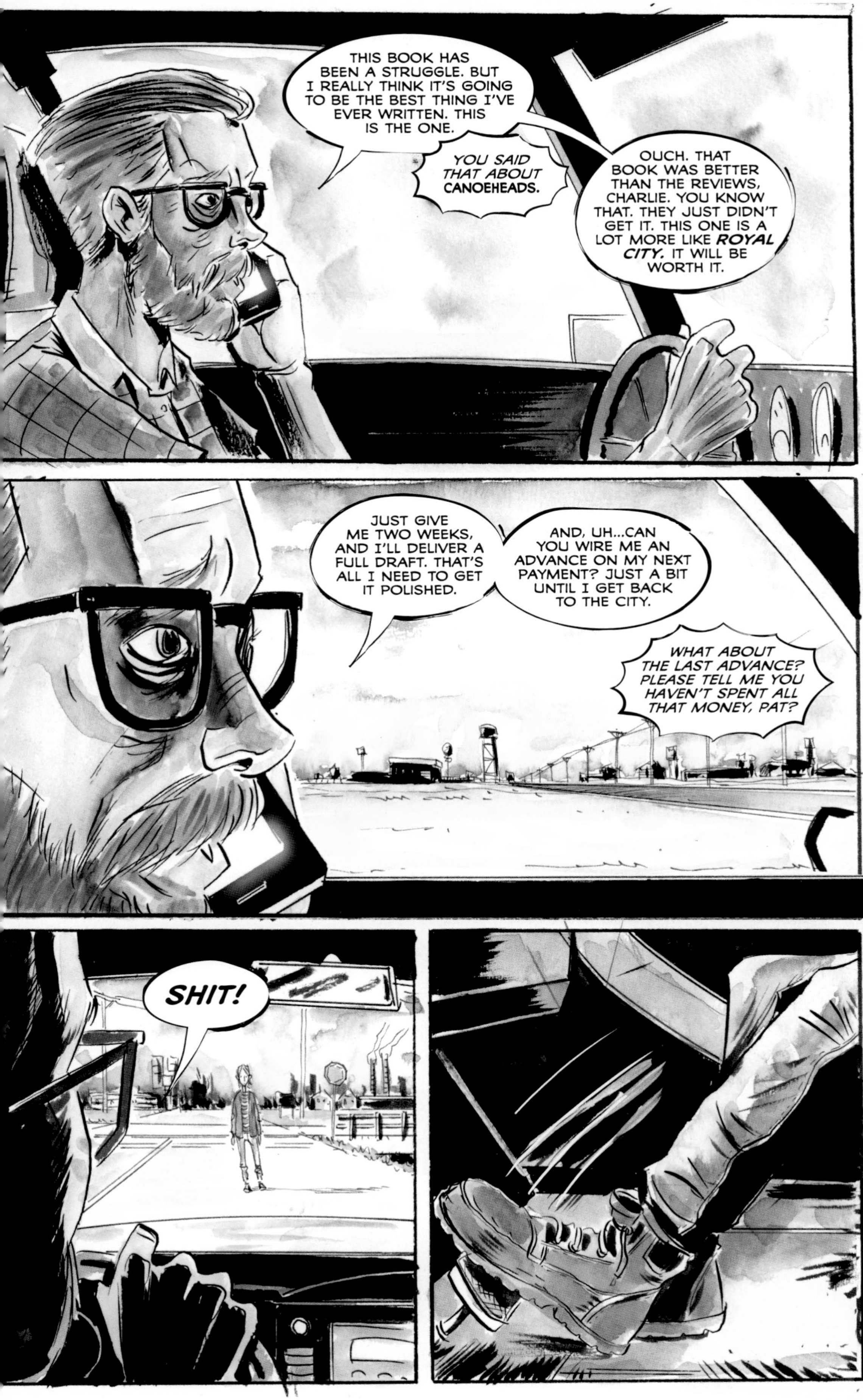
THIS BOOK HAS BEEN A STRUGGLE. BUT I REALLY THINK IT'S GOING TO BE THE BEST THING I'VE EVER WRITTEN. THIS IS THE ONE.
YOU SAID THAT ABOUT CANOEHEADS.
OUCH. THAT BOOK WAS BETTER THAN THE REVIEWS, CHARLIE. YOU KNOW THAT. THEY JUST DIDN'T GET IT. THIS ONE IS A LOT MORE LIKE ROYAL CITY. IT WILL BE WORTH IT.
JUST GIVE ME TWO WEEKS, AND I'LL DELIVER A FULL DRAFT. THAT'S ALL I NEED TO GET IT POLISHED.
AND, UH...CAN YOU WIRE ME AN ADVANCE ON MY NEXT PAYMENT? JUST A BIT UNTIL I GET BACK TO THE CITY.
WHAT ABOUT THE LAST ADVANCE? PLEASE TELL ME YOU HAVEN'T SPENT ALL THAT MONEY, PAT?
SHIT!

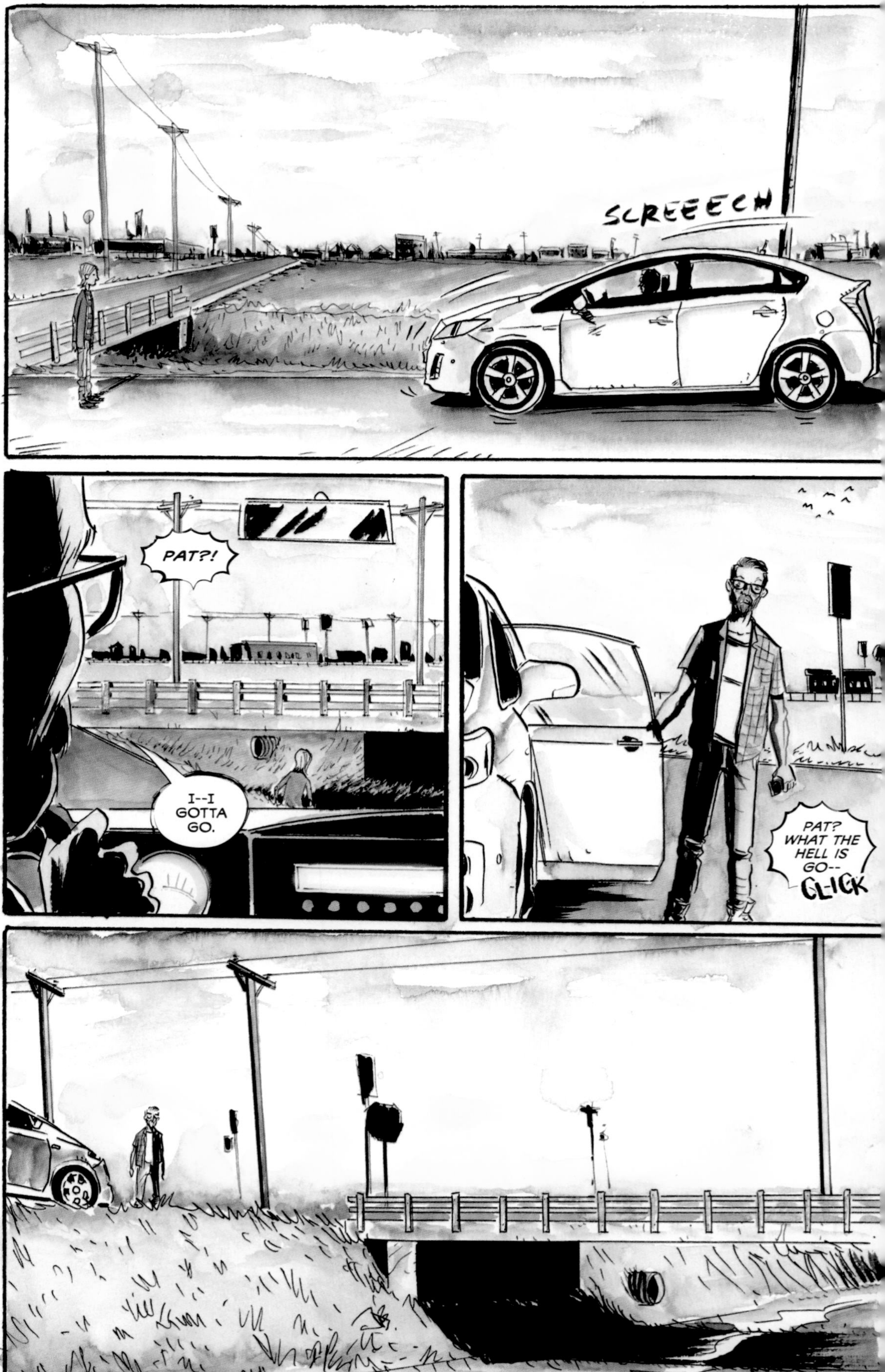
SCREEECH
PAT?!
I--I GOTTA GO.
PAT? WHAT THE HELL IS GO--
CLICK

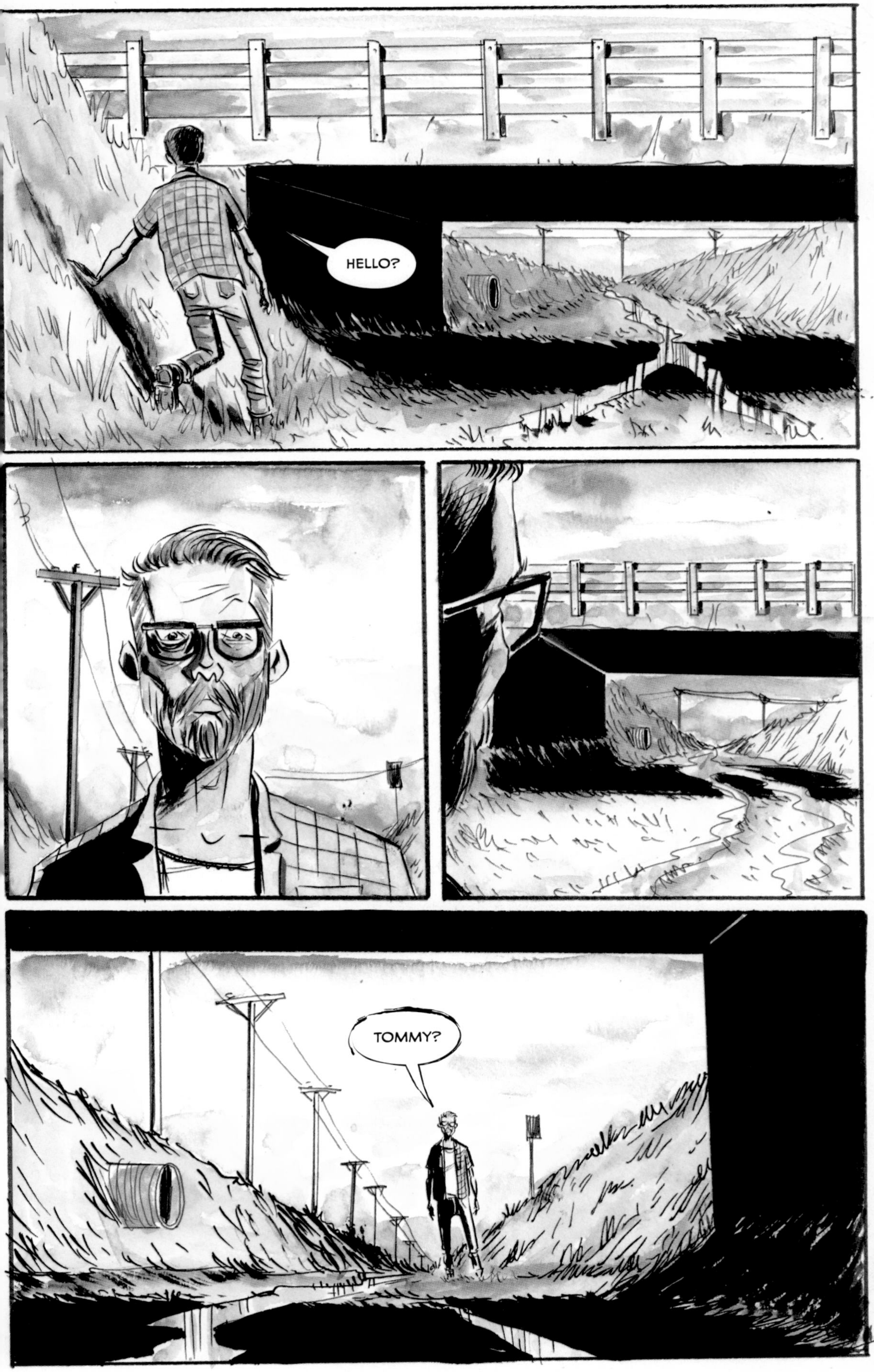
HELLO?
TOMMY?

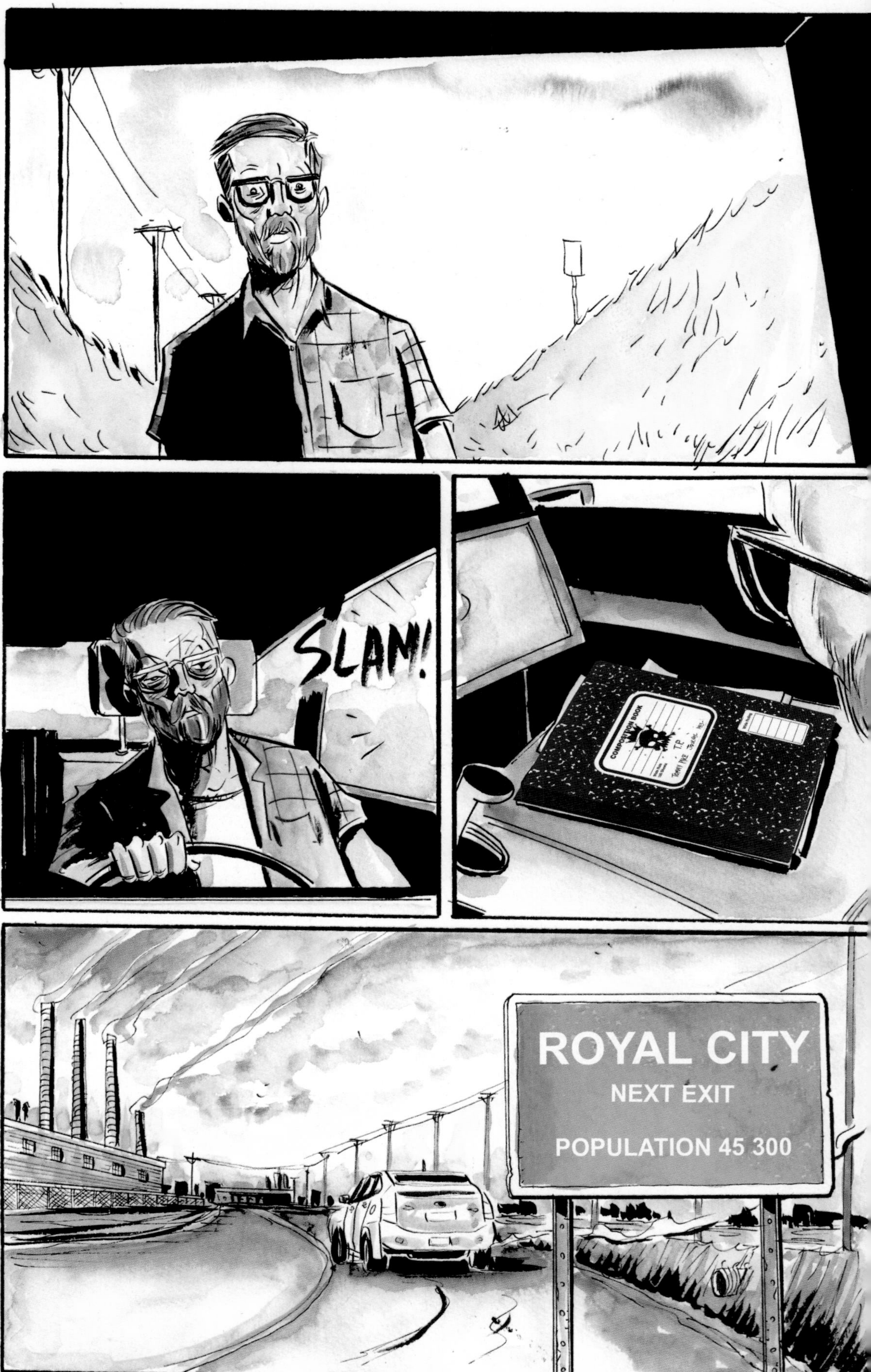
SLAM!
ROYAL CITY
NEXT EXIT
POPULATION 45 300

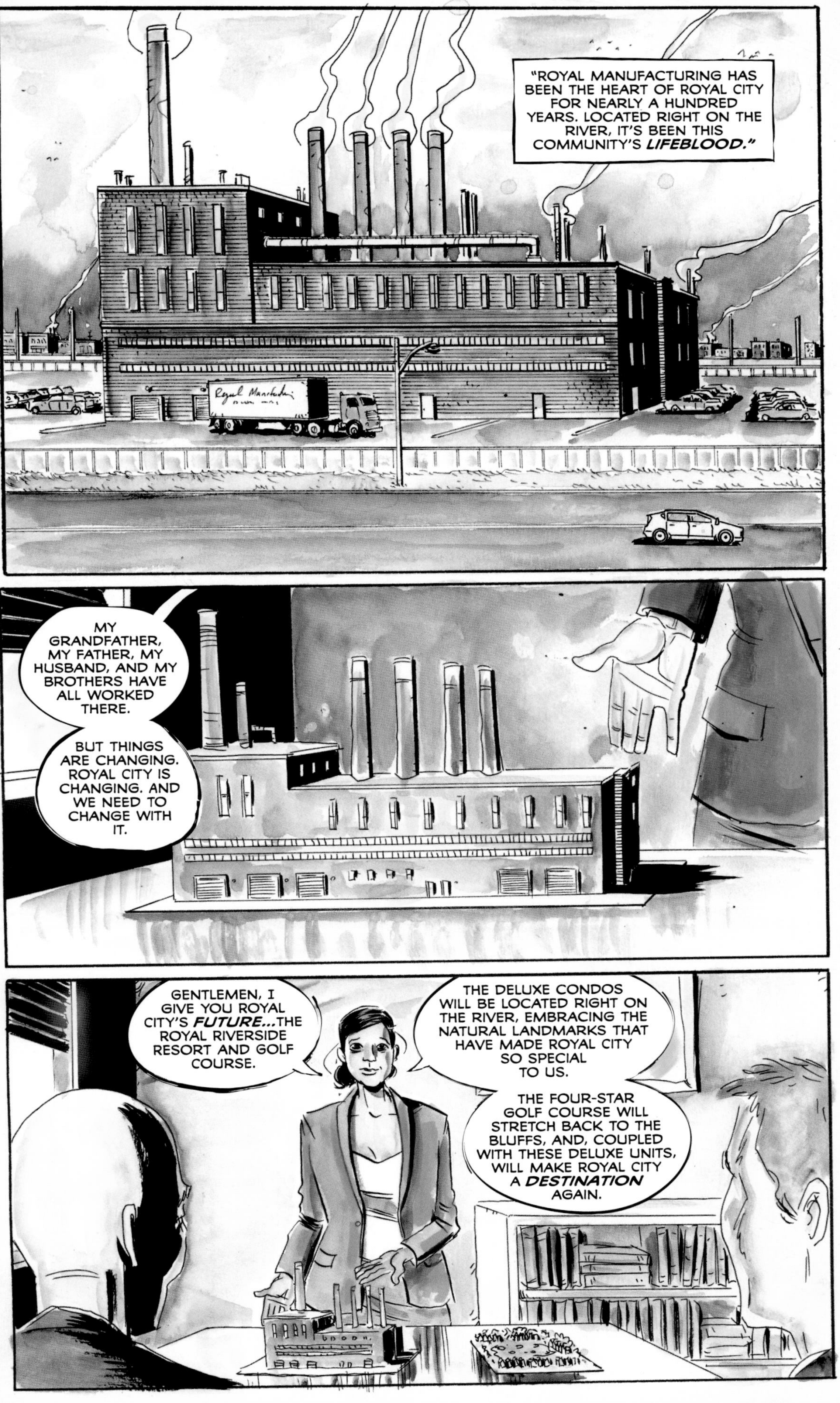
"ROYAL MANUFACTURING HAS BEEN THE HEART OF ROYAL CITY FOR NEARLY A HUNDRED YEARS. LOCATED RIGHT ON THE RIVER, IT'S BEEN THIS COMMUNITY'S *LIFEBLOOD.*"
Royal Manufacturing
MY GRANDFATHER, MY FATHER, MY HUSBAND, AND MY BROTHERS HAVE ALL WORKED THERE.
BUT THINGS ARE CHANGING. ROYAL CITY IS CHANGING. AND WE NEED TO CHANGE WITH IT.
GENTLEMEN, I GIVE YOU ROYAL CITY'S *FUTURE...*THE ROYAL RIVERSIDE RESORT AND GOLF COURSE.
THE DELUXE CONDOS WILL BE LOCATED RIGHT ON THE RIVER, EMBRACING THE NATURAL LANDMARKS THAT HAVE MADE ROYAL CITY SO SPECIAL TO US.
THE FOUR-STAR GOLF COURSE WILL STRETCH BACK TO THE BLUFFS, AND, COUPLED WITH THESE DELUXE UNITS, WILL MAKE ROYAL CITY A *DESTINATION* AGAIN.

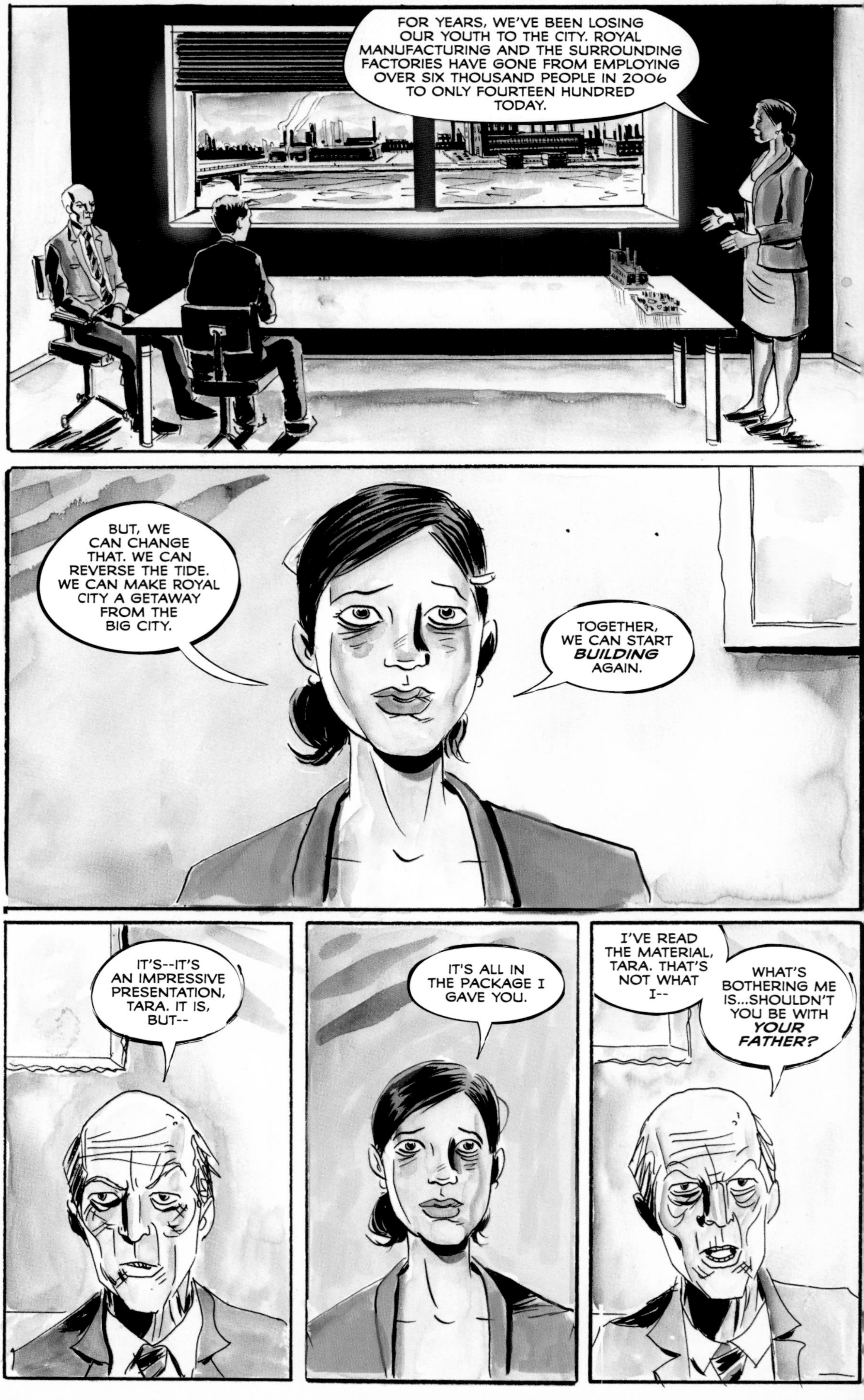
FOR YEARS, WE'VE BEEN LOSING OUR YOUTH TO THE CITY. ROYAL MANUFACTURING AND THE SURROUNDING FACTORIES HAVE GONE FROM EMPLOYING OVER SIX THOUSAND PEOPLE IN 2006 TO ONLY FOURTEEN HUNDRED TODAY.
BUT, WE CAN CHANGE THAT. WE CAN REVERSE THE TIDE. WE CAN MAKE ROYAL CITY A GETAWAY FROM THE BIG CITY.
TOGETHER, WE CAN START *BUILDING* AGAIN.
IT'S--IT'S AN IMPRESSIVE PRESENTATION, TARA. IT IS, BUT--
IT'S ALL IN THE PACKAGE I GAVE YOU.
I'VE READ THE MATERIAL, TARA. THAT'S NOT WHAT I--
WHAT'S BOTHERING ME IS...SHOULDN'T YOU BE WITH *YOUR FATHER?*

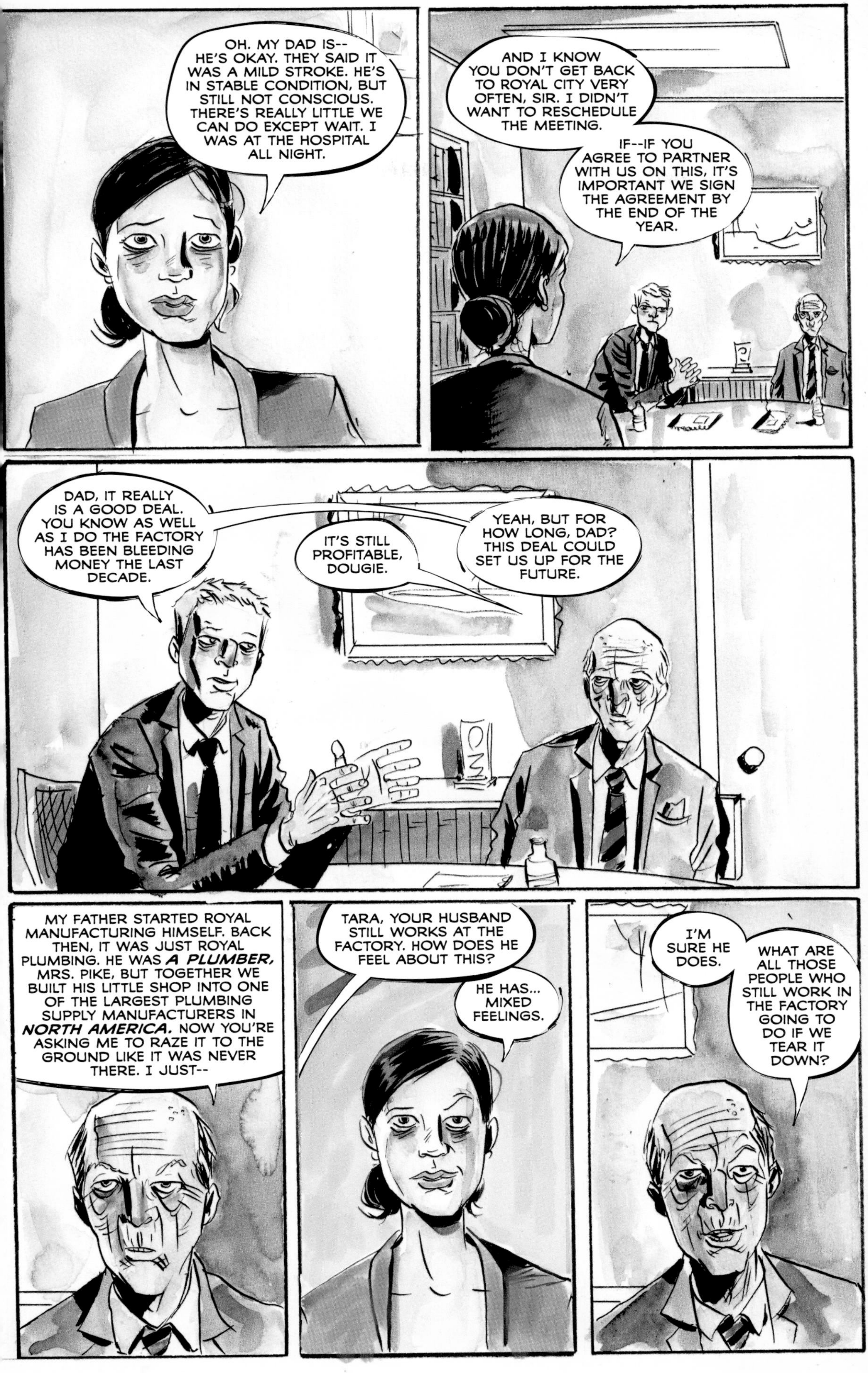
OH. MY DAD IS-- HE'S OKAY. THEY SAID IT WAS A MILD STROKE. HE'S IN STABLE CONDITION, BUT STILL NOT CONSCIOUS. THERE'S REALLY LITTLE WE CAN DO EXCEPT WAIT. I WAS AT THE HOSPITAL ALL NIGHT.
AND I KNOW YOU DON'T GET BACK TO ROYAL CITY VERY OFTEN, SIR. I DIDN'T WANT TO RESCHEDULE THE MEETING.
IF--IF YOU AGREE TO PARTNER WITH US ON THIS, IT'S IMPORTANT WE SIGN THE AGREEMENT BY THE END OF THE YEAR.
DAD, IT REALLY IS A GOOD DEAL. YOU KNOW AS WELL AS I DO THE FACTORY HAS BEEN BLEEDING MONEY THE LAST DECADE.
IT'S STILL PROFITABLE, DOUGIE.
YEAH, BUT FOR HOW LONG, DAD? THIS DEAL COULD SET US UP FOR THE FUTURE.
MY FATHER STARTED ROYAL MANUFACTURING HIMSELF. BACK THEN, IT WAS JUST ROYAL PLUMBING. HE WAS ***A PLUMBER,*** MRS. PIKE, BUT TOGETHER WE BUILT HIS LITTLE SHOP INTO ONE OF THE LARGEST PLUMBING SUPPLY MANUFACTURERS IN ***NORTH AMERICA.*** NOW YOU'RE ASKING ME TO RAZE IT TO THE GROUND LIKE IT WAS NEVER THERE. I JUST--
TARA, YOUR HUSBAND STILL WORKS AT THE FACTORY. HOW DOES HE FEEL ABOUT THIS?
HE HAS... MIXED FEELINGS.
I'M SURE HE DOES.
WHAT ARE ALL THOSE PEOPLE WHO STILL WORK IN THE FACTORY GOING TO DO IF WE TEAR IT DOWN?

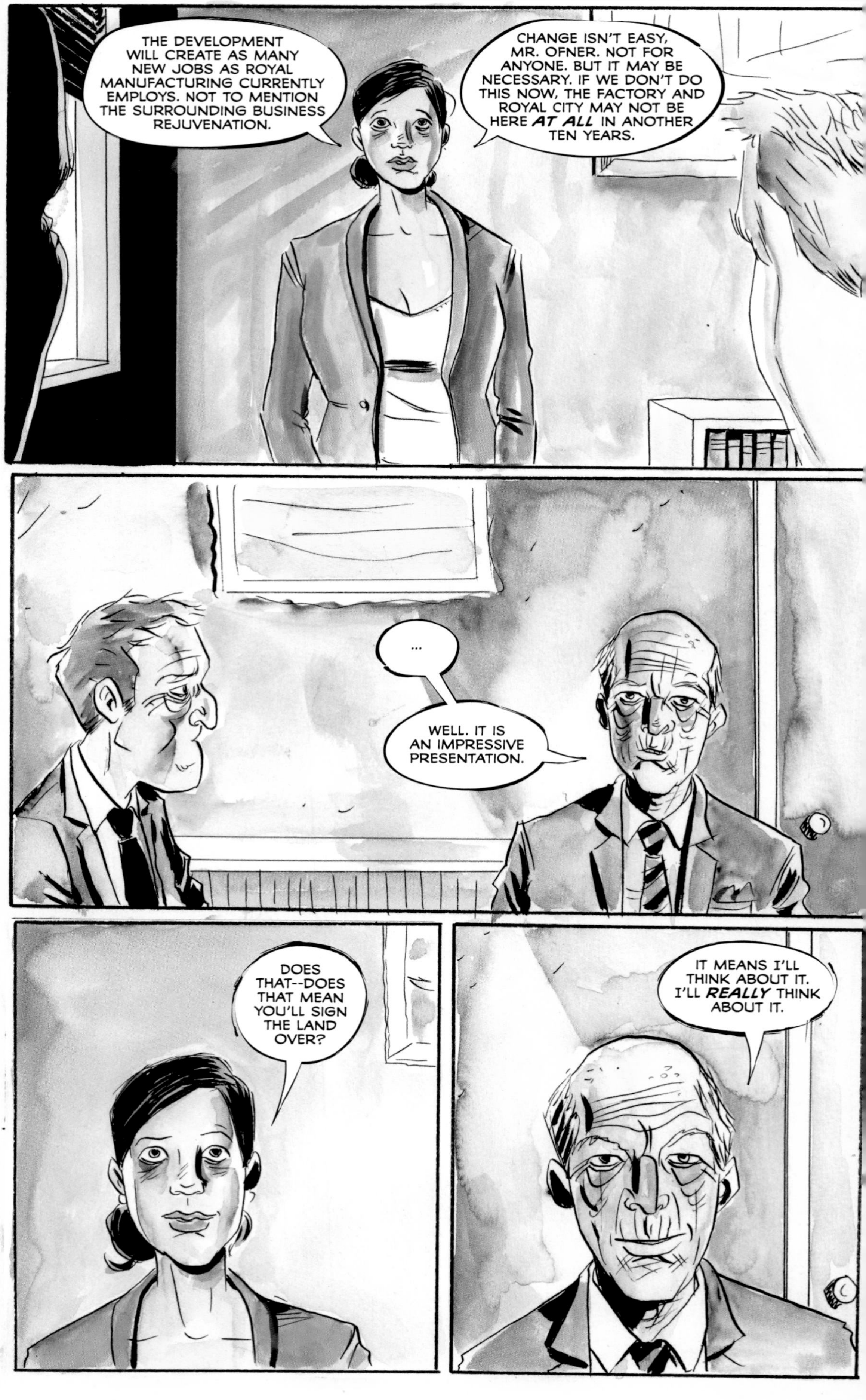
THE DEVELOPMENT WILL CREATE AS MANY NEW JOBS AS ROYAL MANUFACTURING CURRENTLY EMPLOYS. NOT TO MENTION THE SURROUNDING BUSINESS REJUVENATION.
CHANGE ISN'T EASY, MR. OFNER. NOT FOR ANYONE. BUT IT MAY BE NECESSARY. IF WE DON'T DO THIS NOW, THE FACTORY AND ROYAL CITY MAY NOT BE HERE *AT ALL* IN ANOTHER TEN YEARS.
...
WELL. IT IS AN IMPRESSIVE PRESENTATION.
DOES THAT--DOES THAT MEAN YOU'LL SIGN THE LAND OVER?
IT MEANS I'LL THINK ABOUT IT. I'LL *REALLY* THINK ABOUT IT.

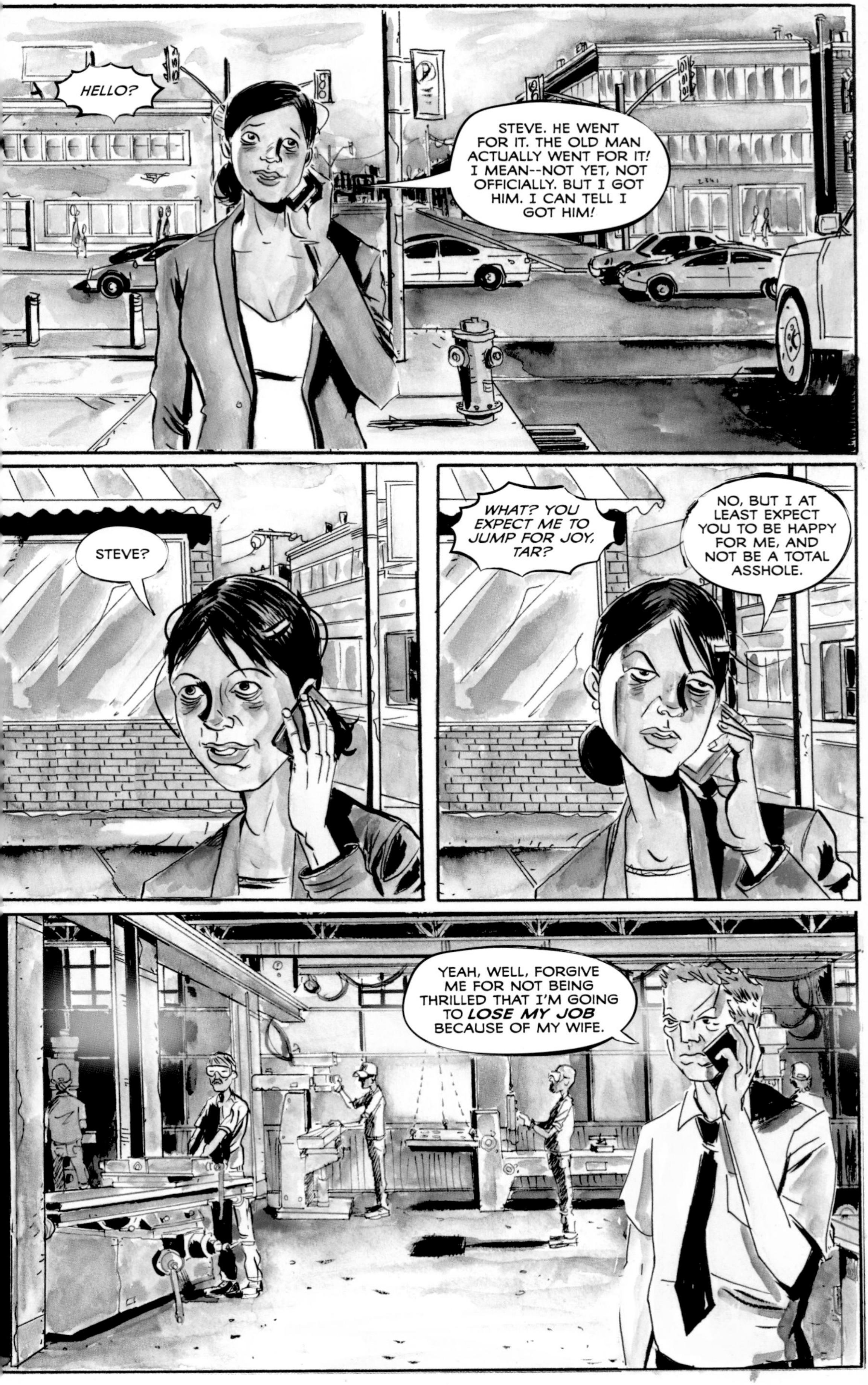
HELLO?
STEVE. HE WENT FOR IT. THE OLD MAN ACTUALLY WENT FOR IT! I MEAN--NOT YET, NOT OFFICIALLY. BUT I GOT HIM. I CAN TELL I GOT HIM!
STEVE?
WHAT? YOU EXPECT ME TO JUMP FOR JOY, TAR?
NO, BUT I AT LEAST EXPECT YOU TO BE HAPPY FOR ME, AND NOT BE A TOTAL ASSHOLE.
YEAH, WELL, FORGIVE ME FOR NOT BEING THRILLED THAT I'M GOING TO LOSE MY JOB BECAUSE OF MY WIFE.

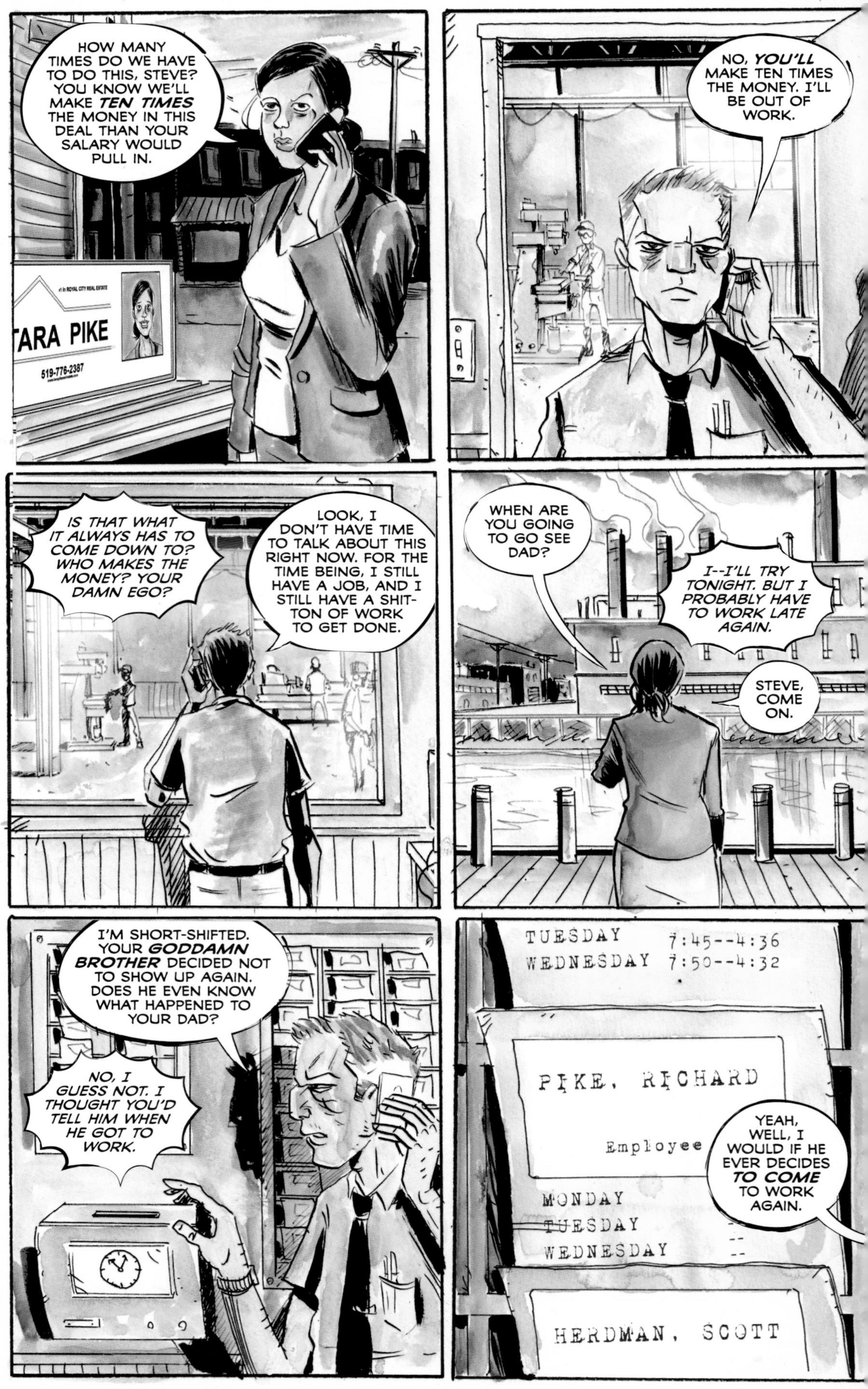
HOW MANY TIMES DO WE HAVE TO DO THIS, STEVE? YOU KNOW WE'LL MAKE ***TEN TIMES*** THE MONEY IN THIS DEAL THAN YOUR SALARY WOULD PULL IN.
TARA PIKE
519-776-2387
NO, ***YOU'LL*** MAKE TEN TIMES THE MONEY. I'LL BE OUT OF WORK.
IS THAT WHAT IT ALWAYS HAS TO COME DOWN TO? WHO MAKES THE MONEY? YOUR DAMN EGO?
LOOK, I DON'T HAVE TIME TO TALK ABOUT THIS RIGHT NOW. FOR THE TIME BEING, I STILL HAVE A JOB, AND I STILL HAVE A SHIT-TON OF WORK TO GET DONE.
WHEN ARE YOU GOING TO GO SEE DAD?
I--I'LL TRY TONIGHT. BUT I PROBABLY HAVE TO WORK LATE AGAIN.
STEVE, COME ON.
I'M SHORT-SHIFTED. YOUR ***GODDAMN BROTHER*** DECIDED NOT TO SHOW UP AGAIN. DOES HE EVEN KNOW WHAT HAPPENED TO YOUR DAD?
NO, I GUESS NOT. I THOUGHT YOU'D TELL HIM WHEN HE GOT TO WORK.
TUESDAY 7:45--4:36
WEDNESDAY 7:50--4:32
PIKE, RICHARD
Employee
MONDAY
TUESDAY
WEDNESDAY
YEAH, WELL, I WOULD IF HE EVER DECIDES ***TO COME*** TO WORK AGAIN.
HERDMAN, SCOTT

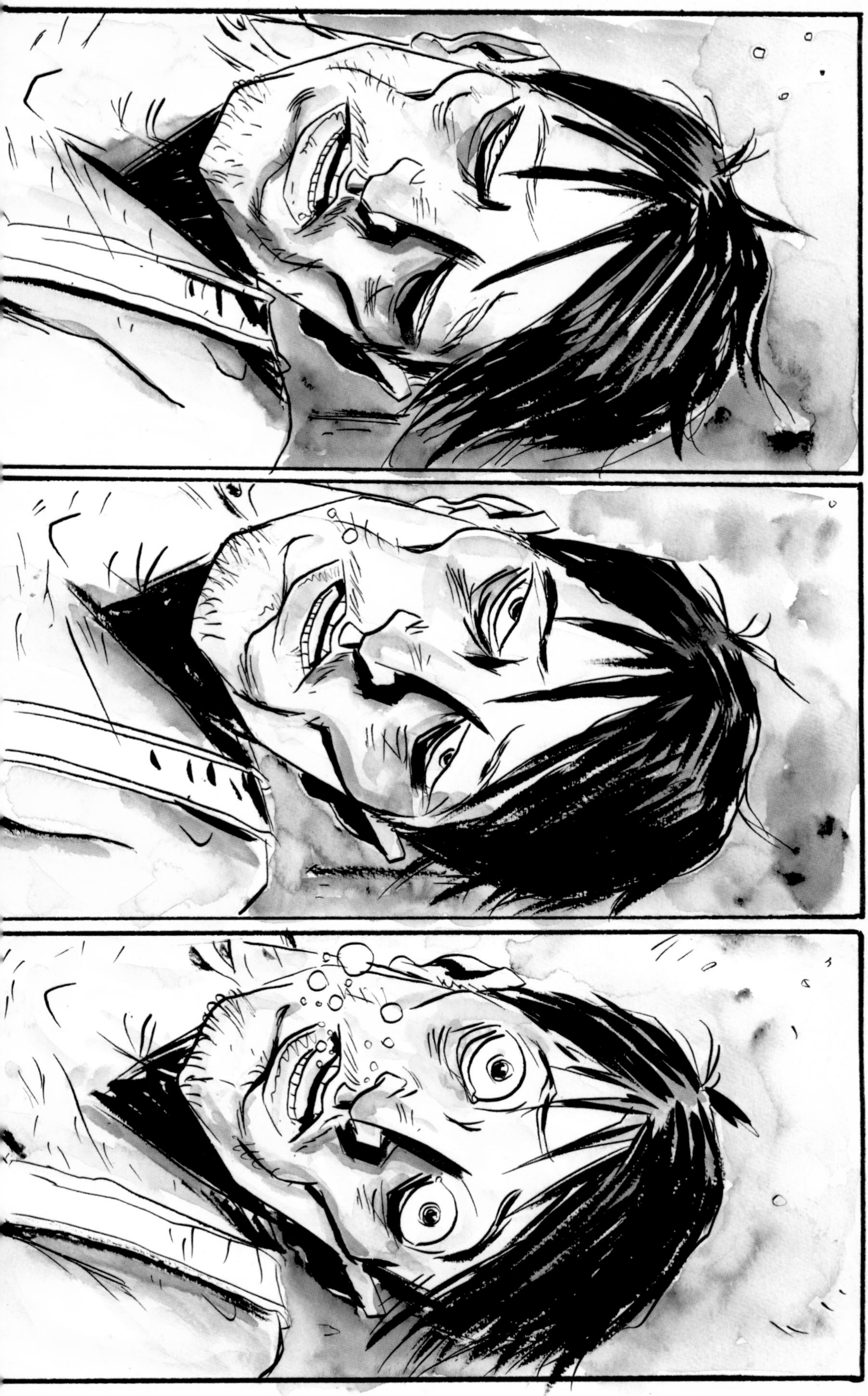

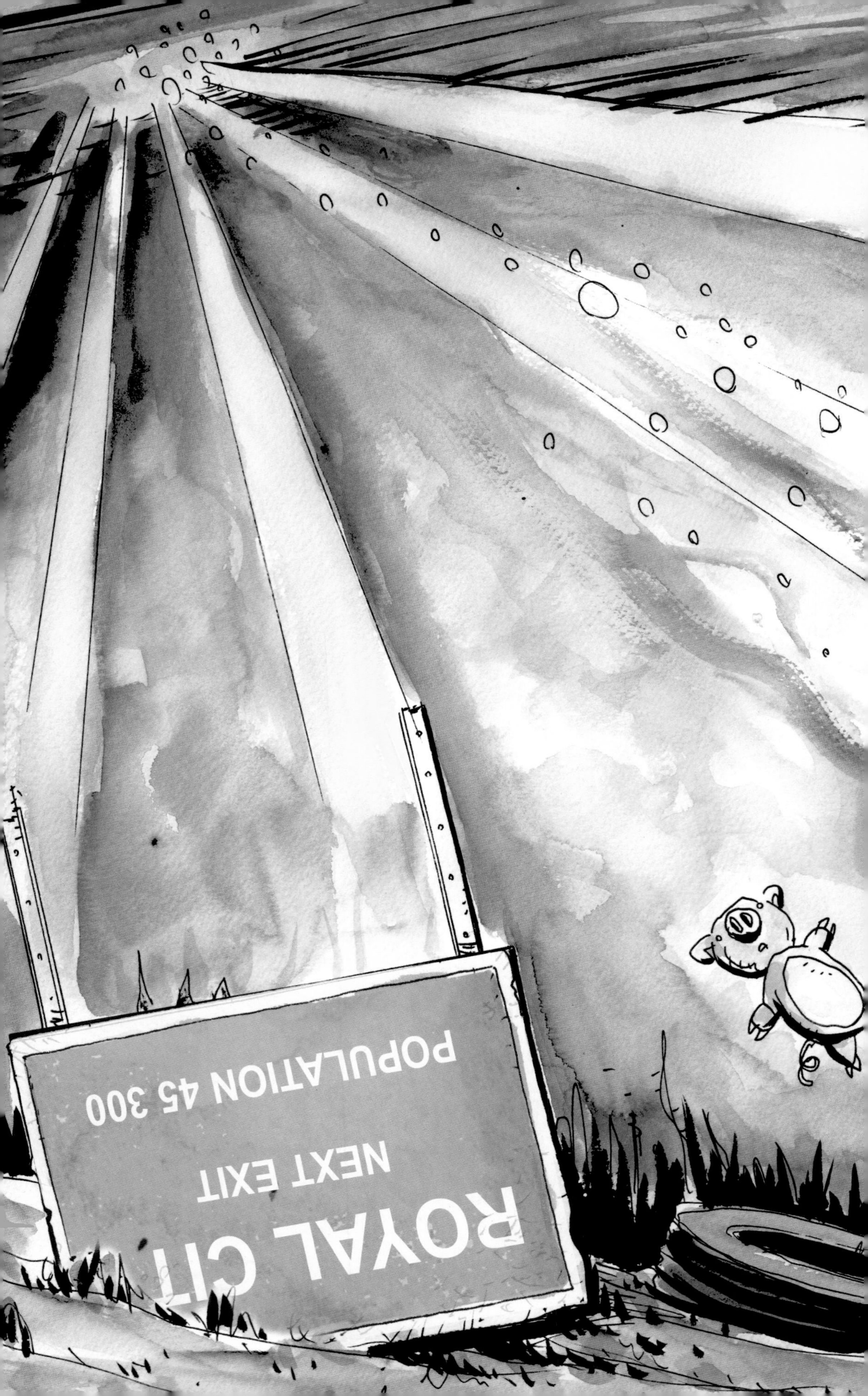
ROYAL CIT
NEXT EXIT
POPULATION 45 300

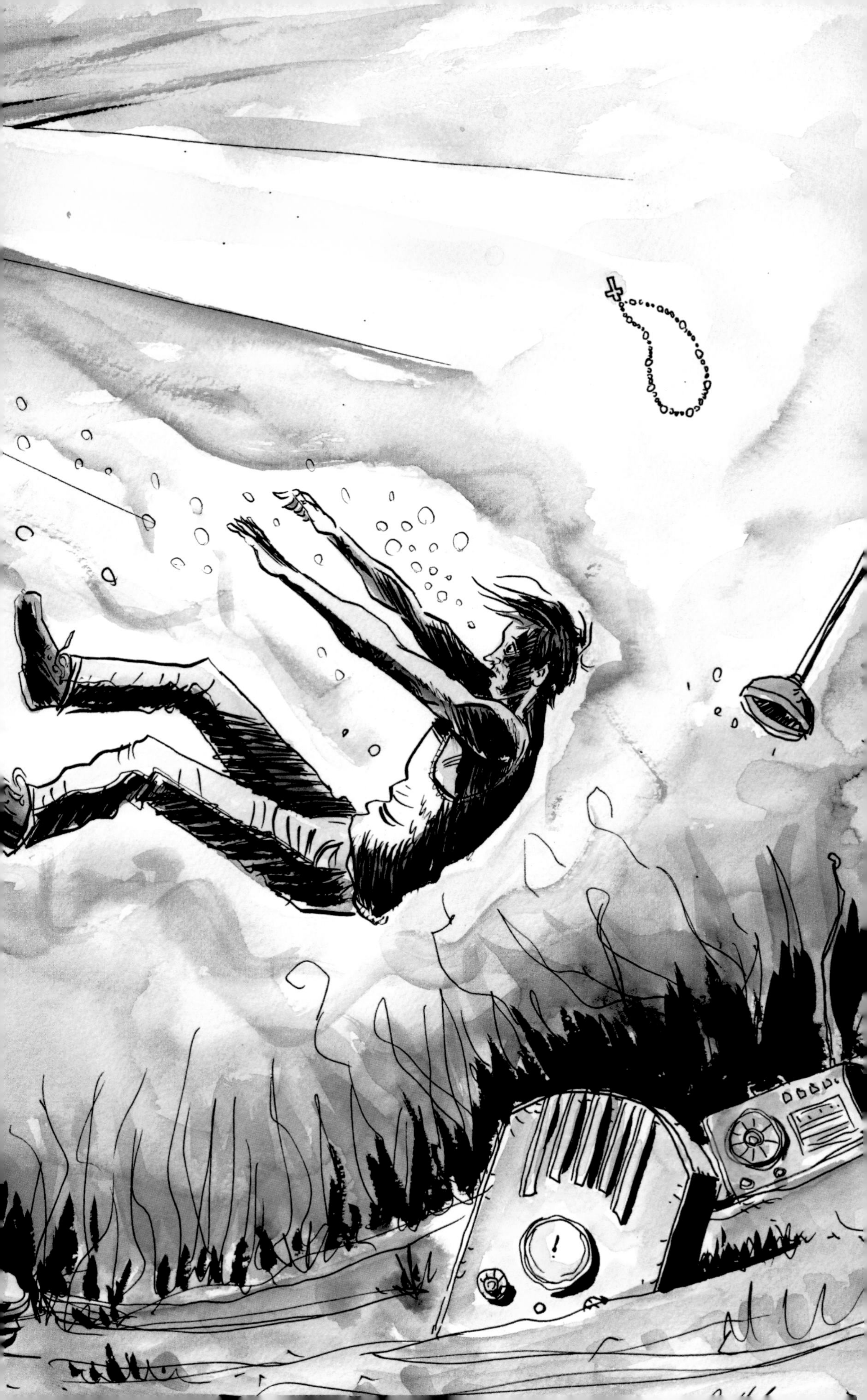

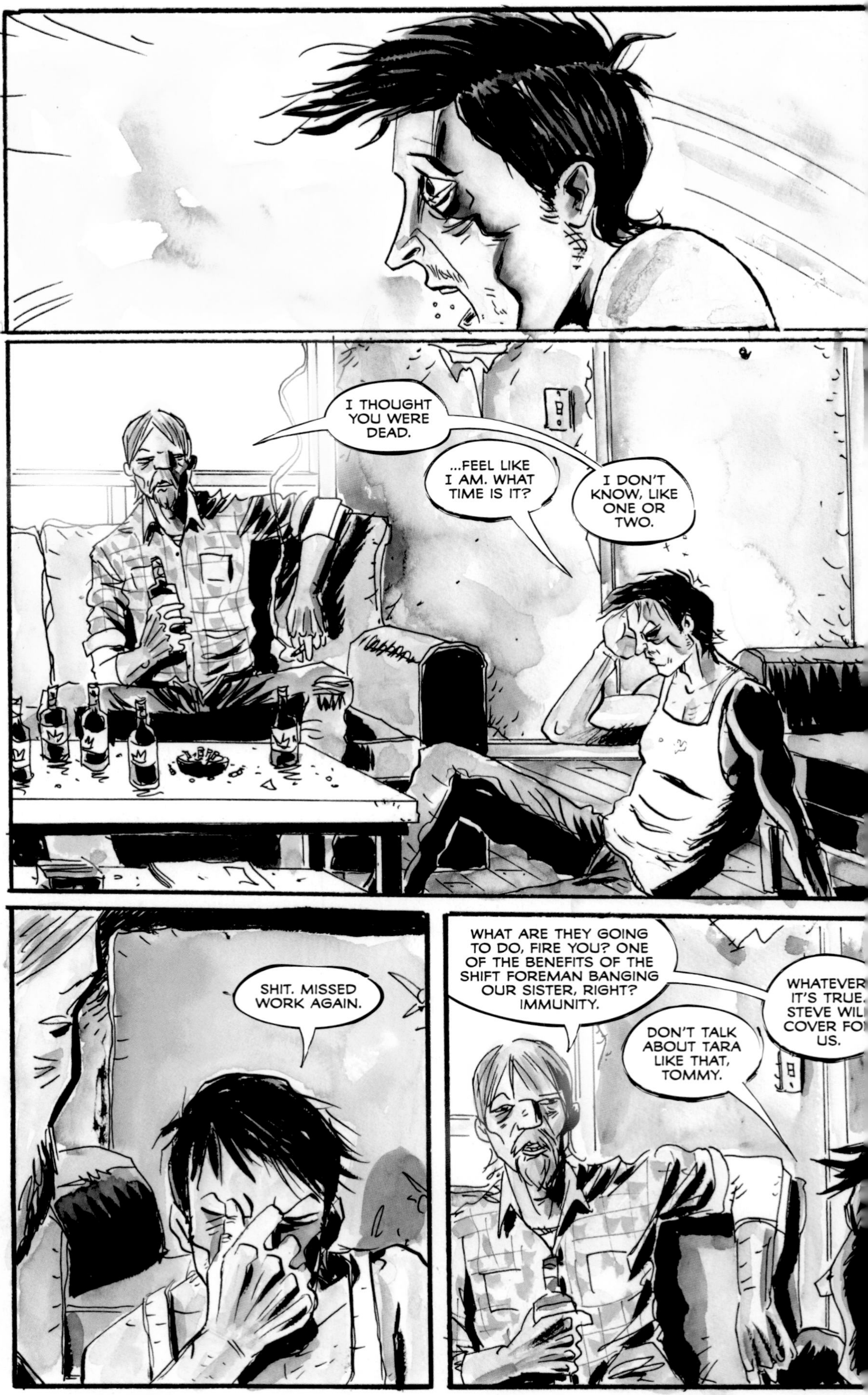
I THOUGHT YOU WERE DEAD.
...FEEL LIKE I AM. WHAT TIME IS IT?
I DON'T KNOW, LIKE ONE OR TWO.
SHIT. MISSED WORK AGAIN.
WHAT ARE THEY GOING TO DO, FIRE YOU? ONE OF THE BENEFITS OF THE SHIFT FOREMAN BANGING OUR SISTER, RIGHT? IMMUNITY.
DON'T TALK ABOUT TARA LIKE THAT, TOMMY.
WHATEVER IT'S TRUE. STEVE WIL COVER FO US.

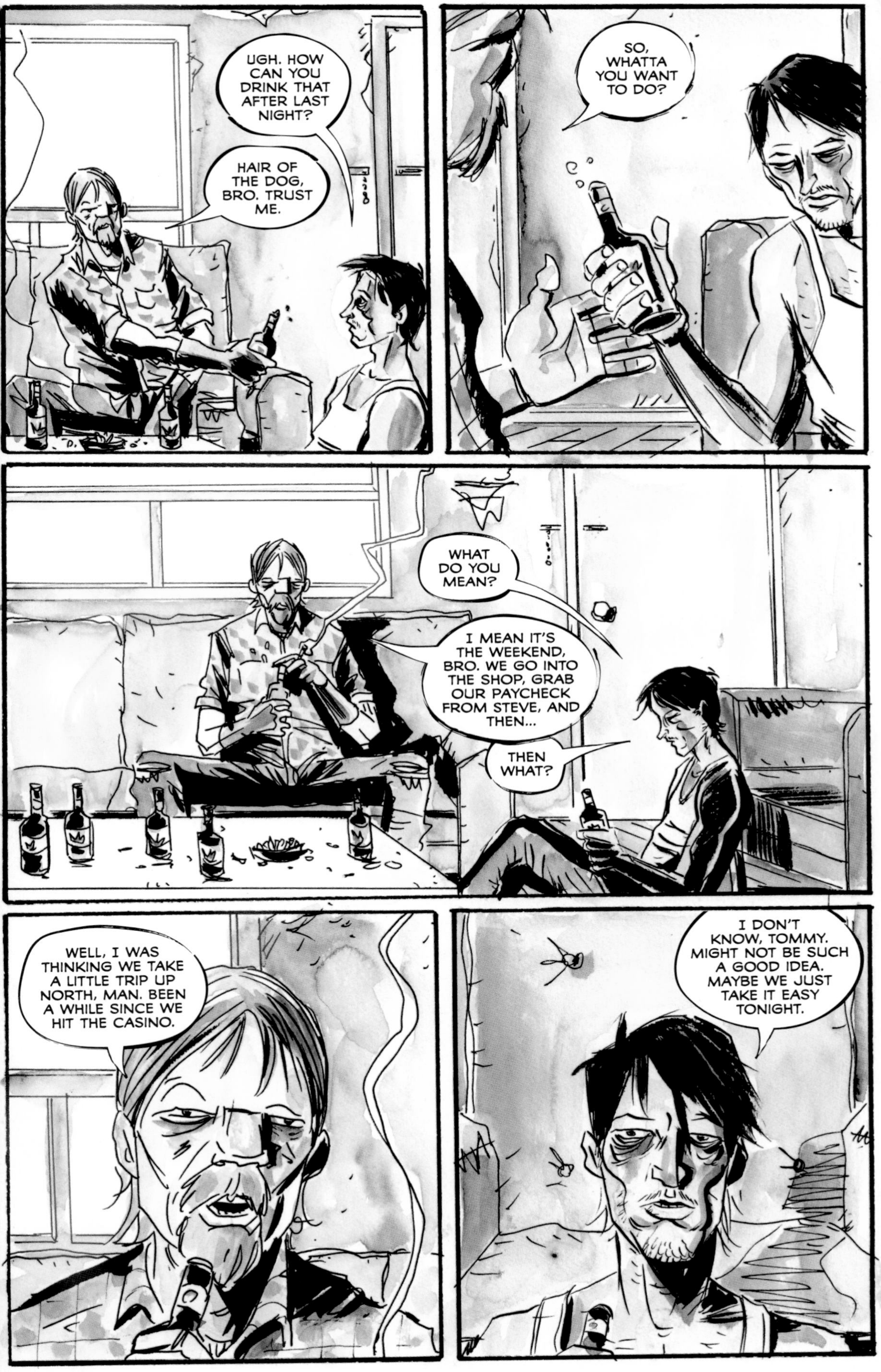
UGH. HOW CAN YOU DRINK THAT AFTER LAST NIGHT?
HAIR OF THE DOG, BRO. TRUST ME.
SO, WHATTA YOU WANT TO DO?
WHAT DO YOU MEAN?
I MEAN IT'S THE WEEKEND, BRO. WE GO INTO THE SHOP, GRAB OUR PAYCHECK FROM STEVE, AND THEN...
THEN WHAT?
WELL, I WAS THINKING WE TAKE A LITTLE TRIP UP NORTH, MAN. BEEN A WHILE SINCE WE HIT THE CASINO.
I DON'T KNOW, TOMMY. MIGHT NOT BE SUCH A GOOD IDEA. MAYBE WE JUST TAKE IT EASY TONIGHT.

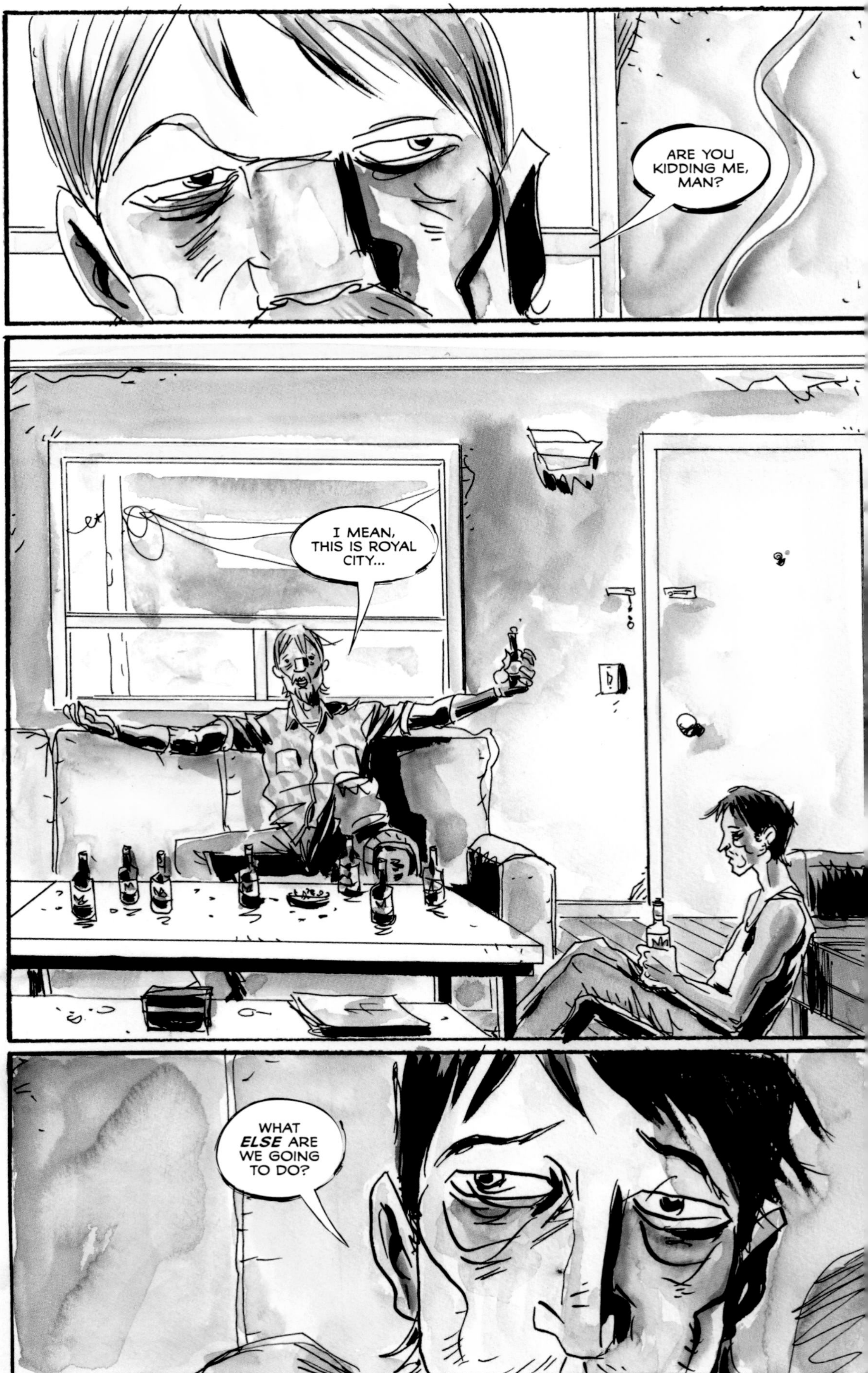
ARE YOU KIDDING ME, MAN?
I MEAN, THIS IS ROYAL CITY...
WHAT *ELSE* ARE WE GOING TO DO?

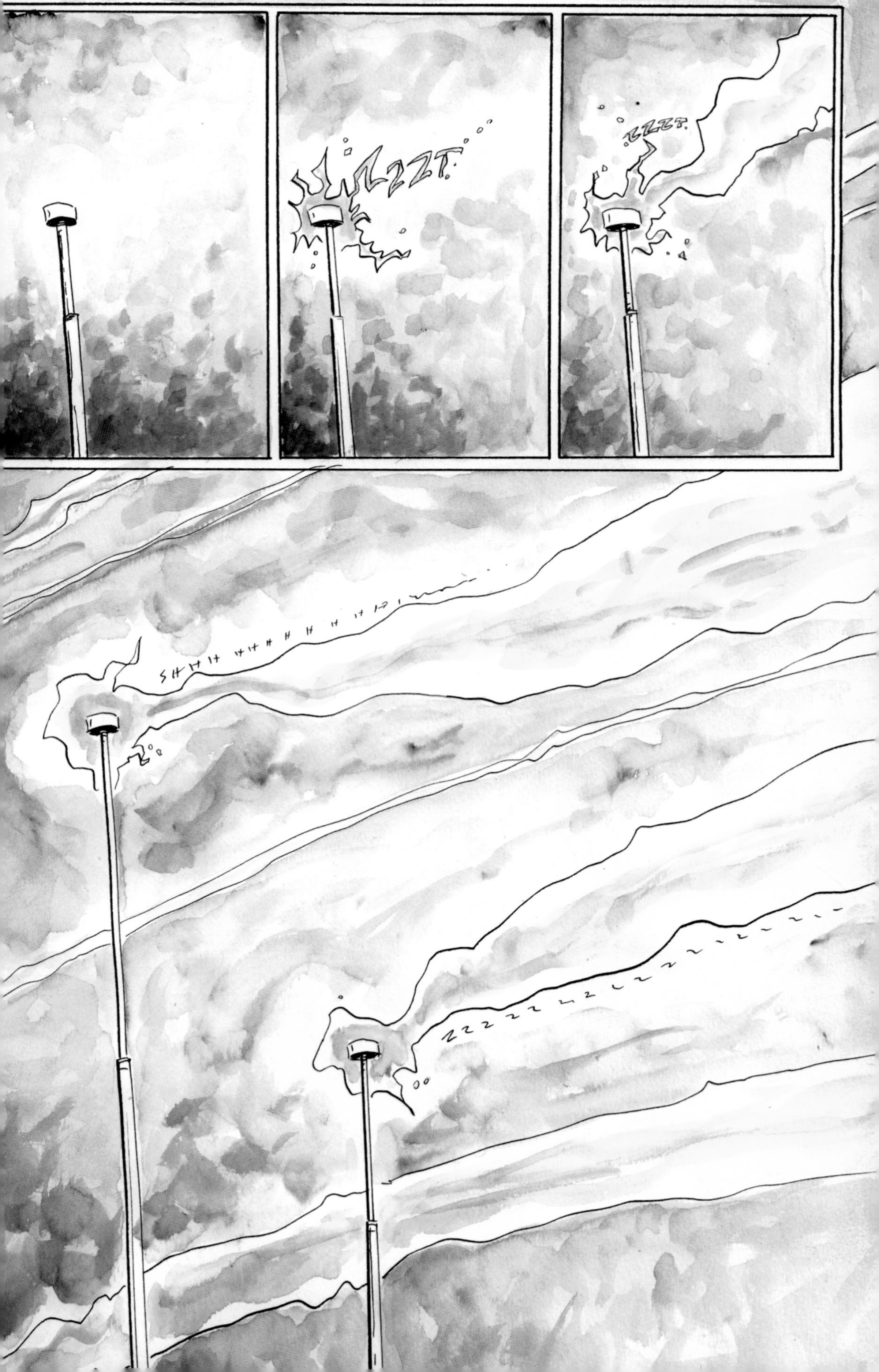
ZZZT.
ZZZT.

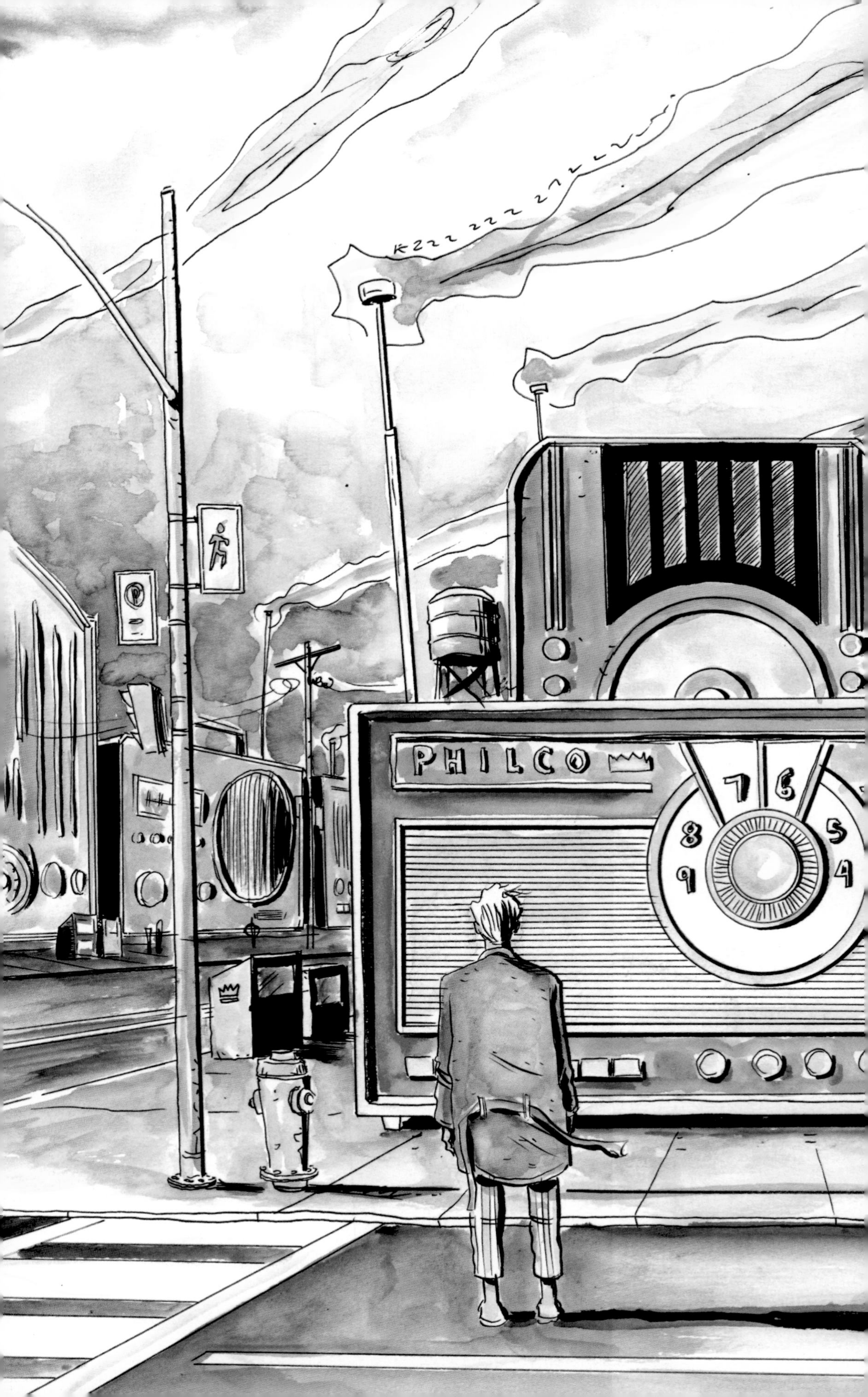
PHILCO

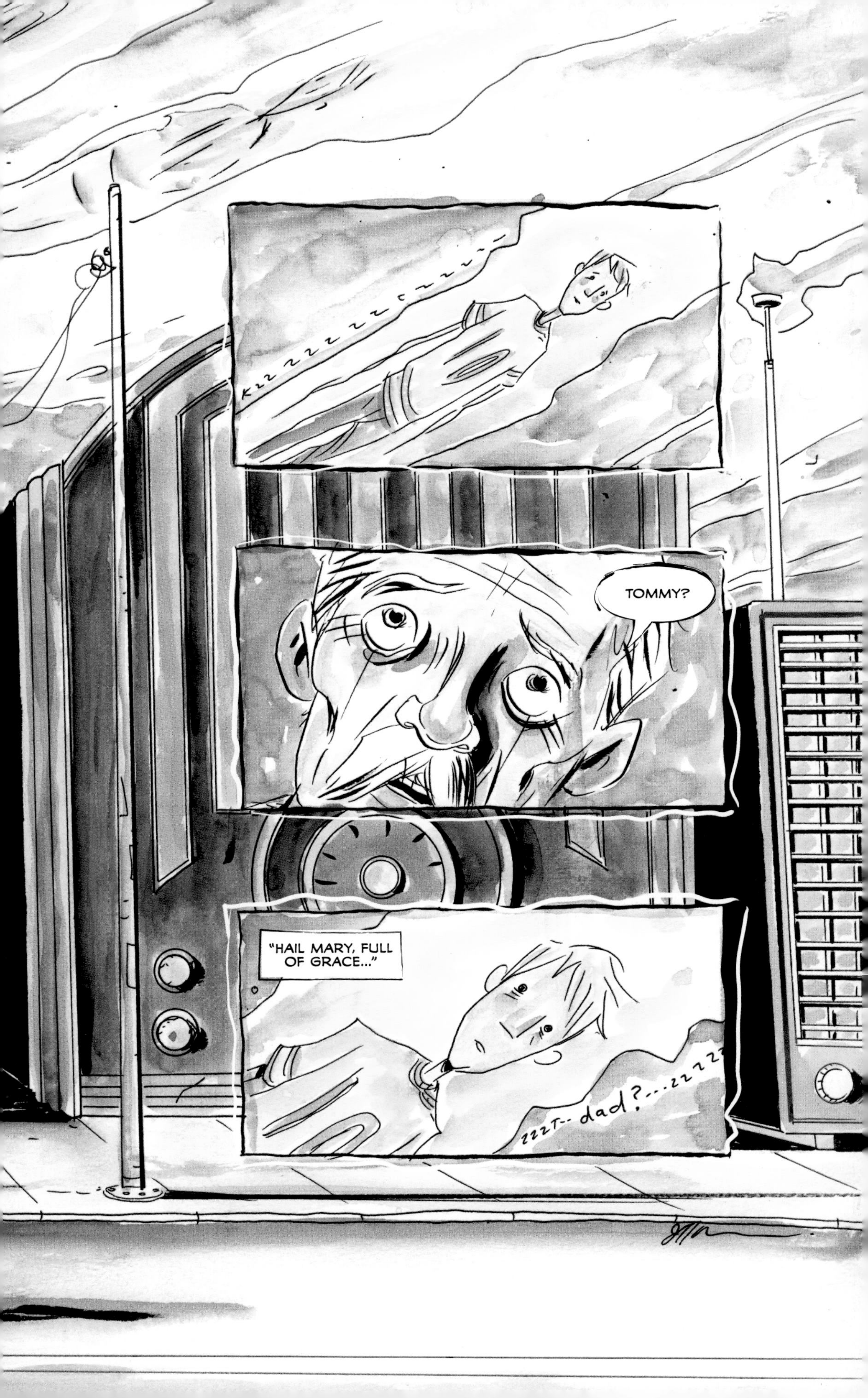
KZZZZZZZZZZZZZZZZ
TOMMY?
"HAIL MARY, FULL OF GRACE..."
ZZZT-- dad?...ZZZZZ

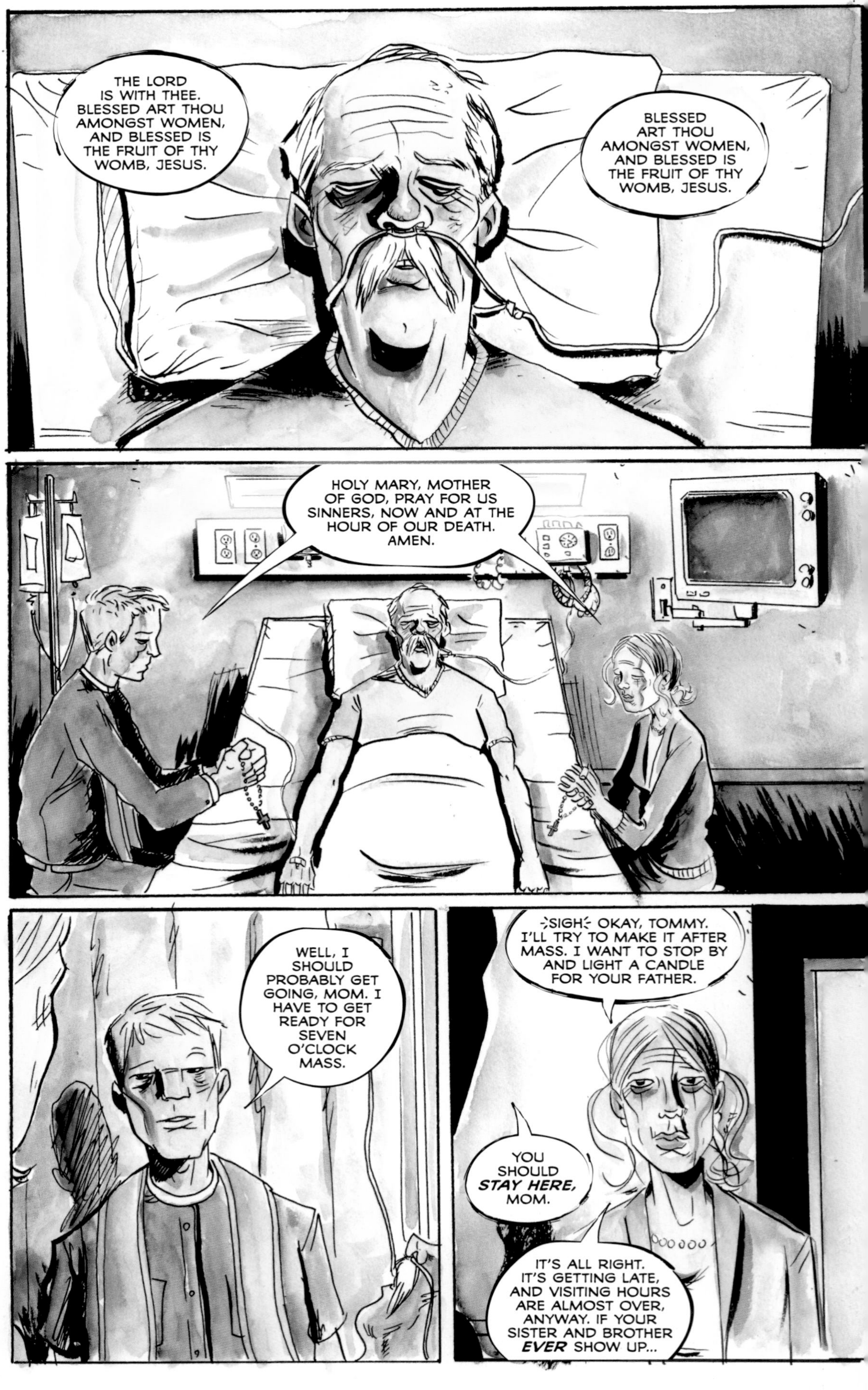
THE LORD IS WITH THEE. BLESSED ART THOU AMONGST WOMEN, AND BLESSED IS THE FRUIT OF THY WOMB, JESUS.
BLESSED ART THOU AMONGST WOMEN, AND BLESSED IS THE FRUIT OF THY WOMB, JESUS.
HOLY MARY, MOTHER OF GOD, PRAY FOR US SINNERS, NOW AND AT THE HOUR OF OUR DEATH. AMEN.
WELL, I SHOULD PROBABLY GET GOING, MOM. I HAVE TO GET READY FOR SEVEN O'CLOCK MASS.
-SIGH- OKAY, TOMMY. I'LL TRY TO MAKE IT AFTER MASS. I WANT TO STOP BY AND LIGHT A CANDLE FOR YOUR FATHER.
YOU SHOULD *STAY HERE,* MOM.
IT'S ALL RIGHT. IT'S GETTING LATE, AND VISITING HOURS ARE ALMOST OVER, ANYWAY. IF YOUR SISTER AND BROTHER *EVER* SHOW UP...

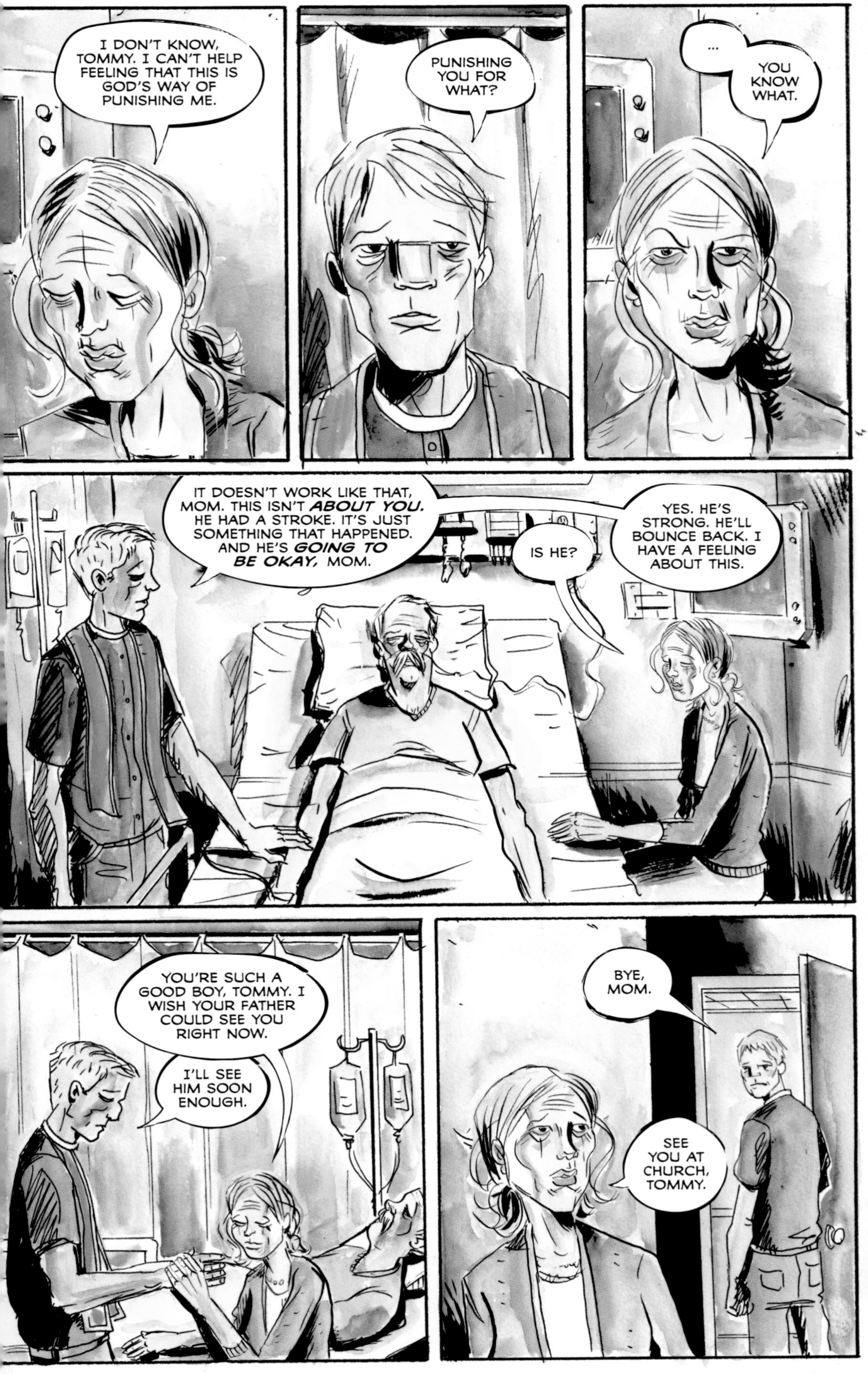
I DON'T KNOW, TOMMY. I CAN'T HELP FEELING THAT THIS IS GOD'S WAY OF PUNISHING ME.
PUNISHING YOU FOR WHAT?
...
YOU KNOW WHAT.
IT DOESN'T WORK LIKE THAT, MOM. THIS ISN'T ***ABOUT YOU.*** HE HAD A STROKE. IT'S JUST SOMETHING THAT HAPPENED. AND HE'S ***GOING TO BE OKAY,*** MOM.
IS HE?
YES. HE'S STRONG. HE'LL BOUNCE BACK. I HAVE A FEELING ABOUT THIS.
YOU'RE SUCH A GOOD BOY, TOMMY. I WISH YOUR FATHER COULD SEE YOU RIGHT NOW.
I'LL SEE HIM SOON ENOUGH.
BYE, MOM.
SEE YOU AT CHURCH, TOMMY.

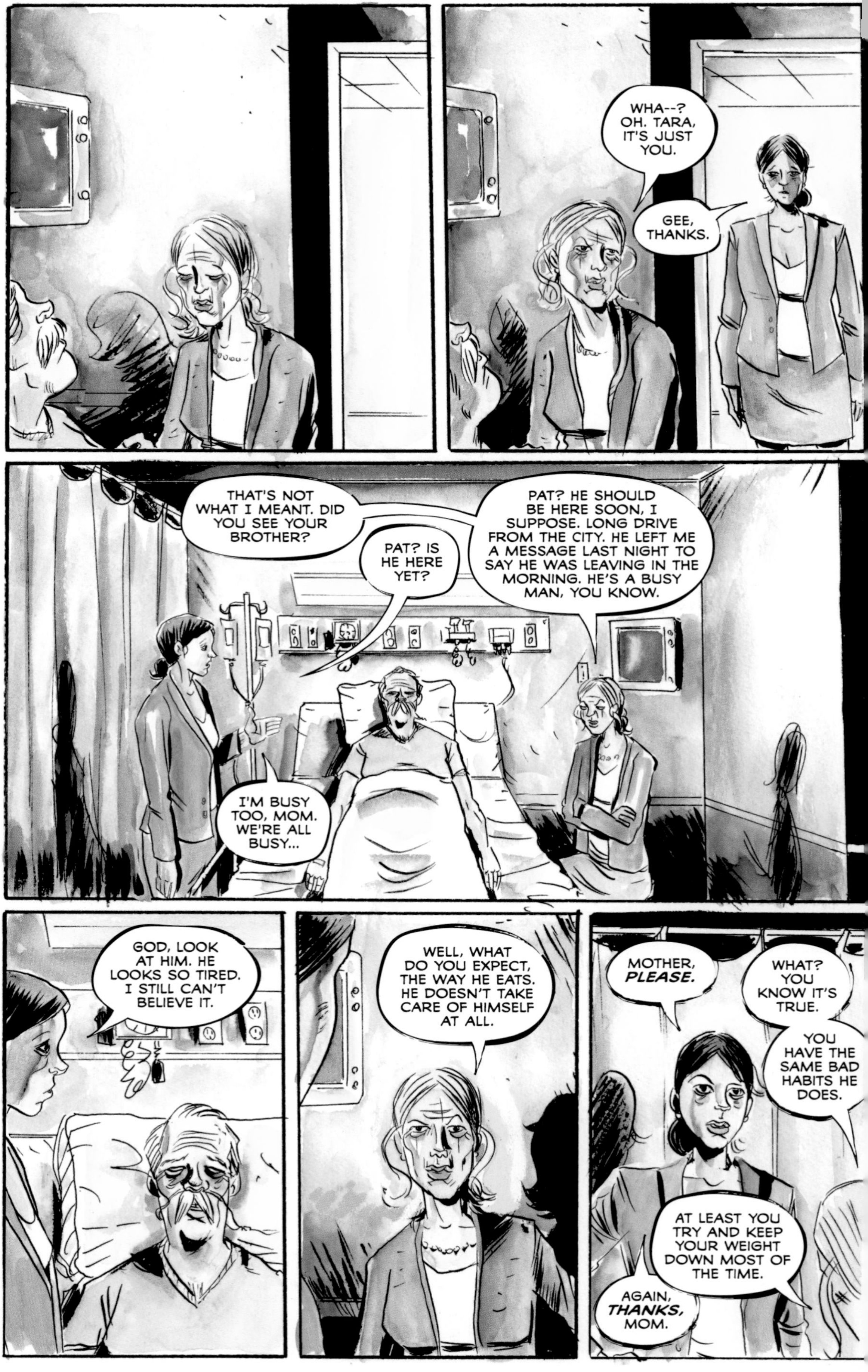
WHA--? OH. TARA, IT'S JUST YOU.
GEE, THANKS.
THAT'S NOT WHAT I MEANT. DID YOU SEE YOUR BROTHER?
PAT? IS HE HERE YET?
PAT? HE SHOULD BE HERE SOON, I SUPPOSE. LONG DRIVE FROM THE CITY. HE LEFT ME A MESSAGE LAST NIGHT TO SAY HE WAS LEAVING IN THE MORNING. HE'S A BUSY MAN, YOU KNOW.
I'M BUSY TOO, MOM. WE'RE ALL BUSY...
GOD, LOOK AT HIM. HE LOOKS SO TIRED. I STILL CAN'T BELIEVE IT.
WELL, WHAT DO YOU EXPECT, THE WAY HE EATS. HE DOESN'T TAKE CARE OF HIMSELF AT ALL.
MOTHER, *PLEASE.*
WHAT? YOU KNOW IT'S TRUE.
YOU HAVE THE SAME BAD HABITS HE DOES.
AT LEAST YOU TRY AND KEEP YOUR WEIGHT DOWN MOST OF THE TIME.
AGAIN, ***THANKS,*** MOM.

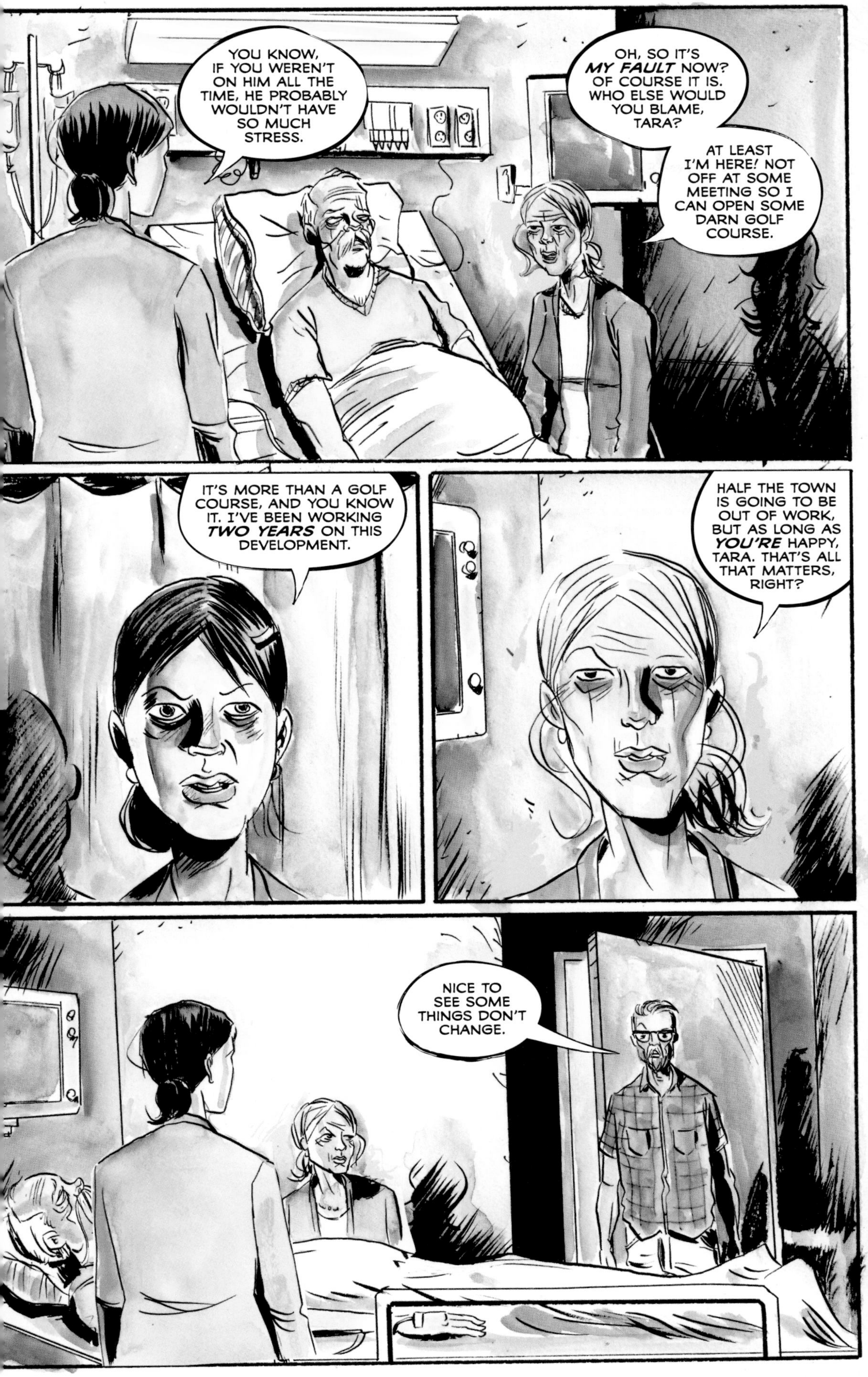
YOU KNOW, IF YOU WEREN'T ON HIM ALL THE TIME, HE PROBABLY WOULDN'T HAVE SO MUCH STRESS.
OH, SO IT'S *MY FAULT* NOW? OF COURSE IT IS. WHO ELSE WOULD YOU BLAME, TARA?
AT LEAST I'M HERE! NOT OFF AT SOME MEETING SO I CAN OPEN SOME DARN GOLF COURSE.
IT'S MORE THAN A GOLF COURSE, AND YOU KNOW IT. I'VE BEEN WORKING *TWO YEARS* ON THIS DEVELOPMENT.
HALF THE TOWN IS GOING TO BE OUT OF WORK, BUT AS LONG AS *YOU'RE* HAPPY, TARA. THAT'S ALL THAT MATTERS, RIGHT?
NICE TO SEE SOME THINGS DON'T CHANGE.

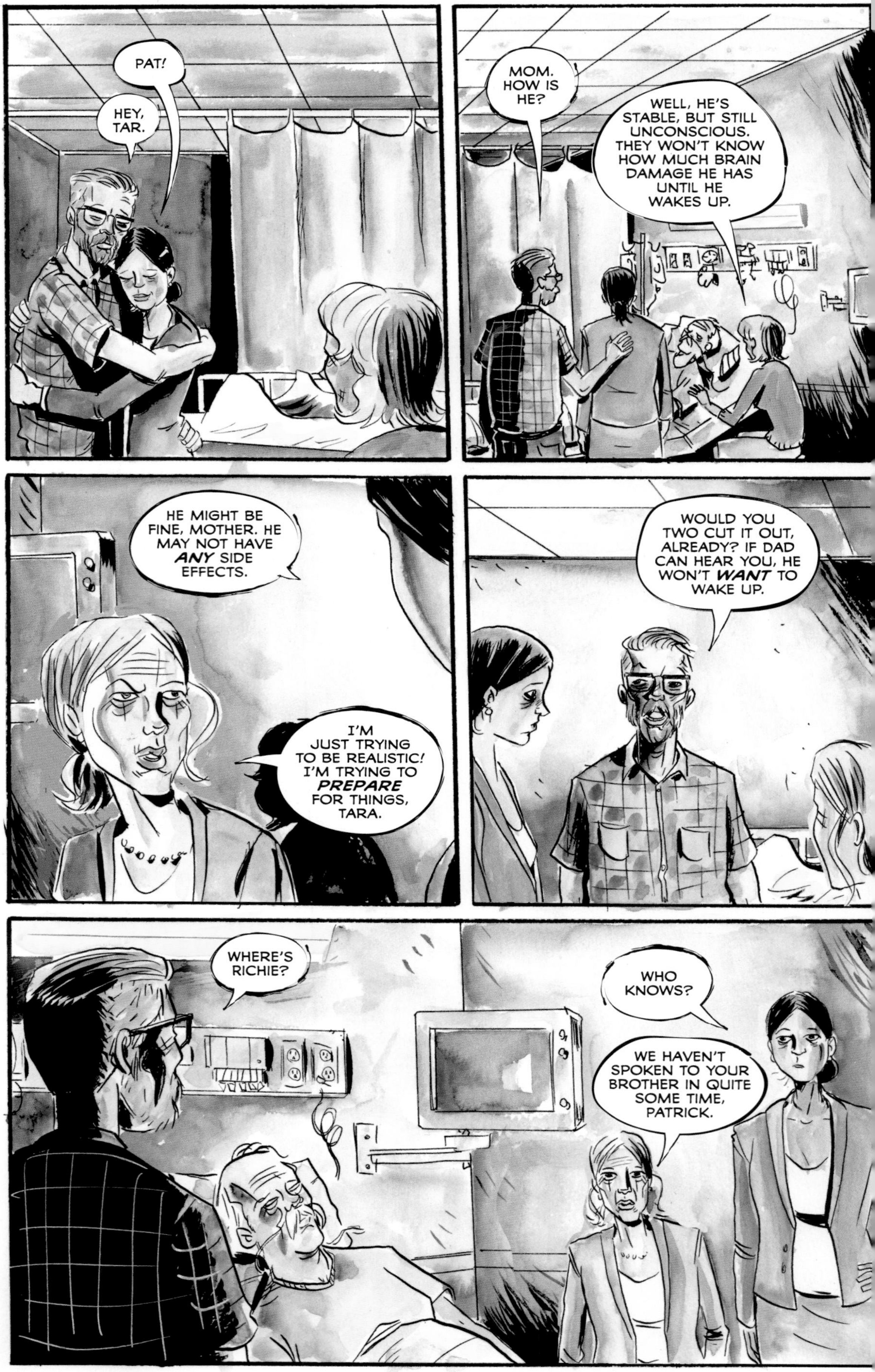
PAT!
HEY, TAR.
MOM. HOW IS HE?
WELL, HE'S STABLE, BUT STILL UNCONSCIOUS. THEY WON'T KNOW HOW MUCH BRAIN DAMAGE HE HAS UNTIL HE WAKES UP.
HE MIGHT BE FINE, MOTHER. HE MAY NOT HAVE ANY SIDE EFFECTS.
I'M JUST TRYING TO BE REALISTIC! I'M TRYING TO PREPARE FOR THINGS, TARA.
WOULD YOU TWO CUT IT OUT, ALREADY? IF DAD CAN HEAR YOU, HE WON'T WANT TO WAKE UP.
WHERE'S RICHIE?
WHO KNOWS?
WE HAVEN'T SPOKEN TO YOUR BROTHER IN QUITE SOME TIME, PATRICK.

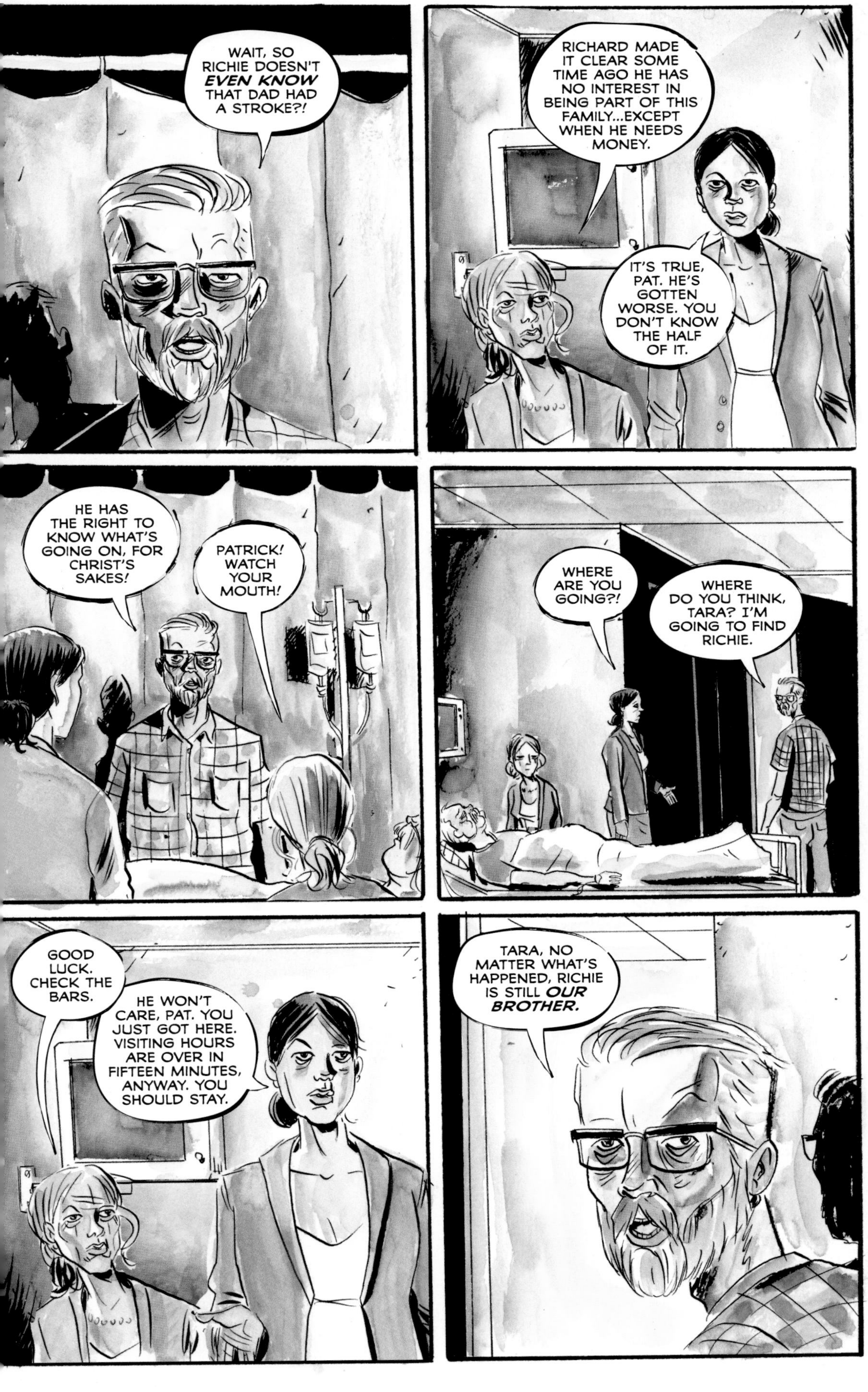
WAIT, SO RICHIE DOESN'T ***EVEN KNOW*** THAT DAD HAD A STROKE?!
RICHARD MADE IT CLEAR SOME TIME AGO HE HAS NO INTEREST IN BEING PART OF THIS FAMILY...EXCEPT WHEN HE NEEDS MONEY.
IT'S TRUE, PAT. HE'S GOTTEN WORSE. YOU DON'T KNOW THE HALF OF IT.
HE HAS THE RIGHT TO KNOW WHAT'S GOING ON, FOR CHRIST'S SAKES!
PATRICK! WATCH YOUR MOUTH!
WHERE ARE YOU GOING?!
WHERE DO YOU THINK, TARA? I'M GOING TO FIND RICHIE.
GOOD LUCK. CHECK THE BARS.
HE WON'T CARE, PAT. YOU JUST GOT HERE. VISITING HOURS ARE OVER IN FIFTEEN MINUTES, ANYWAY. YOU SHOULD STAY.
TARA, NO MATTER WHAT'S HAPPENED, RICHIE IS STILL ***OUR BROTHER.***

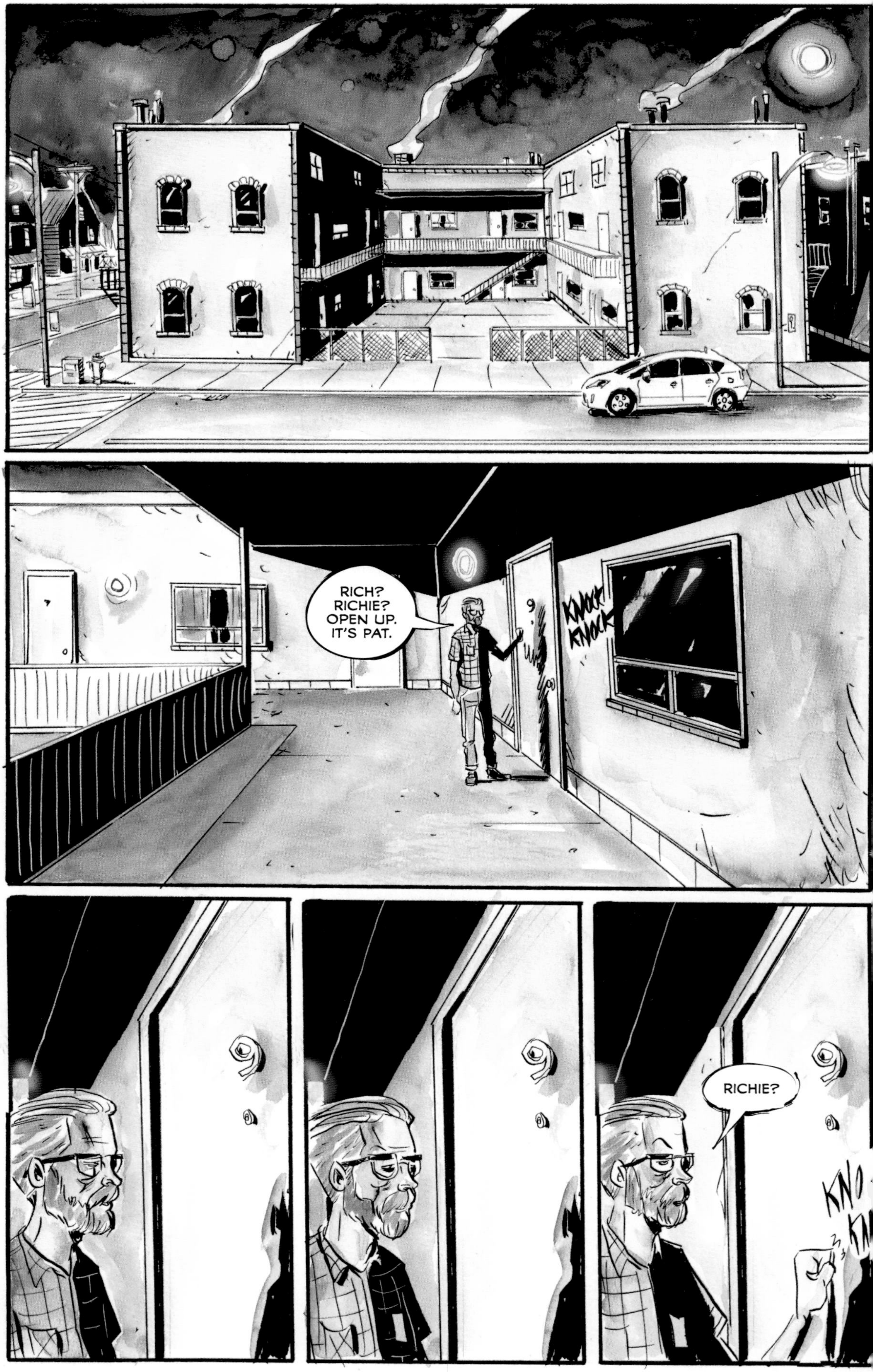
RICH? RICHIE? OPEN UP. IT'S PAT.
KNOCK! KNOCK
RICHIE?

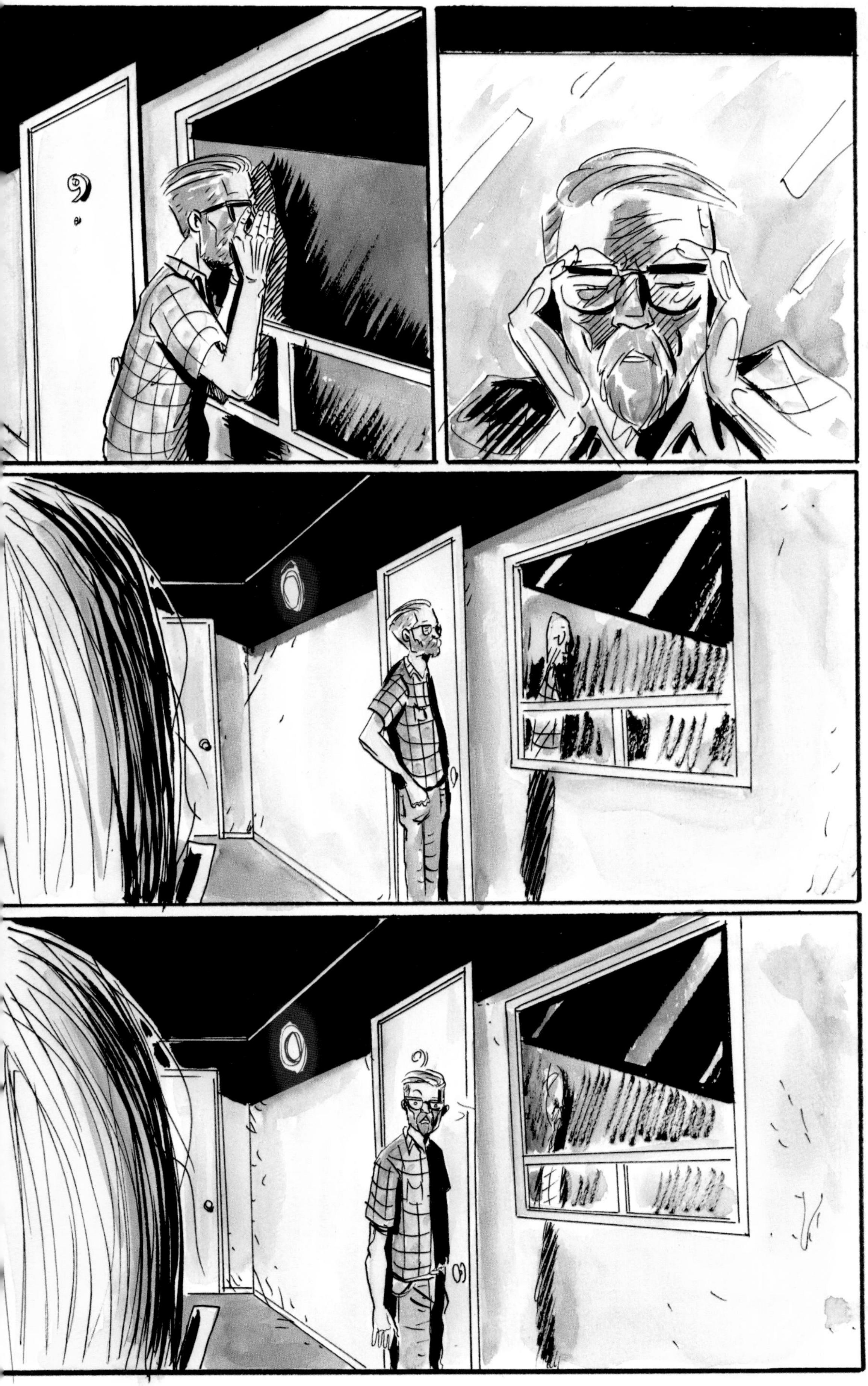

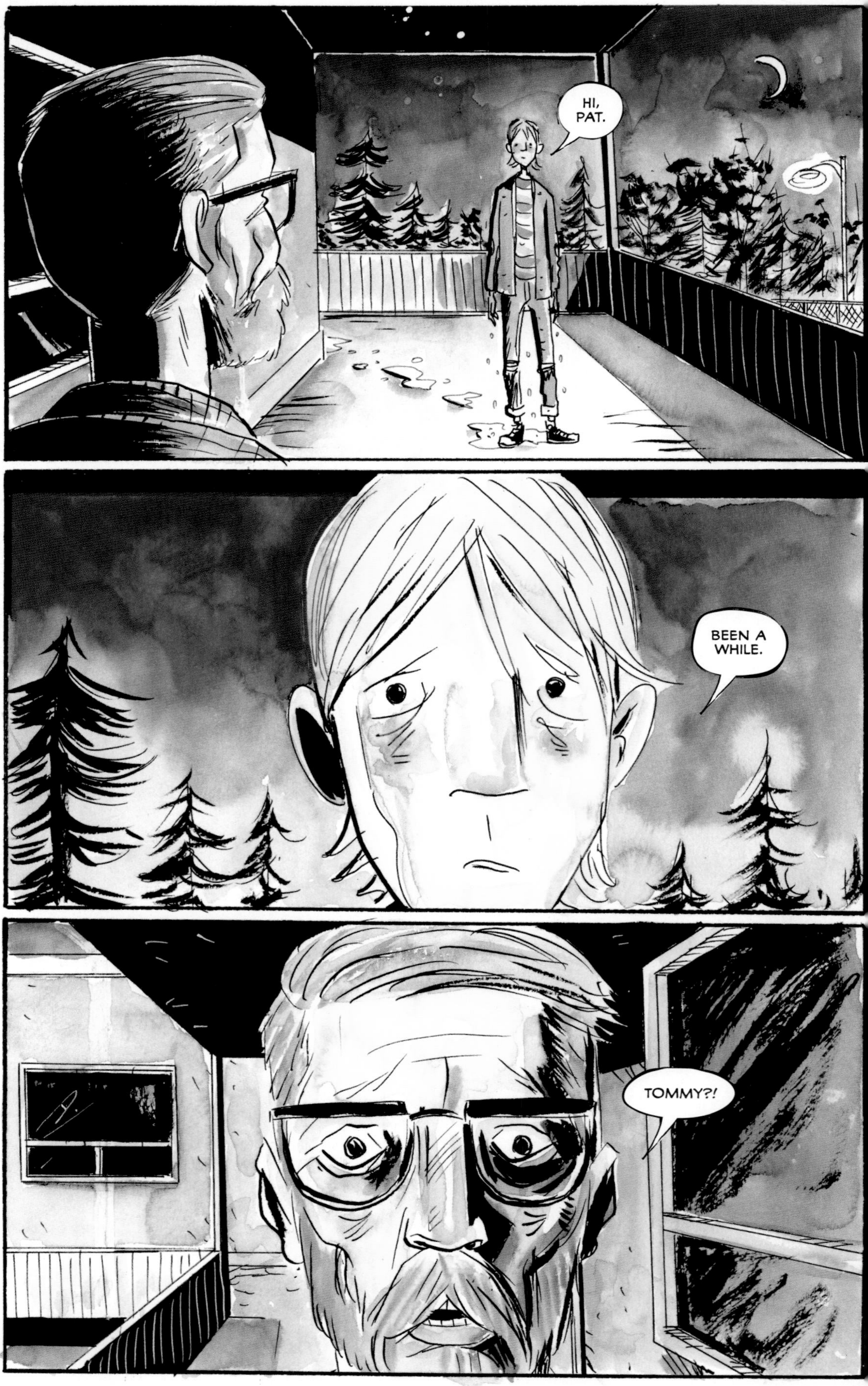
HI, PAT.
BEEN A WHILE.
TOMMY?!

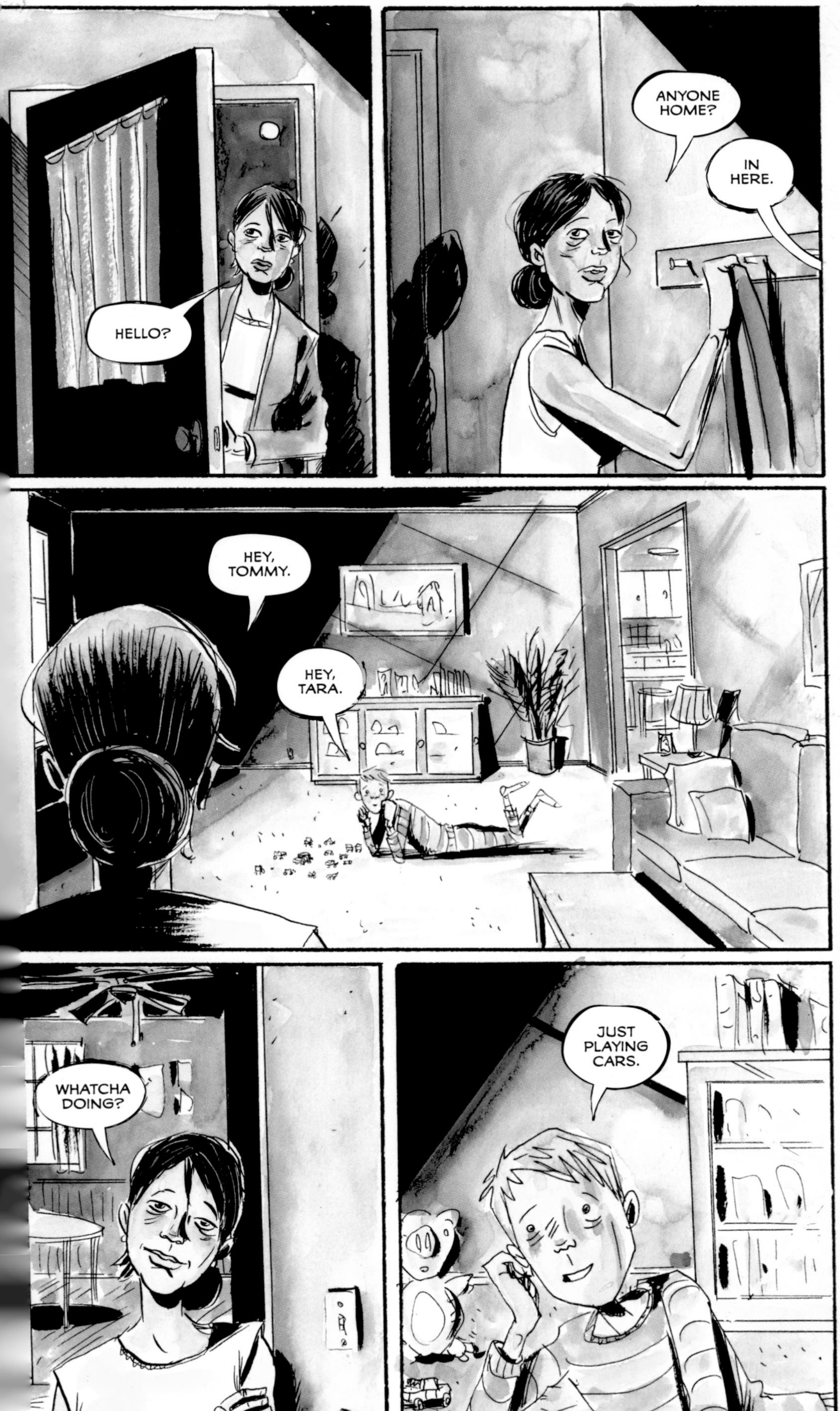
HELLO?
ANYONE HOME?
IN HERE.
HEY, TOMMY.
HEY, TARA.
WHATCHA DOING?
JUST PLAYING CARS.

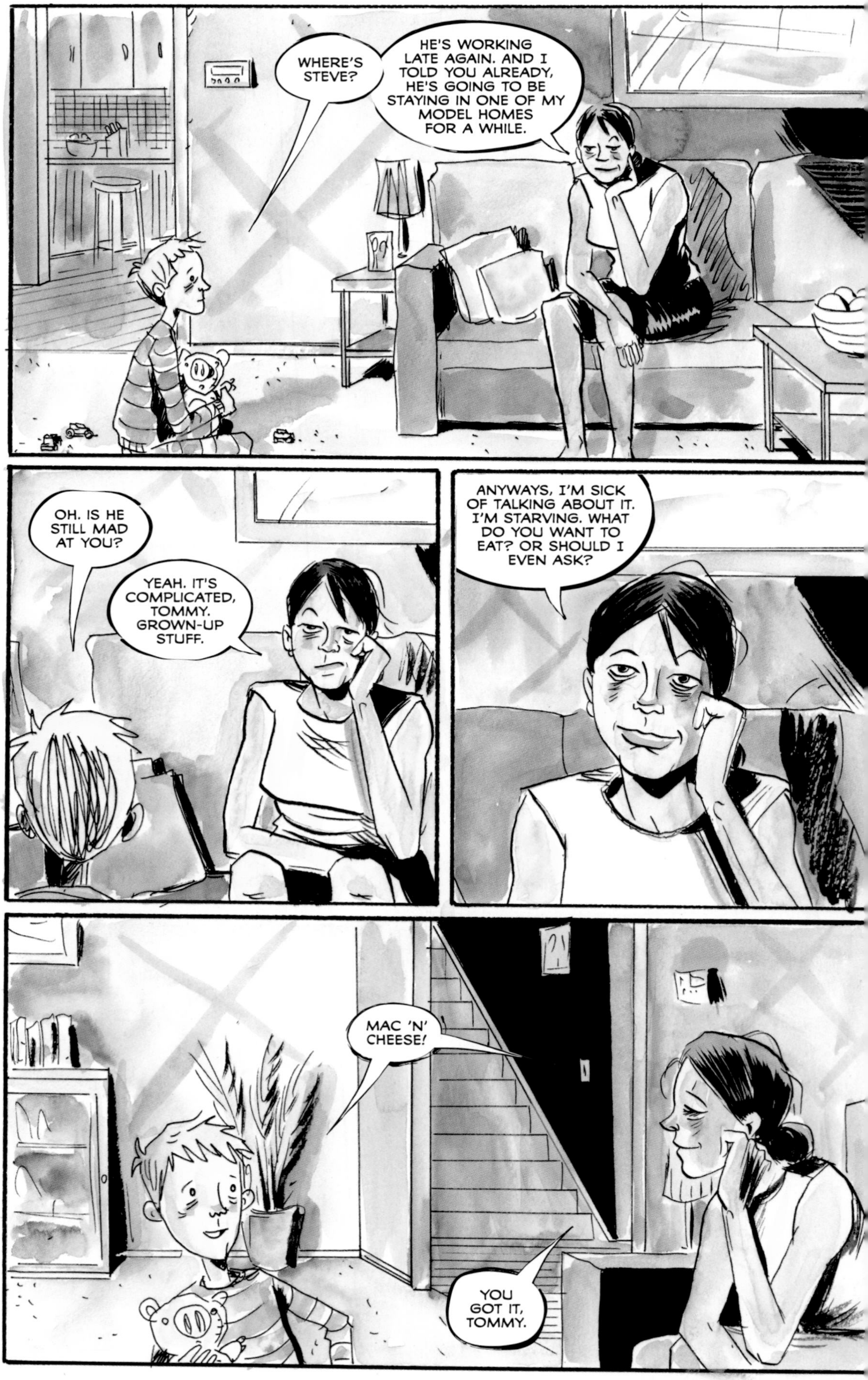
WHERE'S STEVE?
HE'S WORKING LATE AGAIN. AND I TOLD YOU ALREADY, HE'S GOING TO BE STAYING IN ONE OF MY MODEL HOMES FOR A WHILE.
OH. IS HE STILL MAD AT YOU?
YEAH. IT'S COMPLICATED, TOMMY. GROWN-UP STUFF.
ANYWAYS, I'M SICK OF TALKING ABOUT IT. I'M STARVING. WHAT DO YOU WANT TO EAT? OR SHOULD I EVEN ASK?
MAC 'N' CHEESE!
YOU GOT IT, TOMMY.

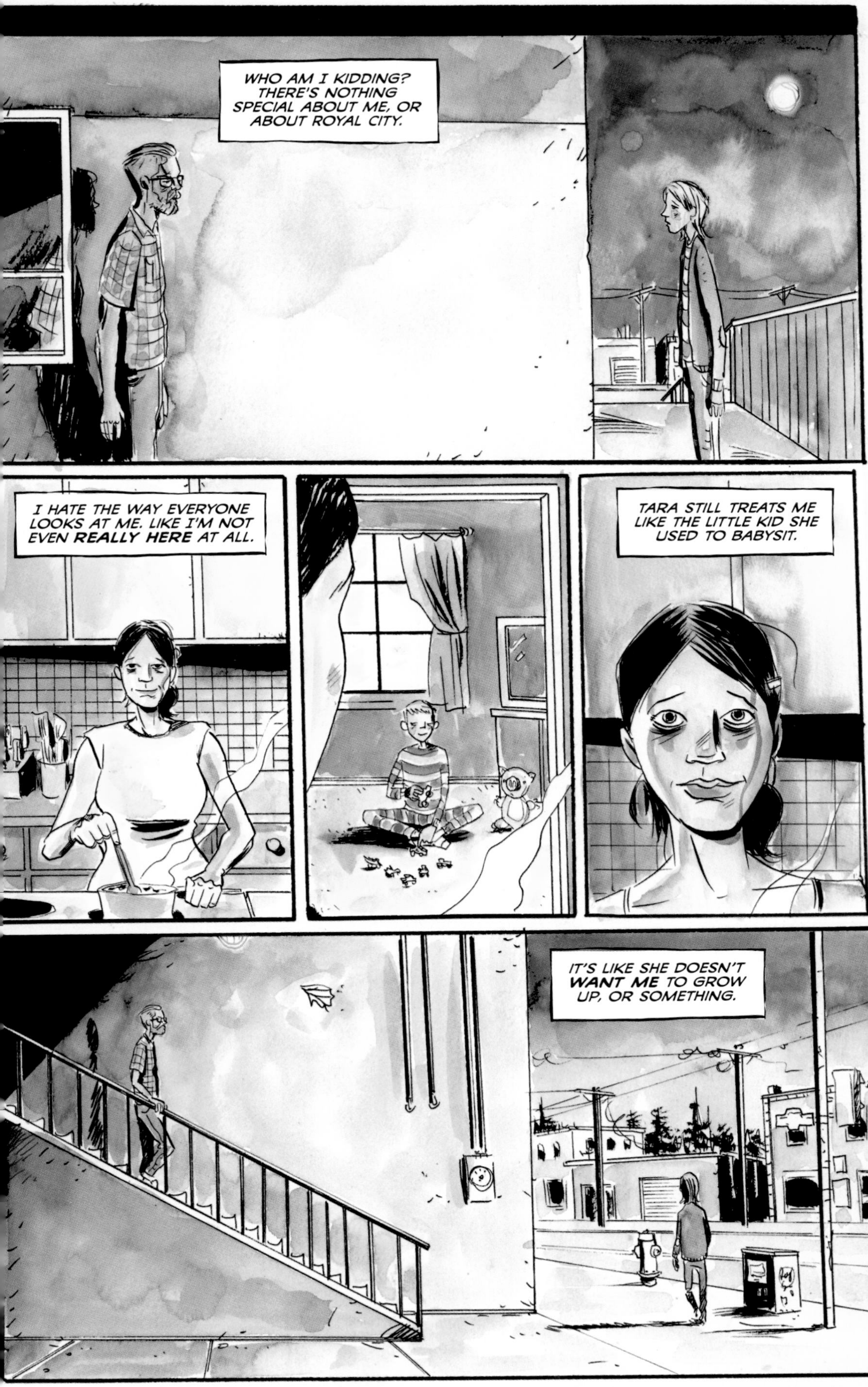
WHO AM I KIDDING? THERE'S NOTHING SPECIAL ABOUT ME, OR ABOUT ROYAL CITY.
I HATE THE WAY EVERYONE LOOKS AT ME. LIKE I'M NOT EVEN **REALLY HERE** AT ALL.
TARA STILL TREATS ME LIKE THE LITTLE KID SHE USED TO BABYSIT.
IT'S LIKE SHE DOESN'T **WANT ME** TO GROW UP, OR SOMETHING.

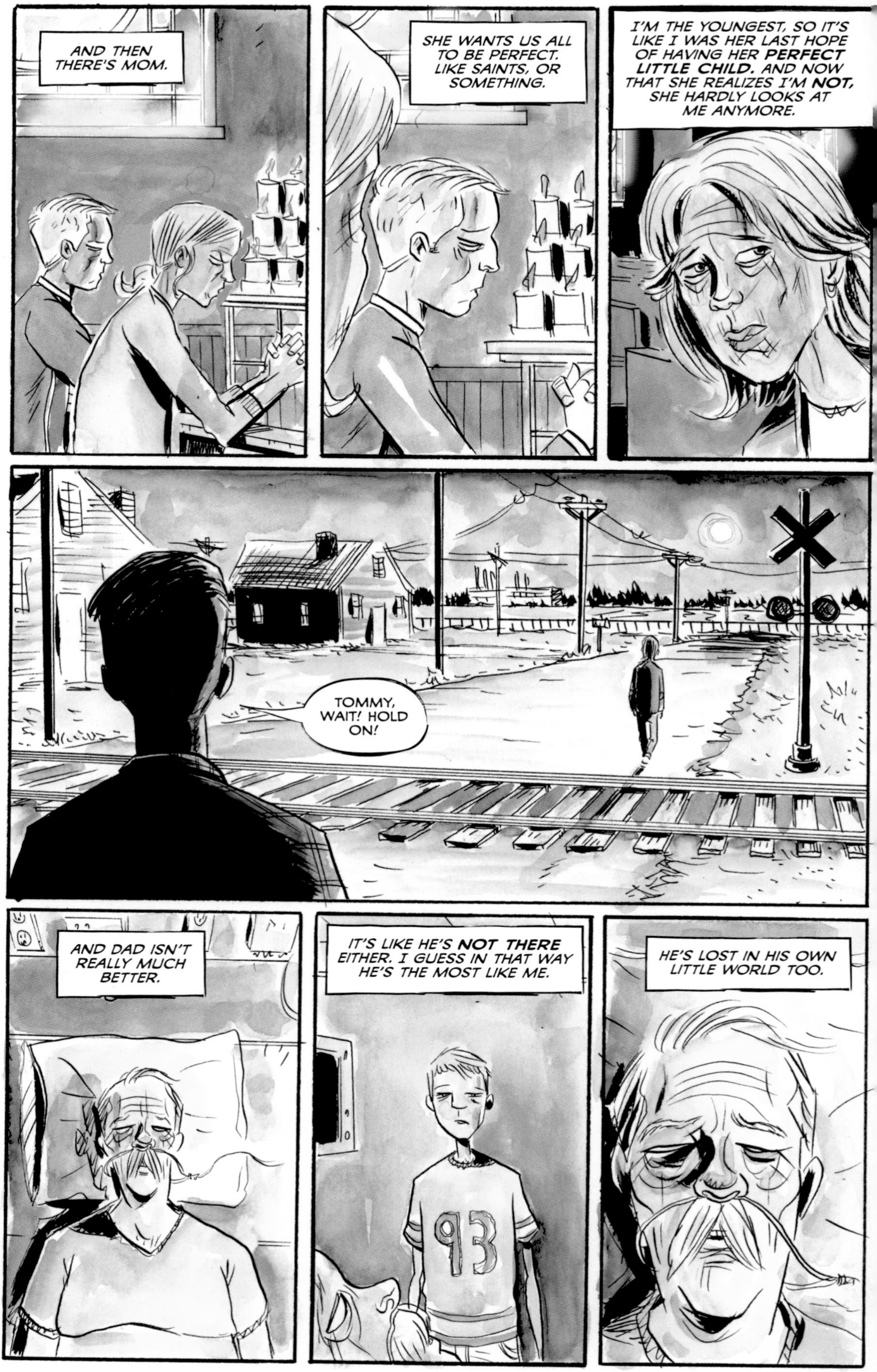
AND THEN THERE'S MOM.
SHE WANTS US ALL TO BE PERFECT. LIKE SAINTS, OR SOMETHING.
I'M THE YOUNGEST, SO IT'S LIKE I WAS HER LAST HOPE OF HAVING HER PERFECT LITTLE CHILD. AND NOW THAT SHE REALIZES I'M NOT, SHE HARDLY LOOKS AT ME ANYMORE.
TOMMY, WAIT! HOLD ON!
AND DAD ISN'T REALLY MUCH BETTER.
IT'S LIKE HE'S NOT THERE EITHER. I GUESS IN THAT WAY HE'S THE MOST LIKE ME.
HE'S LOST IN HIS OWN LITTLE WORLD TOO.

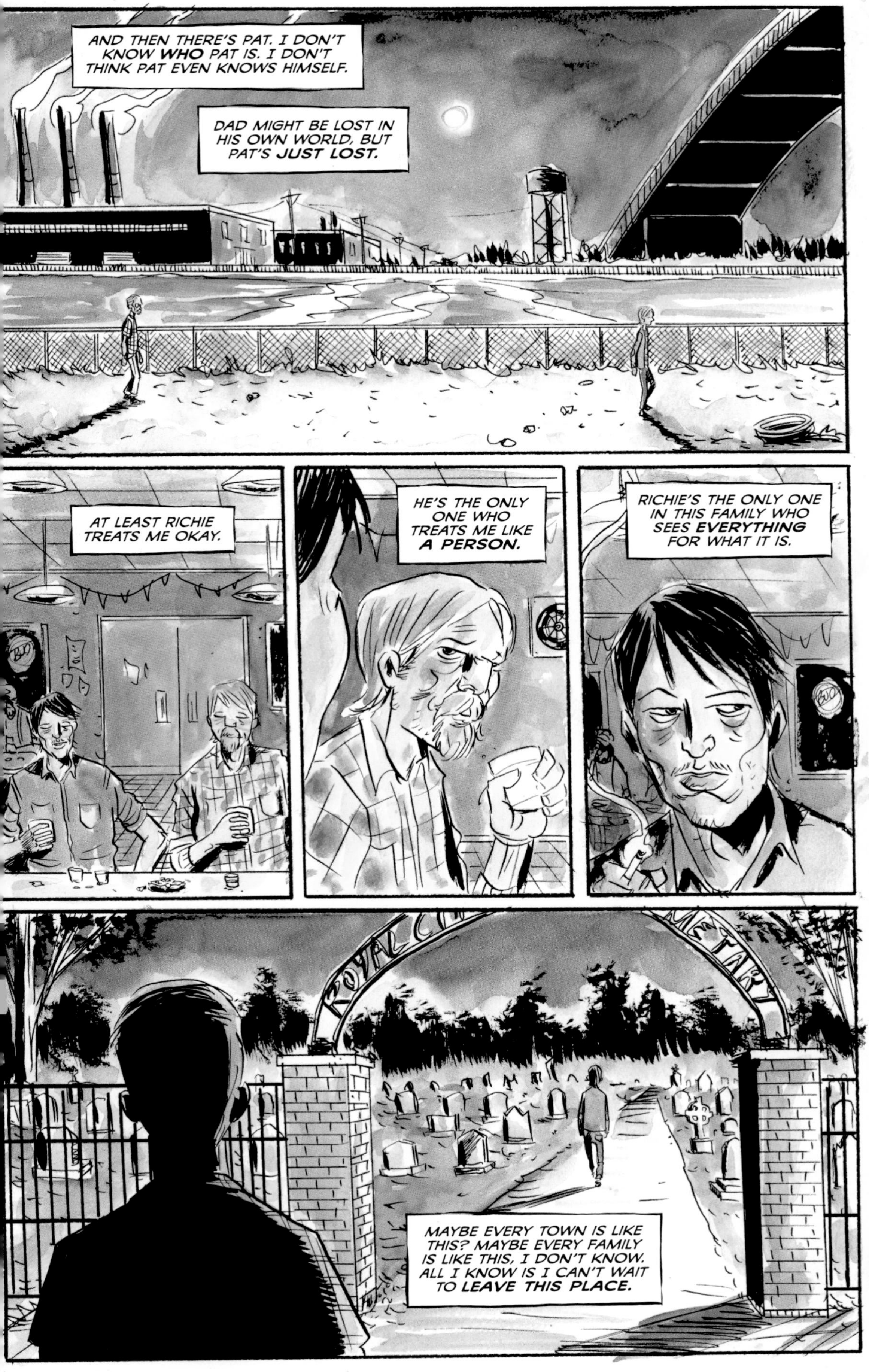
AND THEN THERE'S PAT. I DON'T KNOW WHO PAT IS. I DON'T THINK PAT EVEN KNOWS HIMSELF.
DAD MIGHT BE LOST IN HIS OWN WORLD, BUT PAT'S JUST LOST.
AT LEAST RICHIE TREATS ME OKAY.
HE'S THE ONLY ONE WHO TREATS ME LIKE A PERSON.
RICHIE'S THE ONLY ONE IN THIS FAMILY WHO SEES EVERYTHING FOR WHAT IT IS.
MAYBE EVERY TOWN IS LIKE THIS? MAYBE EVERY FAMILY IS LIKE THIS, I DON'T KNOW. ALL I KNOW IS I CAN'T WAIT TO LEAVE THIS PLACE.

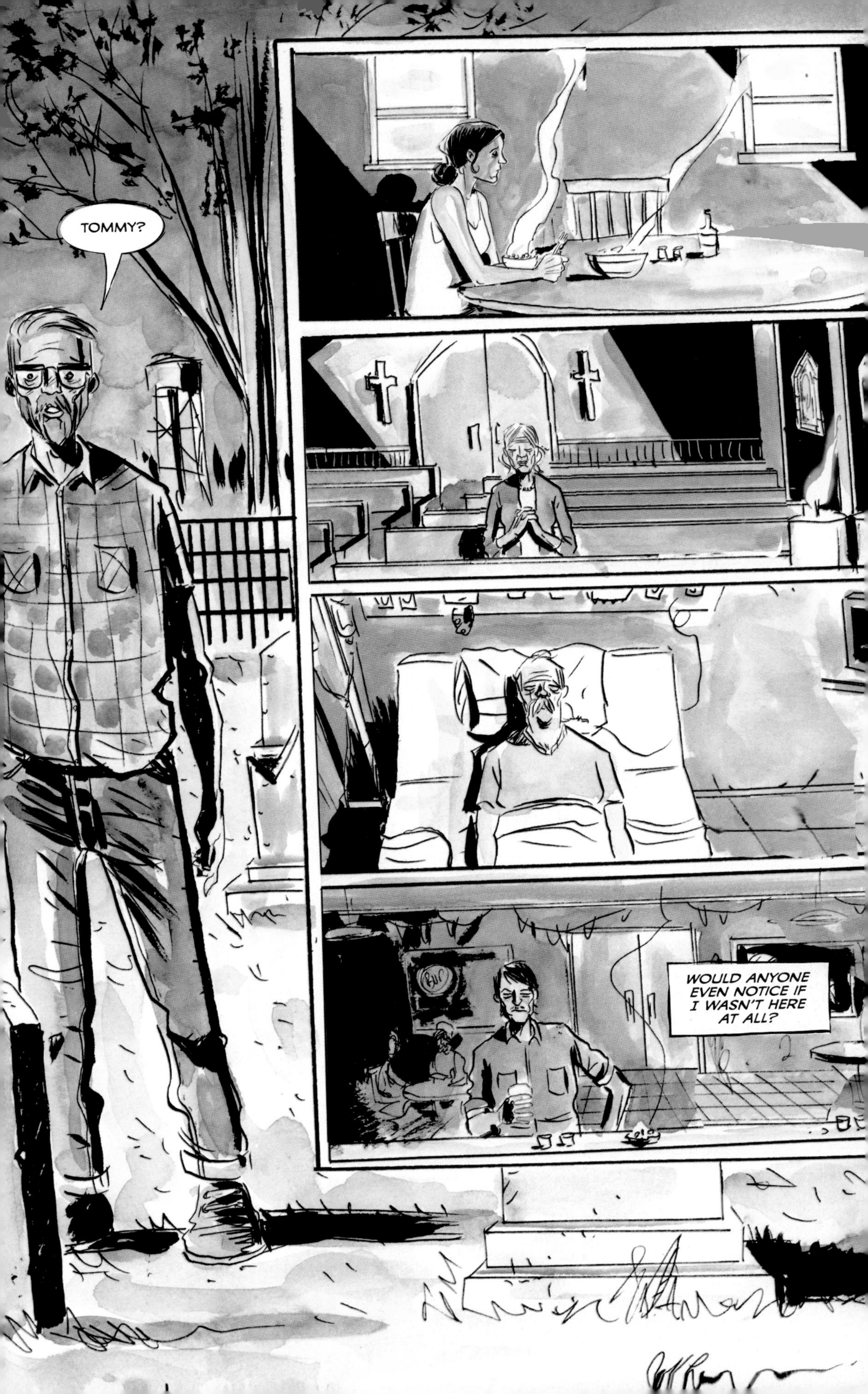
TOMMY?
WOULD ANYONE EVEN NOTICE IF I WASN'T HERE AT ALL?

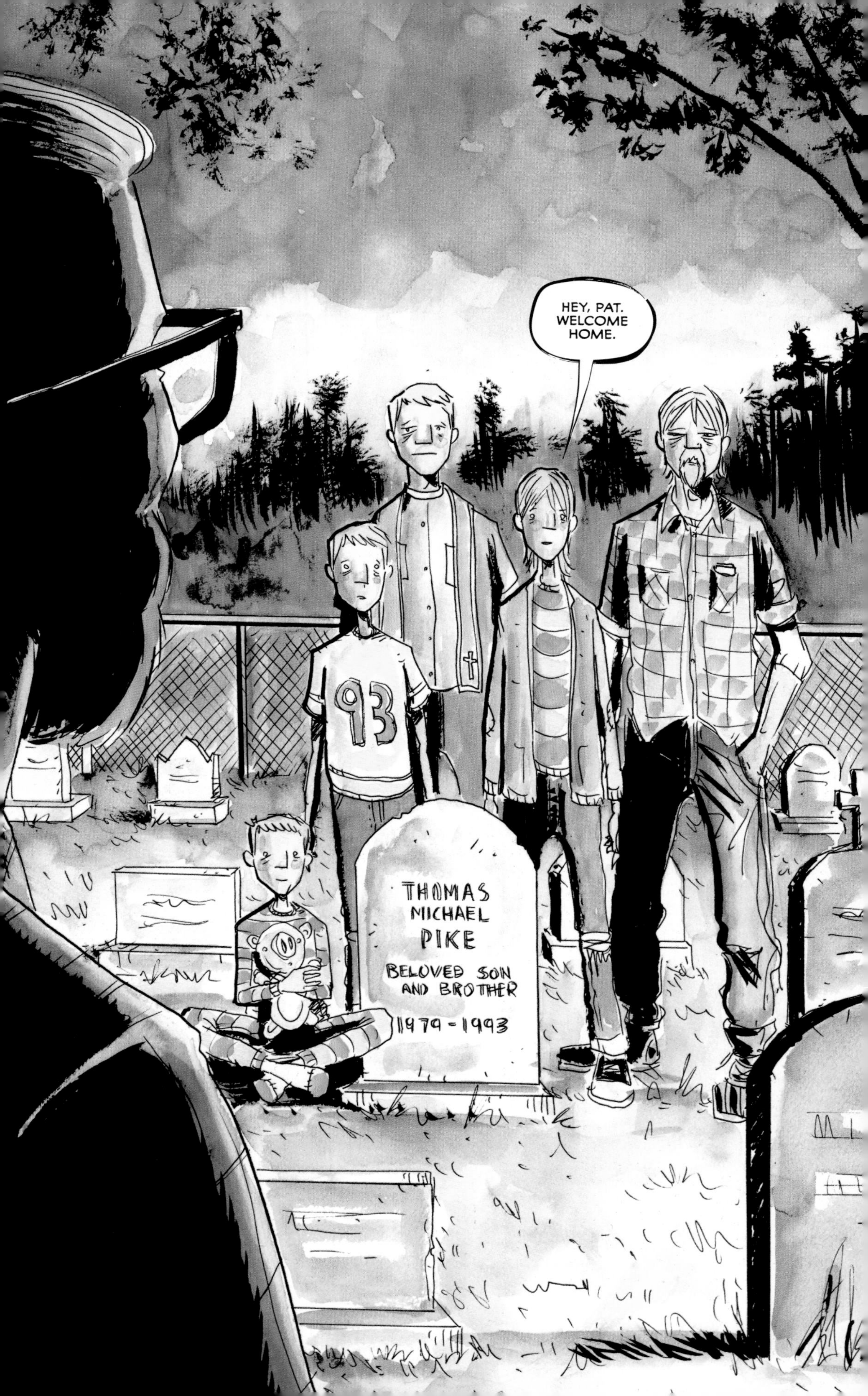
HEY, PAT. WELCOME HOME.
93
THOMAS MICHAEL PIKE
BELOVED SON AND BROTHER
1979 - 1993

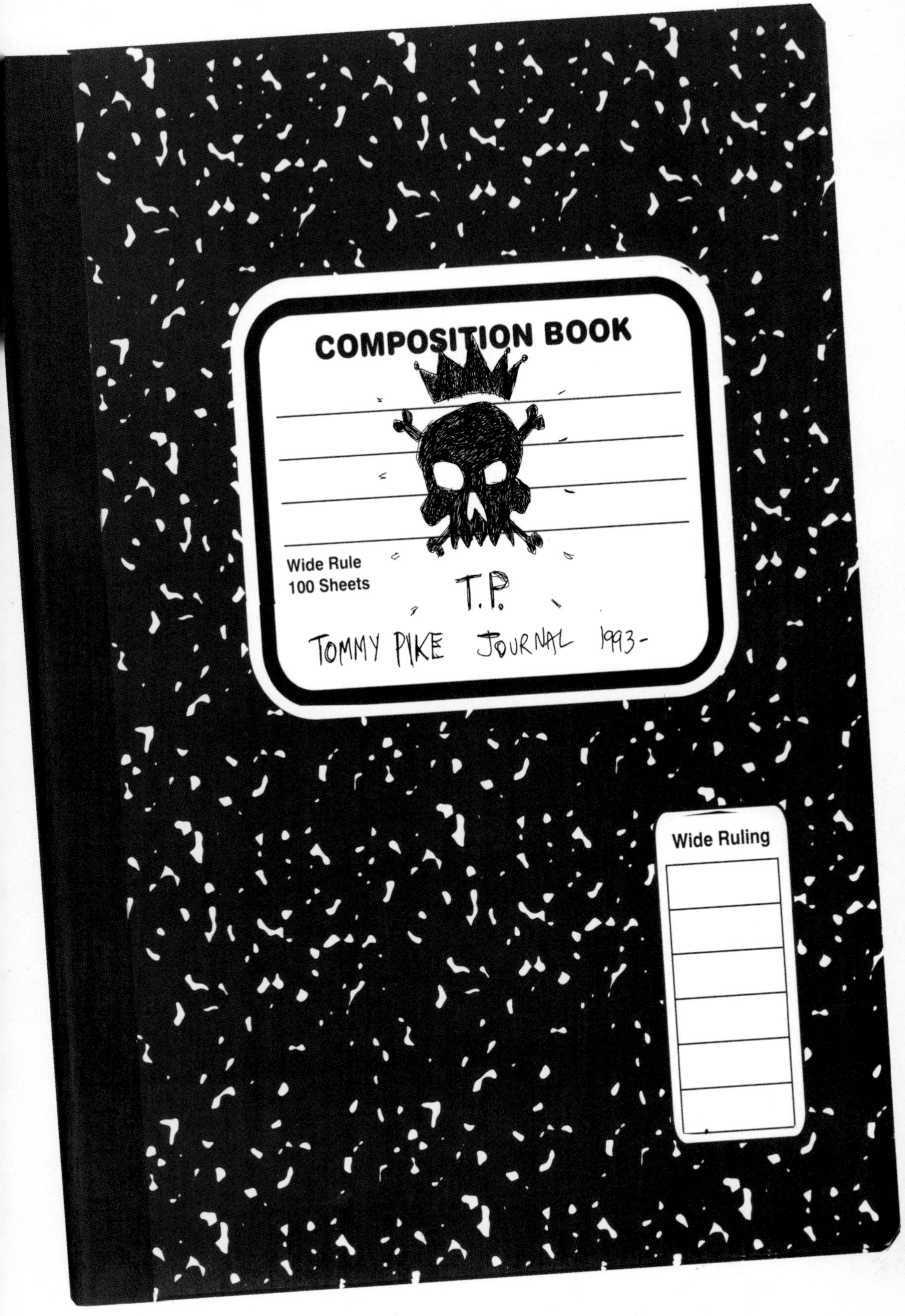
COMPOSITION BOOK
Wide Rule
100 Sheets
T.P.
TOMMY PIKE JOURNAL 1993-
Wide Ruling

Sometimes I wonder if it's hard growing up in Royal City or just hard growing up. I mean there's just something different about this place. I swear you can feel it late at night, a wierdness creeping around the edges of things, keeping you awake and making you feel more alone.

Or maybe that's it. Maybe I am all alone? Maybe I'm the only one who thinks stupid shit like this all the time? The older I get, the less I feel there is any place for me me here. Most of the time I wish I could get on a train and go somewhere far from Royal City. Somewhere where no one knows who I am and I can be whoever I want to be. But then there are days when I think I'm exactly where I need to be. Like there is something different here, Something only I can see, And maybe that makes me special and not fucked up? Maybe there's something I can find no one else can?

But most days I just hate it here. I mean there's something about this place and everyone in it. I hate the way everyone looks at me like I'm not really here at all. Tara still treats me like the little kid she used to babysit. It's like she doesn't want me to grow up or something. And Mom is worse. she wants us all to be perfect like some kind of Saints. I'm the youngest so it's like I was her last hope, at being the perfect little child, and now that she realizes I'm not she hardly looks at me anymore. And Dad isn't really much better. It's like he's not there either I guess, in that way he's the most like me. And then there's Pat. I don't even know who Pat is. I don't think he even knows himself. Dad might be lost in his own little world but Pat is just lost. At least Richie treats me okay. He's the only one who treats me like a person. Richie's the only one in the family who sees everything for what it is. Maybe every town is like this? Maybe every family is like this? I don't know. Sometimes I wonder what would happen if I really did leave? I imagine running away, or worse. Would anybody notice if I wasn't even here at all?

T.P.

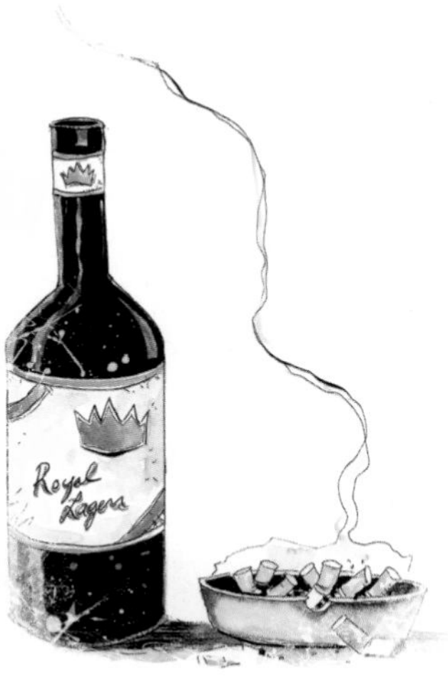
Royal
Lagers

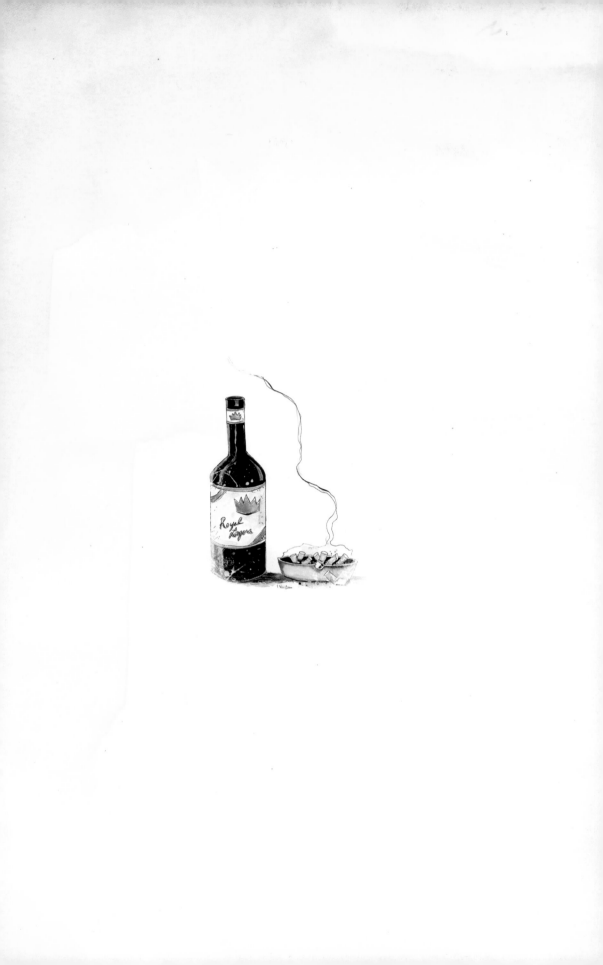

CHAPTER TWO

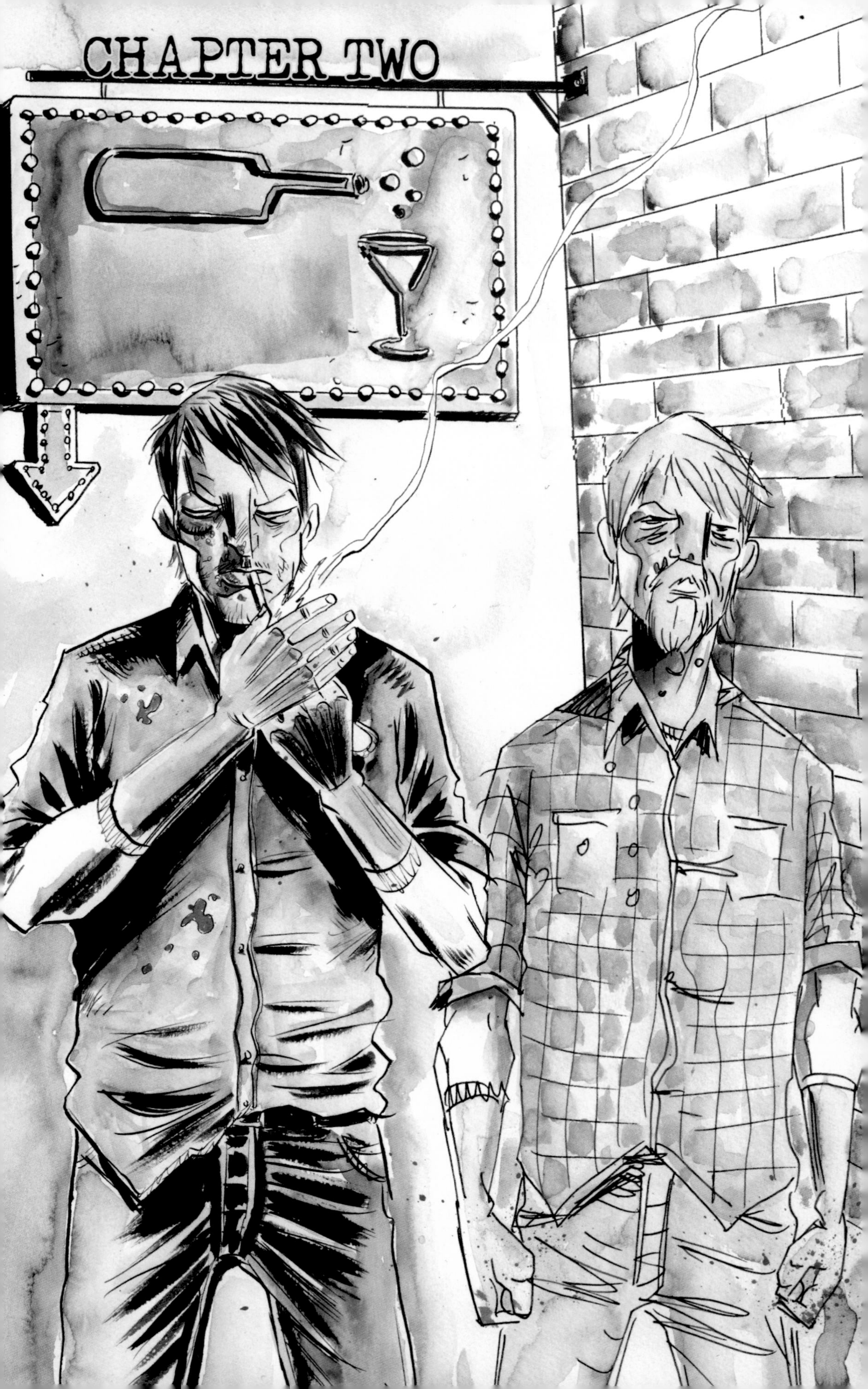

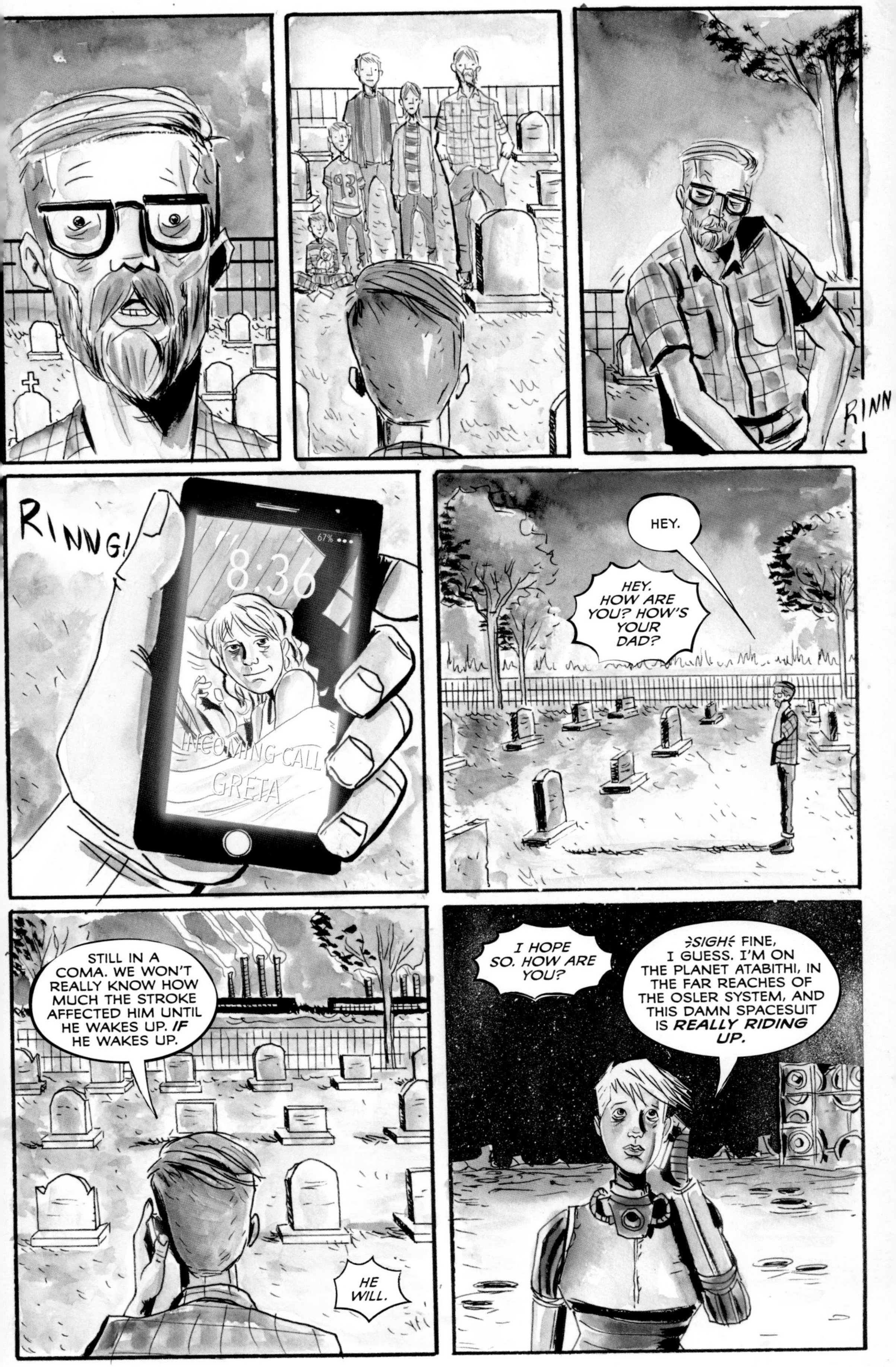
RINN
RINNG!
8:36
INCOMING CALL
GRETA
HEY.
HEY. HOW ARE YOU? HOW'S YOUR DAD?
STILL IN A COMA. WE WON'T REALLY KNOW HOW MUCH THE STROKE AFFECTED HIM UNTIL HE WAKES UP. IF HE WAKES UP.
HE WILL.
I HOPE SO. HOW ARE YOU?
SIGH FINE, I GUESS. I'M ON THE PLANET ATABITHI, IN THE FAR REACHES OF THE OSLER SYSTEM, AND THIS DAMN SPACESUIT IS REALLY RIDING UP.

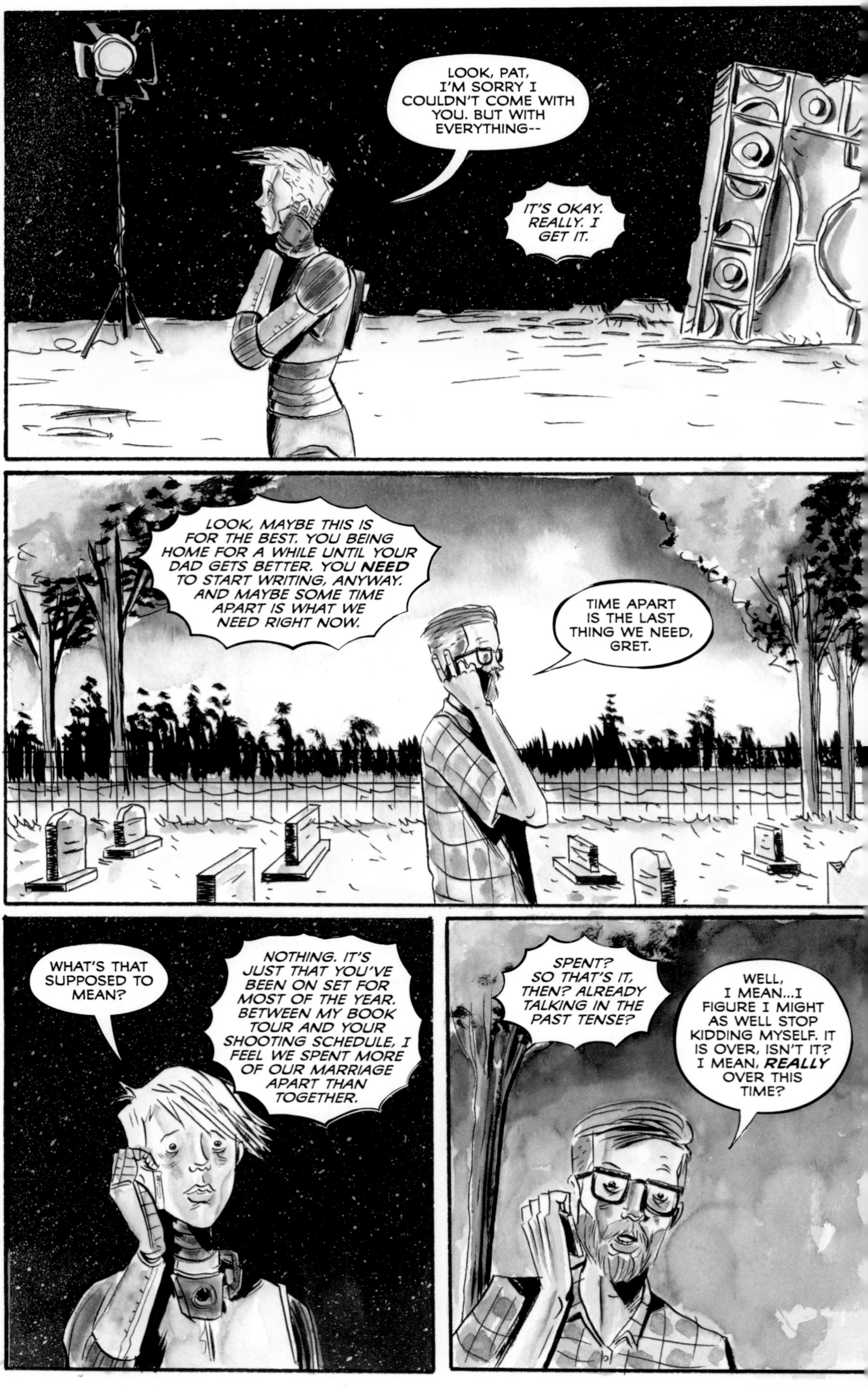
LOOK, PAT, I'M SORRY I COULDN'T COME WITH YOU. BUT WITH EVERYTHING--
IT'S OKAY. REALLY. I GET IT.
LOOK, MAYBE THIS IS FOR THE BEST. YOU BEING HOME FOR A WHILE UNTIL YOUR DAD GETS BETTER. YOU NEED TO START WRITING, ANYWAY. AND MAYBE SOME TIME APART IS WHAT WE NEED RIGHT NOW.
TIME APART IS THE LAST THING WE NEED, GRET.
WHAT'S THAT SUPPOSED TO MEAN?
NOTHING. IT'S JUST THAT YOU'VE BEEN ON SET FOR MOST OF THE YEAR. BETWEEN MY BOOK TOUR AND YOUR SHOOTING SCHEDULE, I FEEL WE SPENT MORE OF OUR MARRIAGE APART THAN TOGETHER.
SPENT? SO THAT'S IT, THEN? ALREADY TALKING IN THE PAST TENSE?
WELL, I MEAN...I FIGURE I MIGHT AS WELL STOP KIDDING MYSELF. IT IS OVER, ISN'T IT? I MEAN, REALLY OVER THIS TIME?

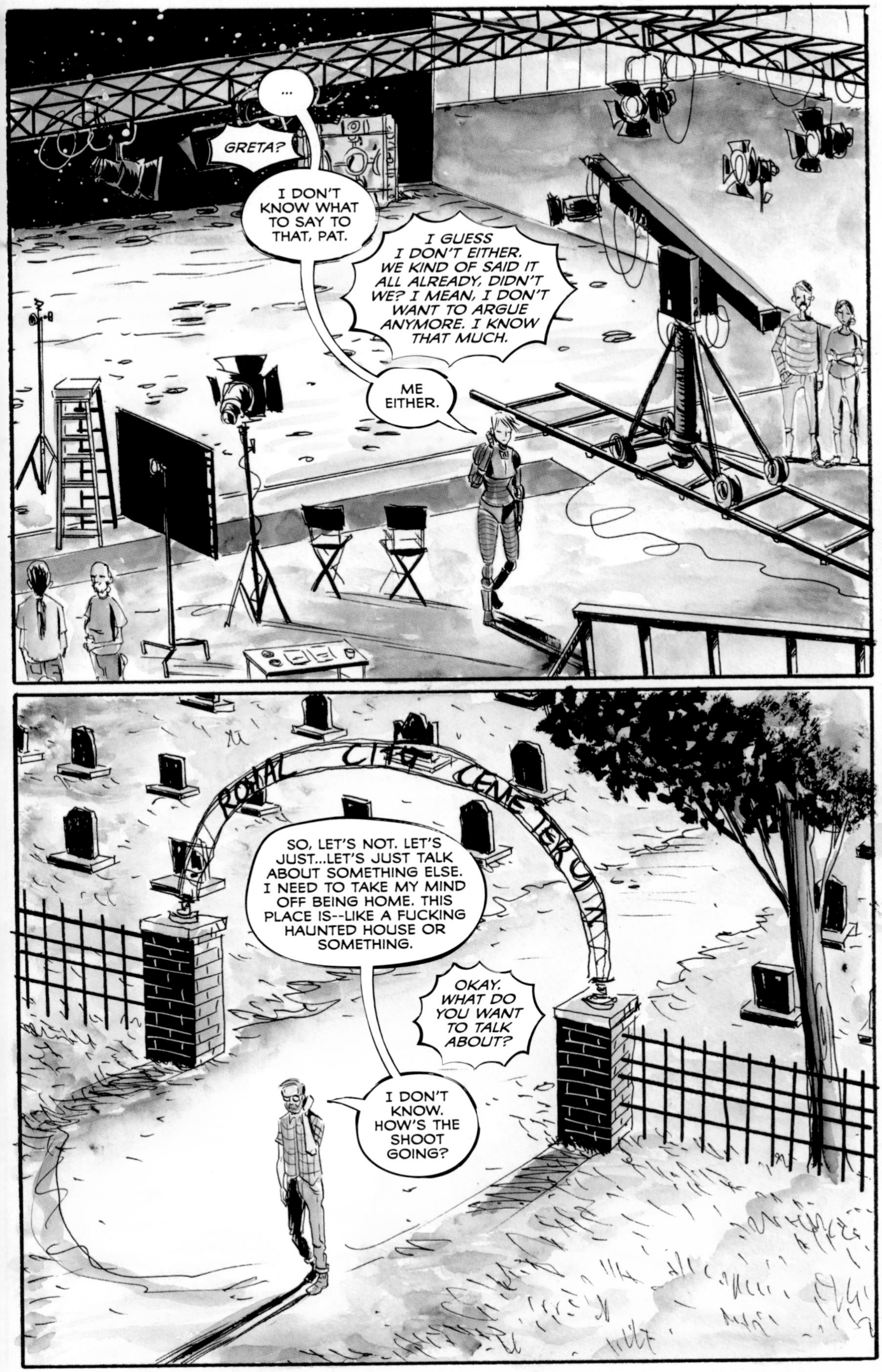
GRETA?
...
I DON'T KNOW WHAT TO SAY TO THAT, PAT.
I GUESS I DON'T EITHER. WE KIND OF SAID IT ALL ALREADY, DIDN'T WE? I MEAN, I DON'T WANT TO ARGUE ANYMORE. I KNOW THAT MUCH.
ME EITHER.
ROYAL CITY CEMETERY
SO, LET'S NOT. LET'S JUST...LET'S JUST TALK ABOUT SOMETHING ELSE. I NEED TO TAKE MY MIND OFF BEING HOME. THIS PLACE IS--LIKE A FUCKING HAUNTED HOUSE OR SOMETHING.
OKAY. WHAT DO YOU WANT TO TALK ABOUT?
I DON'T KNOW. HOW'S THE SHOOT GOING?

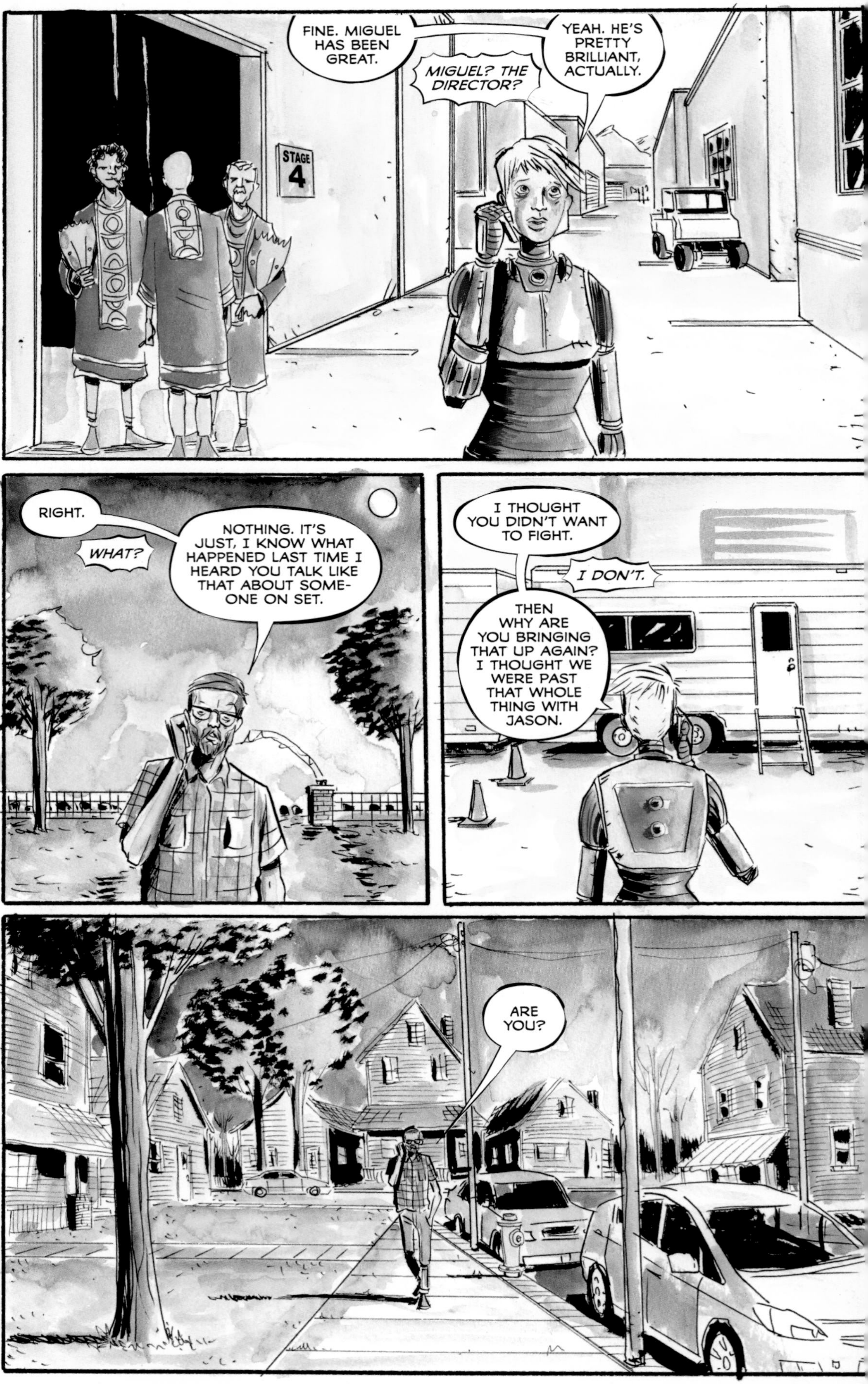
FINE. MIGUEL HAS BEEN GREAT.
MIGUEL? THE DIRECTOR?
YEAH. HE'S PRETTY BRILLIANT, ACTUALLY.
STAGE 4
RIGHT.
WHAT?
NOTHING. IT'S JUST, I KNOW WHAT HAPPENED LAST TIME I HEARD YOU TALK LIKE THAT ABOUT SOME-ONE ON SET.
I THOUGHT YOU DIDN'T WANT TO FIGHT.
I DON'T.
THEN WHY ARE YOU BRINGING THAT UP AGAIN? I THOUGHT WE WERE PAST THAT WHOLE THING WITH JASON.
ARE YOU?

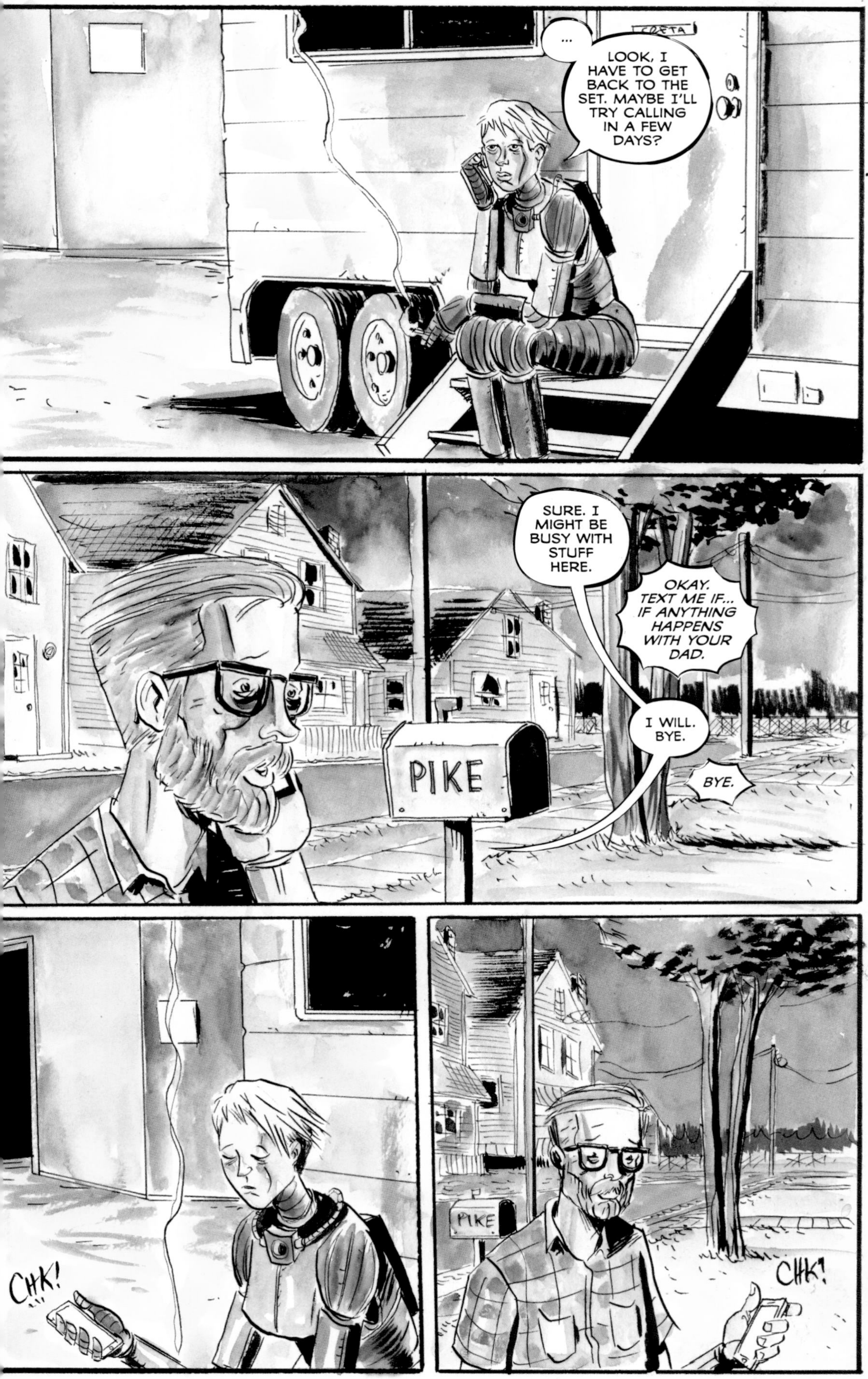
CRETA
...
LOOK, I HAVE TO GET BACK TO THE SET. MAYBE I'LL TRY CALLING IN A FEW DAYS?
SURE. I MIGHT BE BUSY WITH STUFF HERE.
OKAY. TEXT ME IF... IF ANYTHING HAPPENS WITH YOUR DAD.
I WILL. BYE.
BYE.
PIKE
CHK!
PIKE
CHK!

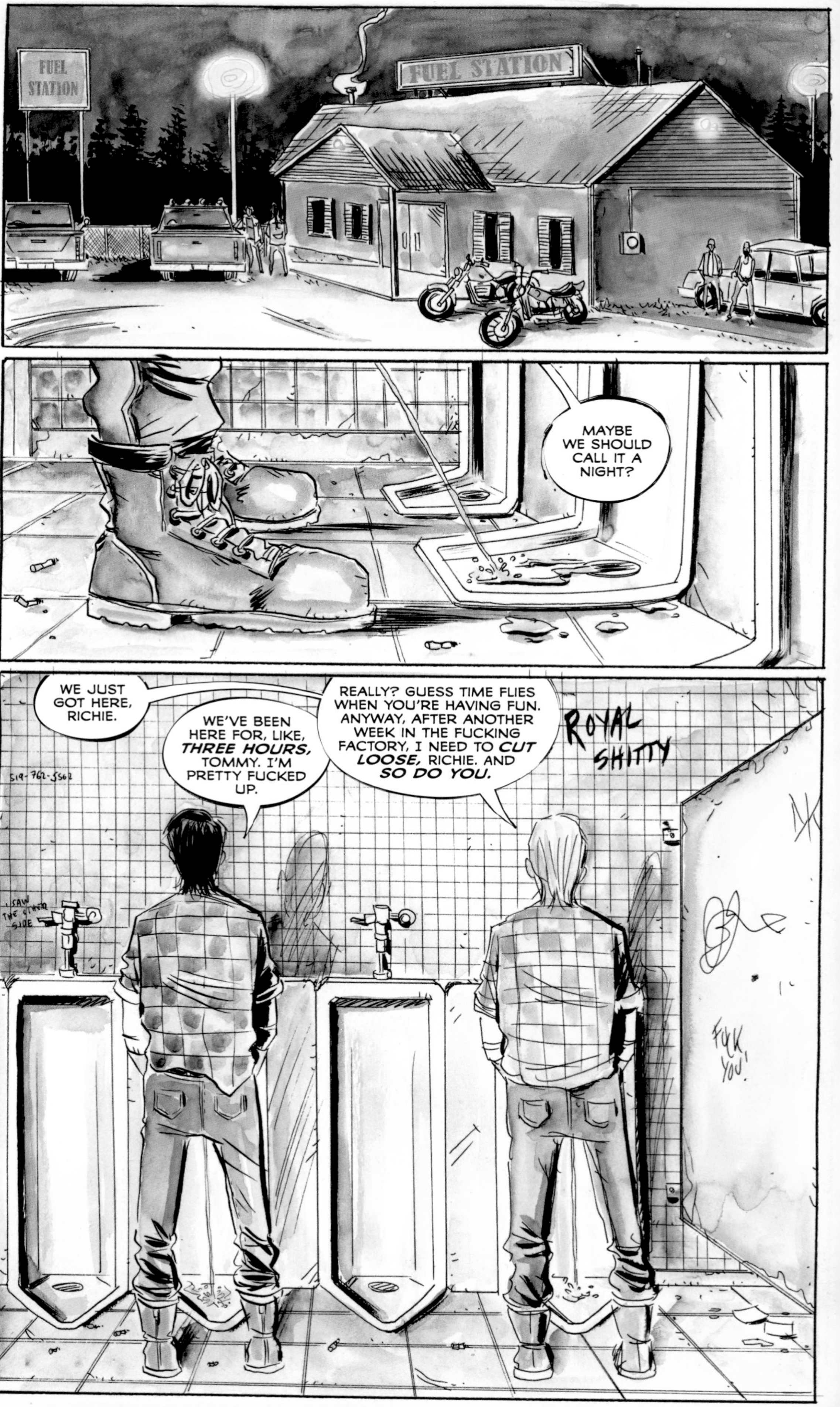

FUEL STATION
FUEL STATION
MAYBE WE SHOULD CALL IT A NIGHT?
WE JUST GOT HERE, RICHIE.
WE'VE BEEN HERE FOR, LIKE, ***THREE HOURS,*** TOMMY. I'M PRETTY FUCKED UP.
REALLY? GUESS TIME FLIES WHEN YOU'RE HAVING FUN. ANYWAY, AFTER ANOTHER WEEK IN THE FUCKING FACTORY, I NEED TO ***CUT LOOSE,*** RICHIE. AND ***SO DO YOU.***
ROYAL SHITTY
519-762-5562
I SAW THE OTHER SIDE
FUCK YOU!

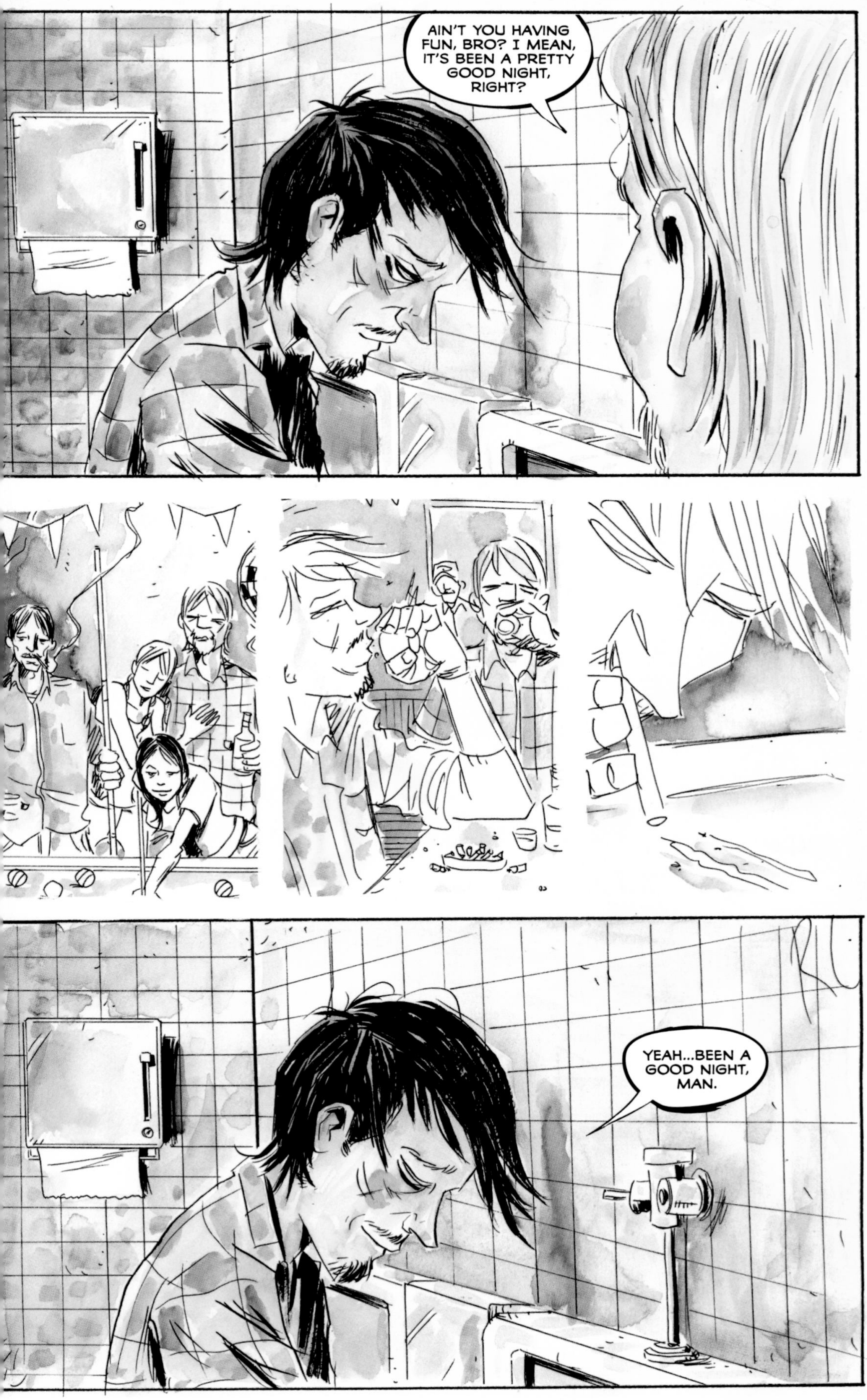
AIN'T YOU HAVING FUN, BRO? I MEAN, IT'S BEEN A PRETTY GOOD NIGHT, RIGHT?
YEAH...BEEN A GOOD NIGHT, MAN.

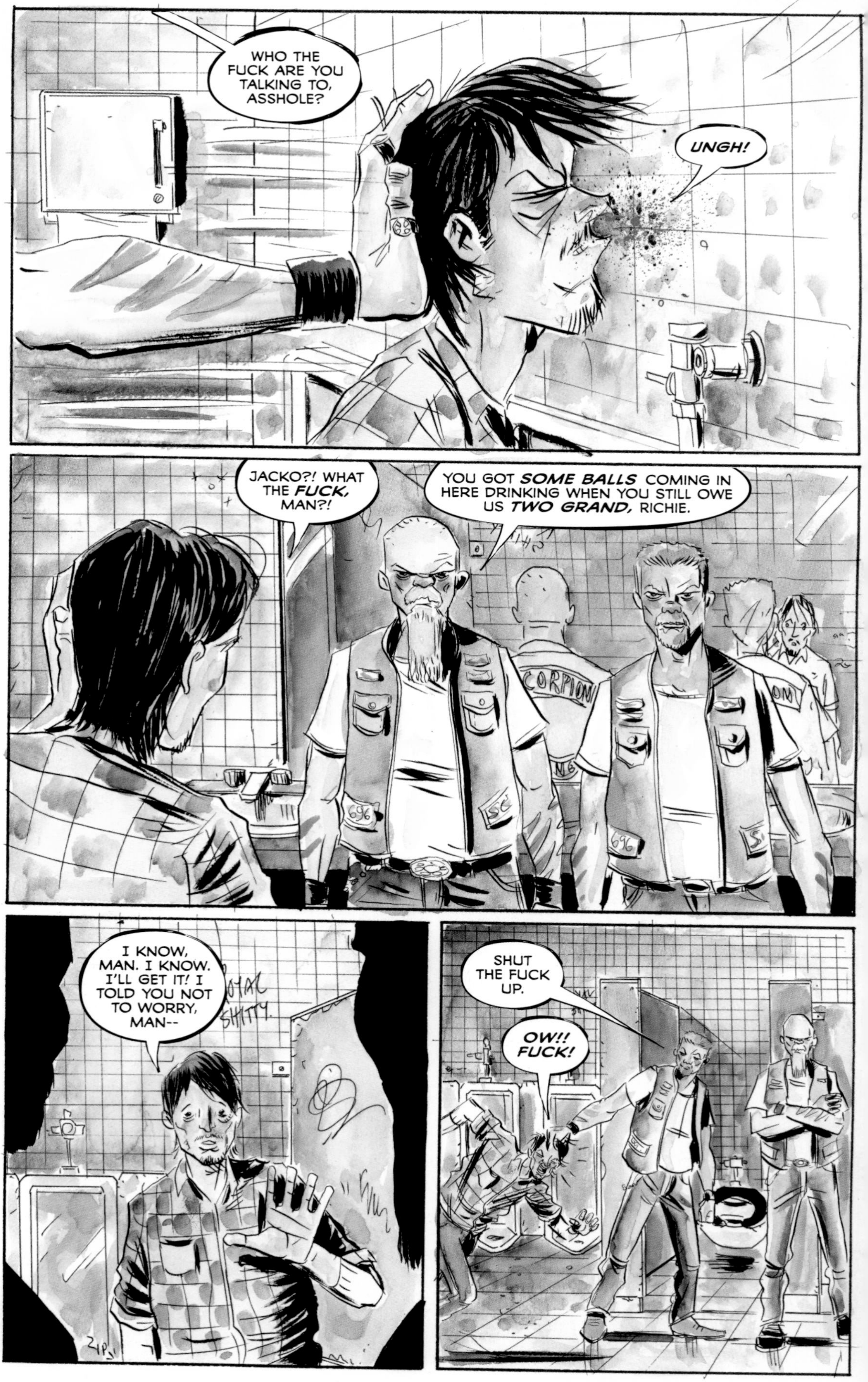
WHO THE FUCK ARE YOU TALKING TO, ASSHOLE?
UNGH!
JACKO?! WHAT THE FUCK, MAN?!
YOU GOT SOME BALLS COMING IN HERE DRINKING WHEN YOU STILL OWE US TWO GRAND, RICHIE.
I KNOW, MAN. I KNOW. I'LL GET IT! I TOLD YOU NOT TO WORRY, MAN--
SHUT THE FUCK UP.
OW!! FUCK!

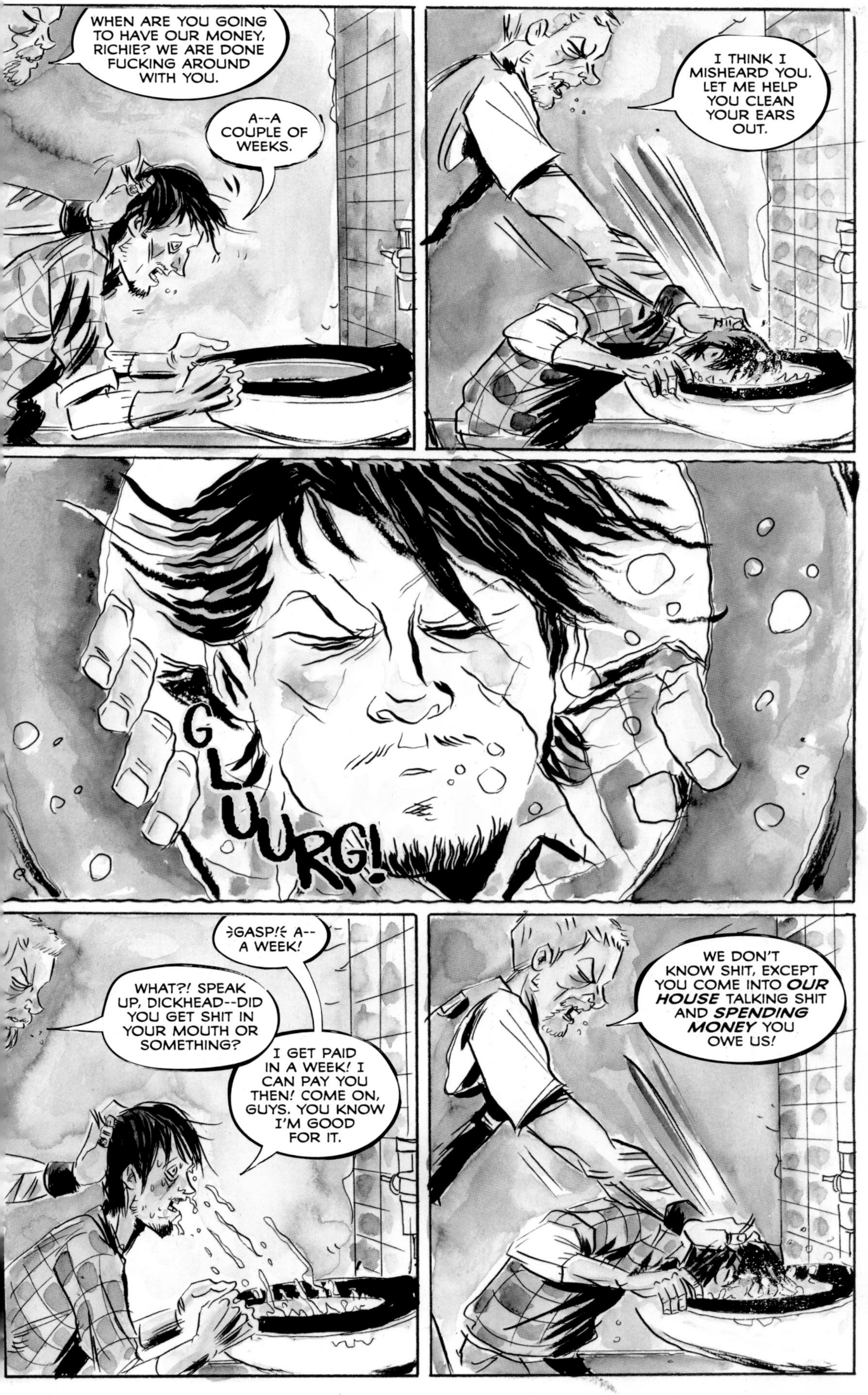
WHEN ARE YOU GOING TO HAVE OUR MONEY, RICHIE? WE ARE DONE FUCKING AROUND WITH YOU.
A--A COUPLE OF WEEKS.
I THINK I MISHEARD YOU. LET ME HELP YOU CLEAN YOUR EARS OUT.
GLUUURG!
GASP! A-- A WEEK!
WHAT?! SPEAK UP, DICKHEAD--DID YOU GET SHIT IN YOUR MOUTH OR SOMETHING?
I GET PAID IN A WEEK! I CAN PAY YOU THEN! COME ON, GUYS. YOU KNOW I'M GOOD FOR IT.
WE DON'T KNOW SHIT, EXCEPT YOU COME INTO OUR HOUSE TALKING SHIT AND SPENDING MONEY YOU OWE US!

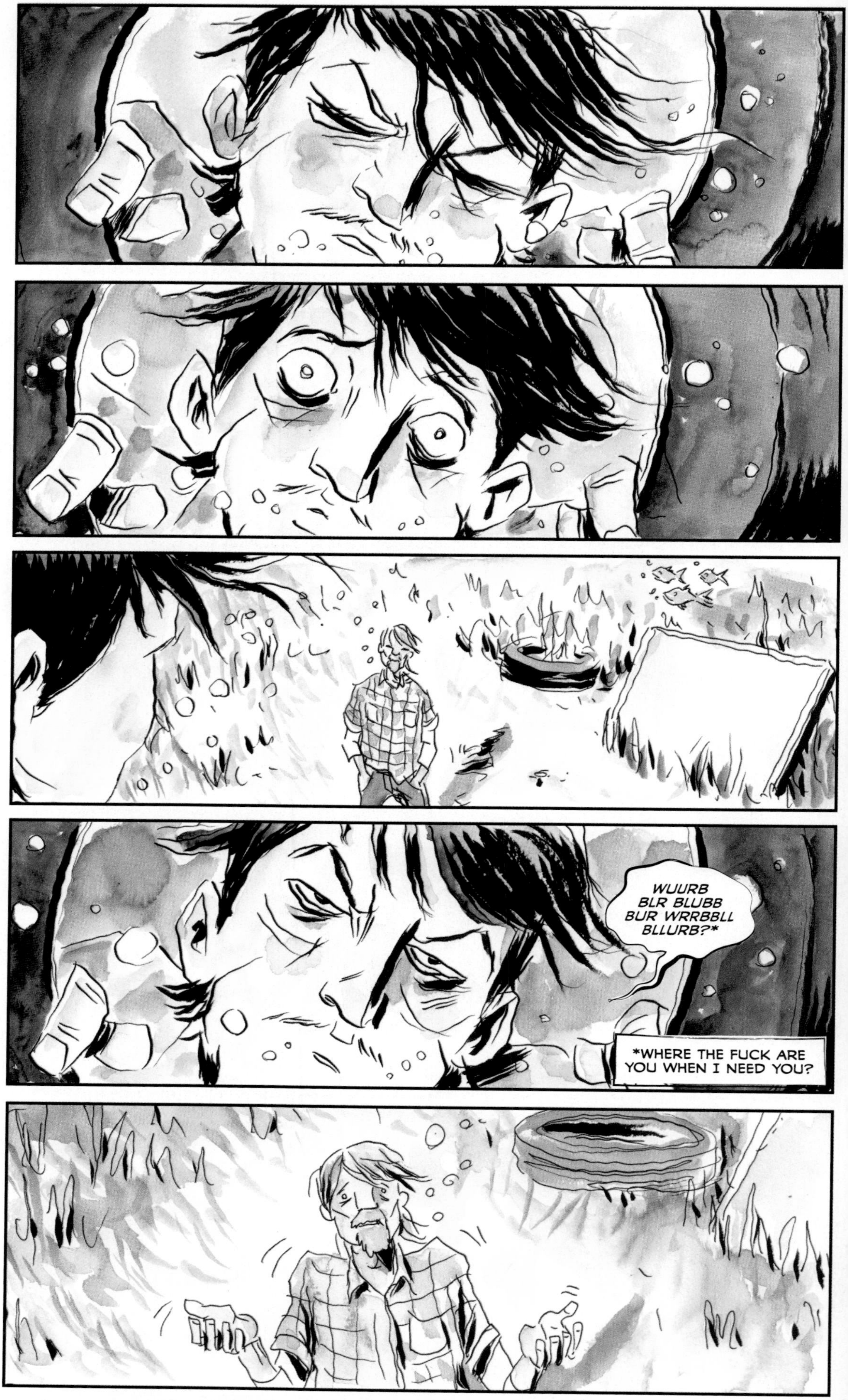
WUURB BLR BLUBB BUR WRRBBLL BLLURB?*
*WHERE THE FUCK ARE YOU WHEN I NEED YOU?

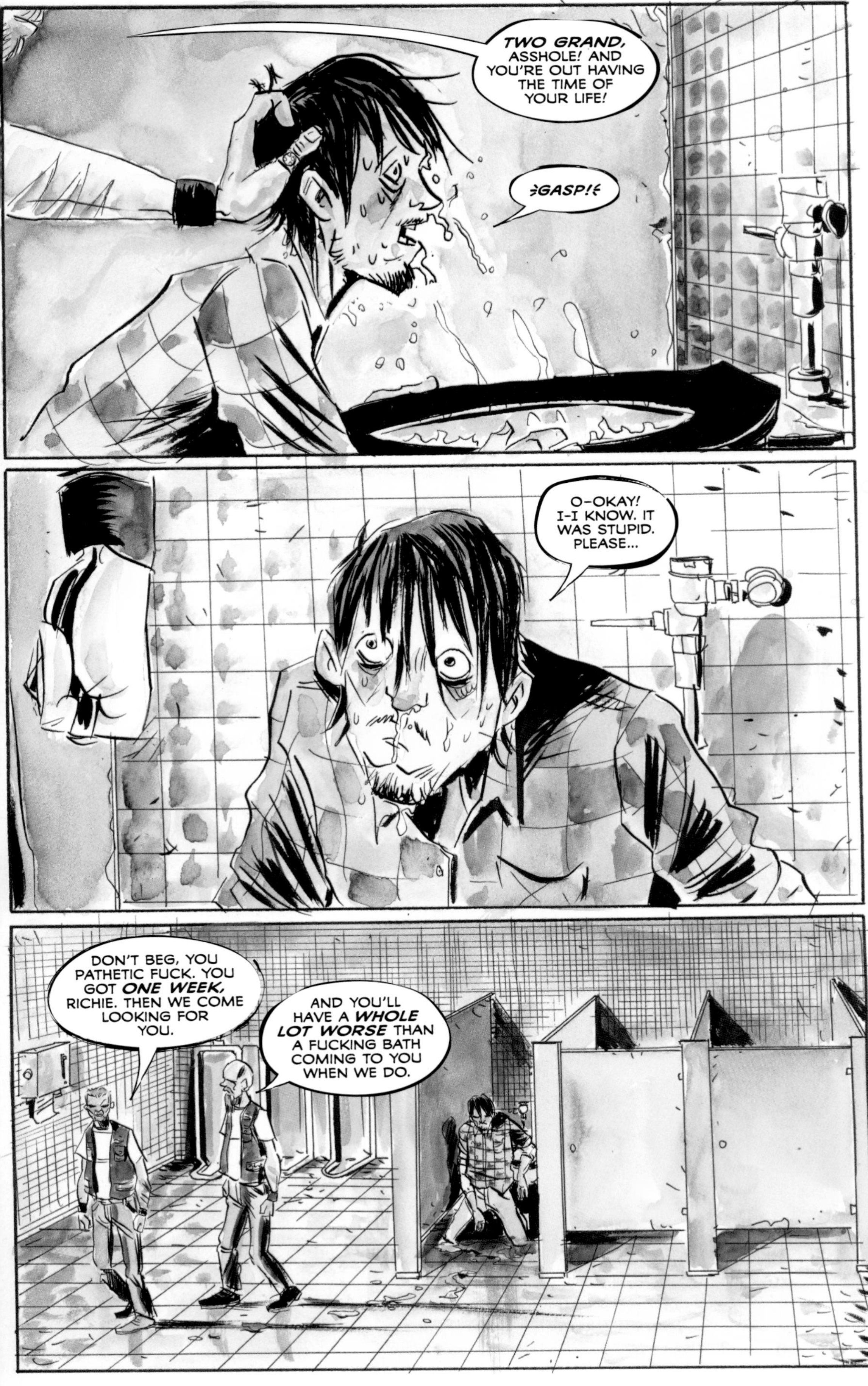
TWO GRAND, ASSHOLE! AND YOU'RE OUT HAVING THE TIME OF YOUR LIFE!
GASP!
O-OKAY! I-I KNOW. IT WAS STUPID. PLEASE...
DON'T BEG, YOU PATHETIC FUCK. YOU GOT ONE WEEK, RICHIE. THEN WE COME LOOKING FOR YOU.
AND YOU'LL HAVE A WHOLE LOT WORSE THAN A FUCKING BATH COMING TO YOU WHEN WE DO.

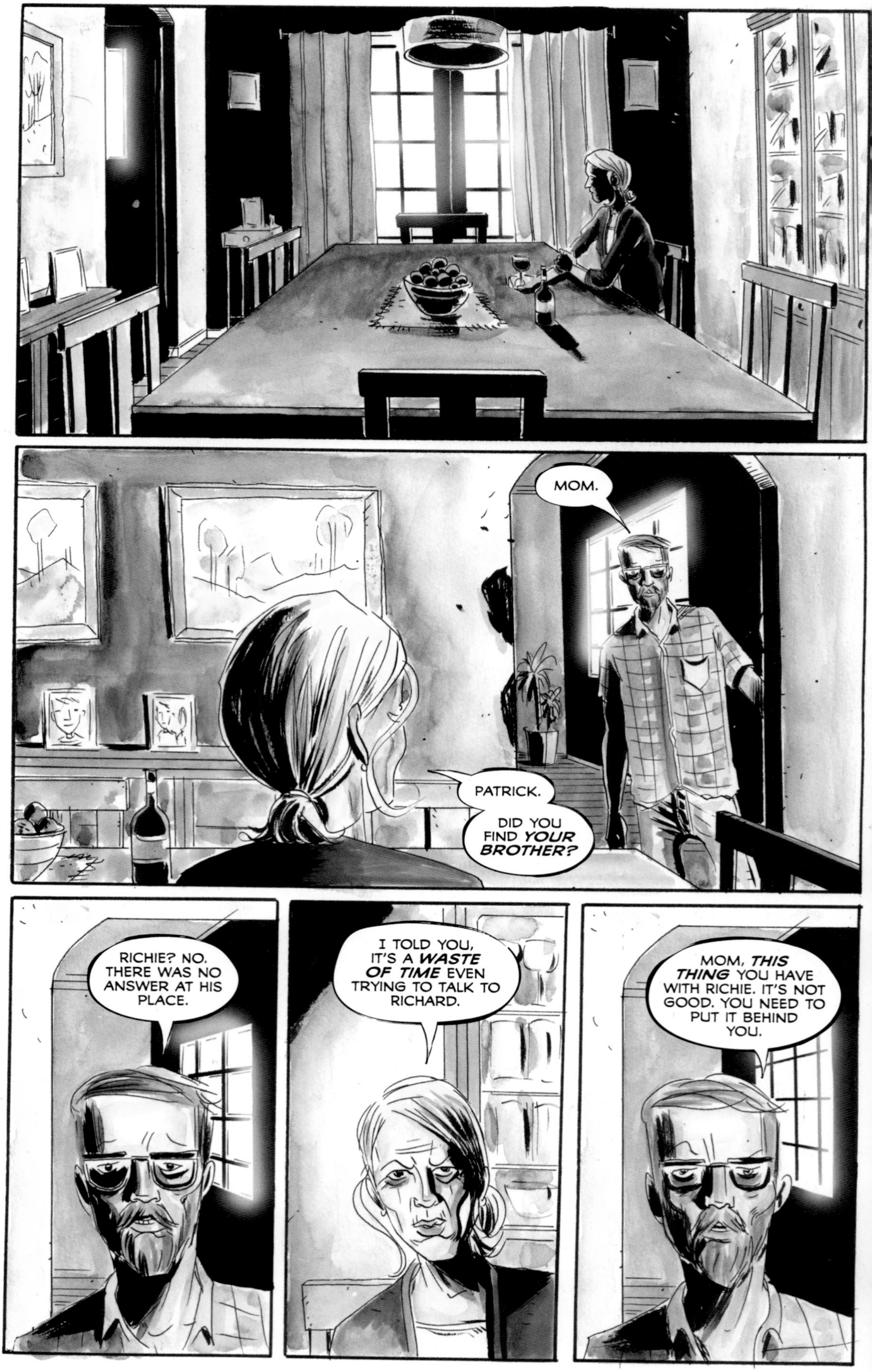
MOM.
PATRICK.
DID YOU FIND *YOUR BROTHER?*
RICHIE? NO. THERE WAS NO ANSWER AT HIS PLACE.
I TOLD YOU, IT'S A *WASTE OF TIME* EVEN TRYING TO TALK TO RICHARD.
MOM, *THIS THING* YOU HAVE WITH RICHIE. IT'S NOT GOOD. YOU NEED TO PUT IT BEHIND YOU.

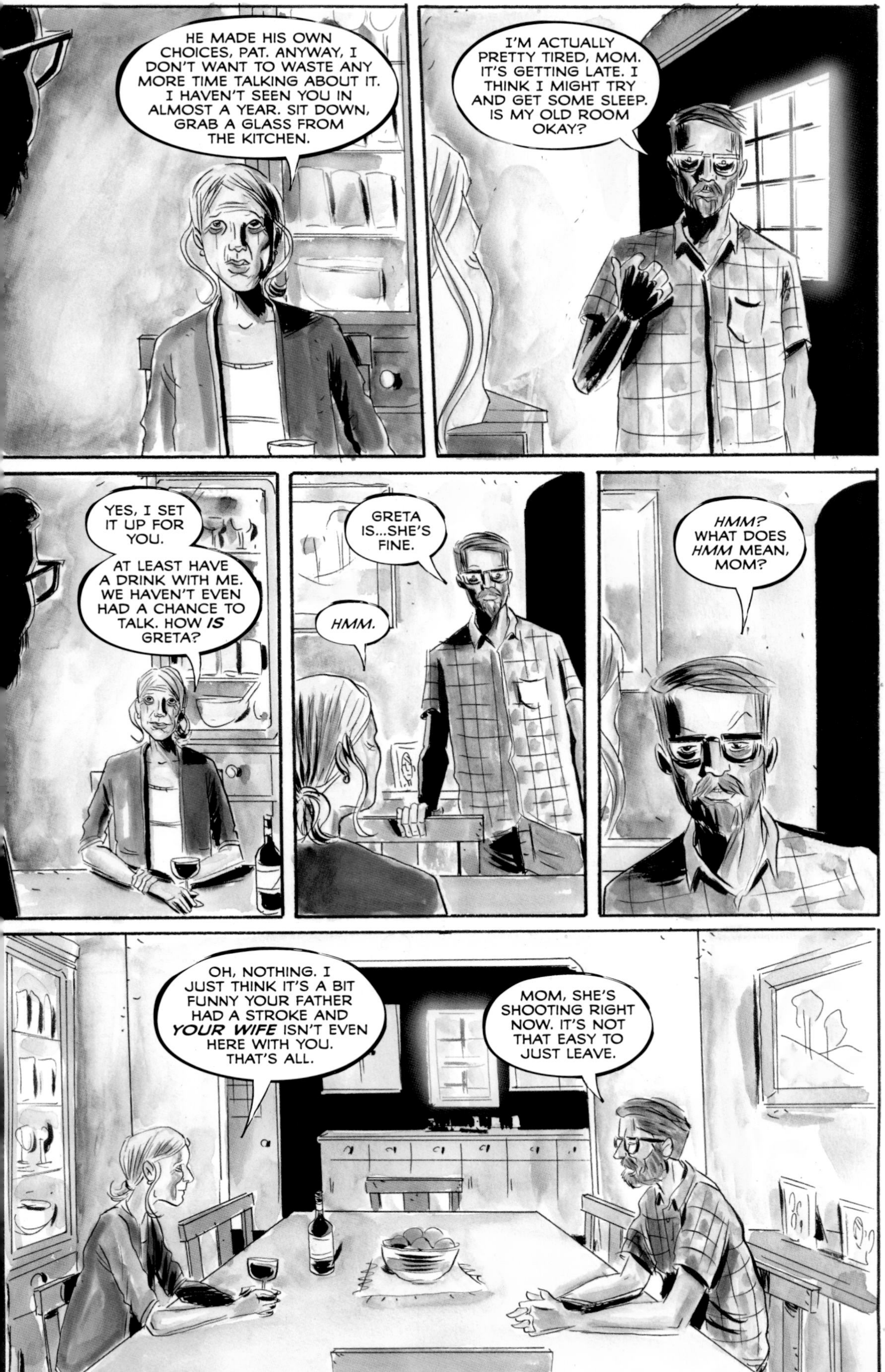
HE MADE HIS OWN CHOICES, PAT. ANYWAY, I DON'T WANT TO WASTE ANY MORE TIME TALKING ABOUT IT. I HAVEN'T SEEN YOU IN ALMOST A YEAR. SIT DOWN, GRAB A GLASS FROM THE KITCHEN.
I'M ACTUALLY PRETTY TIRED, MOM. IT'S GETTING LATE. I THINK I MIGHT TRY AND GET SOME SLEEP. IS MY OLD ROOM OKAY?
YES, I SET IT UP FOR YOU.
AT LEAST HAVE A DRINK WITH ME. WE HAVEN'T EVEN HAD A CHANCE TO TALK. HOW *IS* GRETA?
GRETA IS...SHE'S FINE.
HMM.
HMM? WHAT DOES *HMM* MEAN, MOM?
OH, NOTHING. I JUST THINK IT'S A BIT FUNNY YOUR FATHER HAD A STROKE AND ***YOUR WIFE*** ISN'T EVEN HERE WITH YOU. THAT'S ALL.
MOM, SHE'S SHOOTING RIGHT NOW. IT'S NOT THAT EASY TO JUST LEAVE.

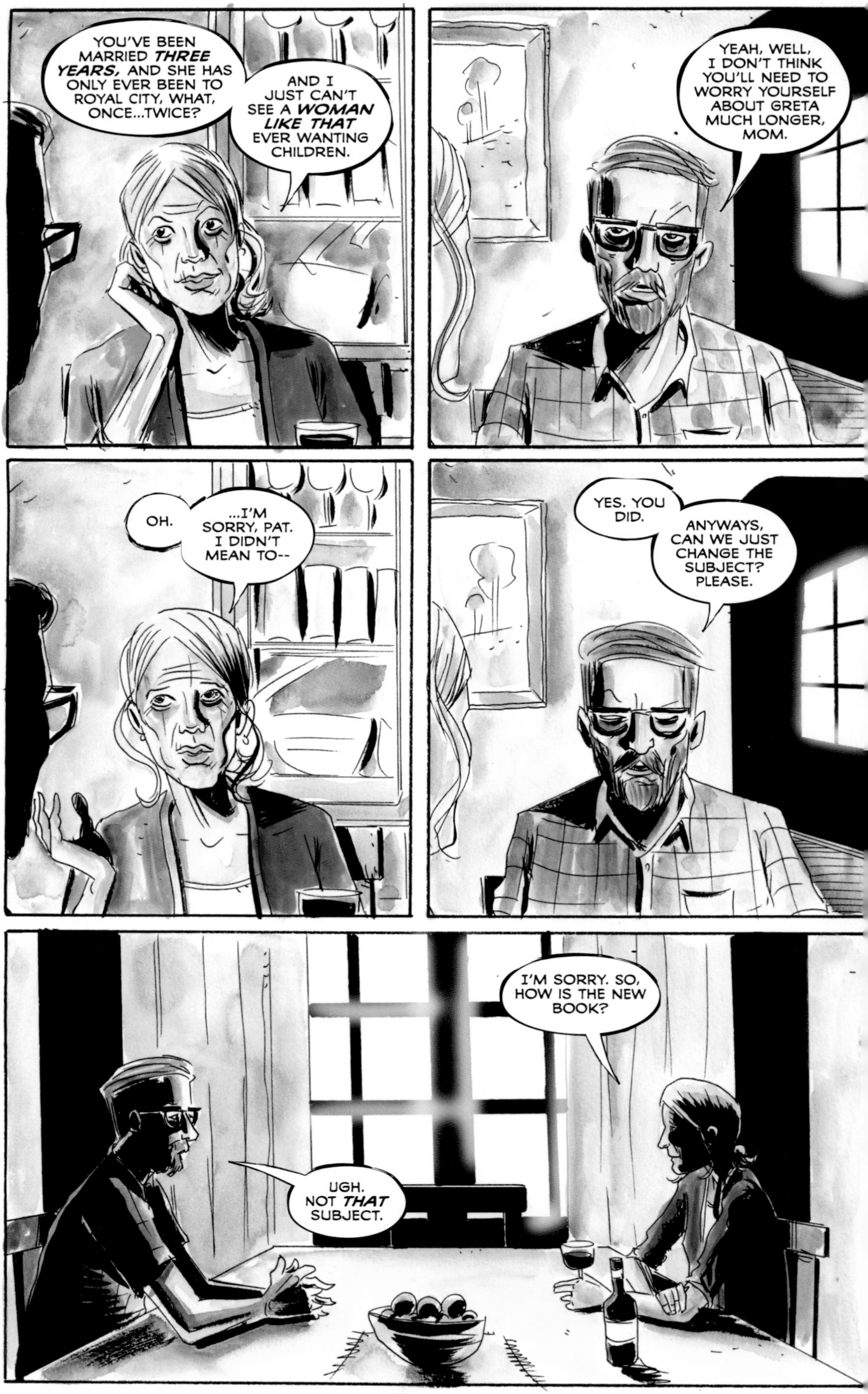
YOU'VE BEEN MARRIED ***THREE YEARS,*** AND SHE HAS ONLY EVER BEEN TO ROYAL CITY, WHAT, ONCE...TWICE?
AND I JUST CAN'T SEE A ***WOMAN LIKE THAT*** EVER WANTING CHILDREN.
YEAH, WELL, I DON'T THINK YOU'LL NEED TO WORRY YOURSELF ABOUT GRETA MUCH LONGER, MOM.
OH.
...I'M SORRY, PAT. I DIDN'T MEAN TO--
YES. YOU DID.
ANYWAYS, CAN WE JUST CHANGE THE SUBJECT? PLEASE.
I'M SORRY. SO, HOW IS THE NEW BOOK?
UGH. NOT ***THAT*** SUBJECT.

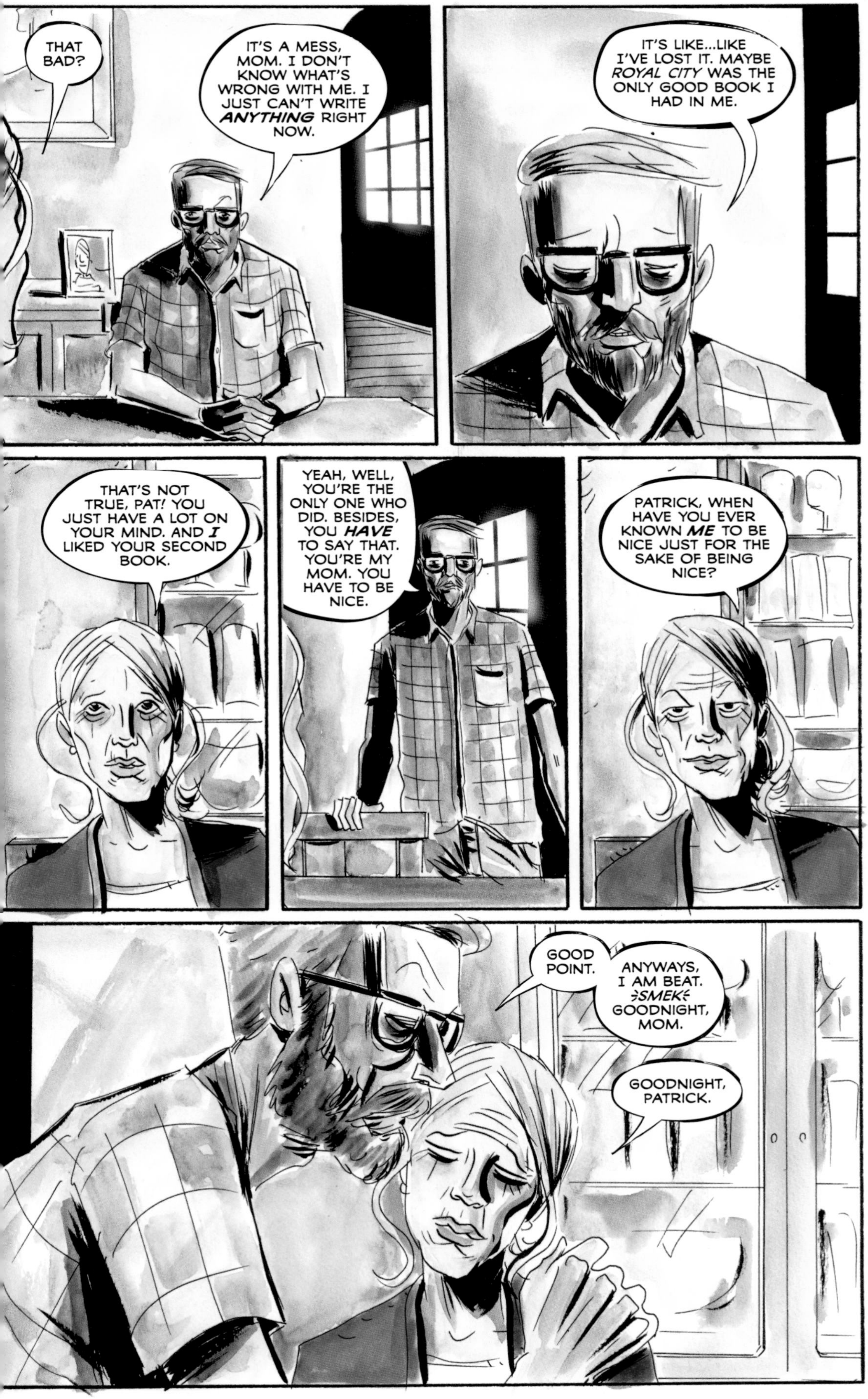
THAT BAD?
IT'S A MESS, MOM. I DON'T KNOW WHAT'S WRONG WITH ME. I JUST CAN'T WRITE ANYTHING RIGHT NOW.
IT'S LIKE...LIKE I'VE LOST IT. MAYBE ROYAL CITY WAS THE ONLY GOOD BOOK I HAD IN ME.
THAT'S NOT TRUE, PAT! YOU JUST HAVE A LOT ON YOUR MIND. AND I LIKED YOUR SECOND BOOK.
YEAH, WELL, YOU'RE THE ONLY ONE WHO DID. BESIDES, YOU HAVE TO SAY THAT. YOU'RE MY MOM. YOU HAVE TO BE NICE.
PATRICK, WHEN HAVE YOU EVER KNOWN ME TO BE NICE JUST FOR THE SAKE OF BEING NICE?
GOOD POINT.
ANYWAYS, I AM BEAT. *SMEK* GOODNIGHT, MOM.
GOODNIGHT, PATRICK.

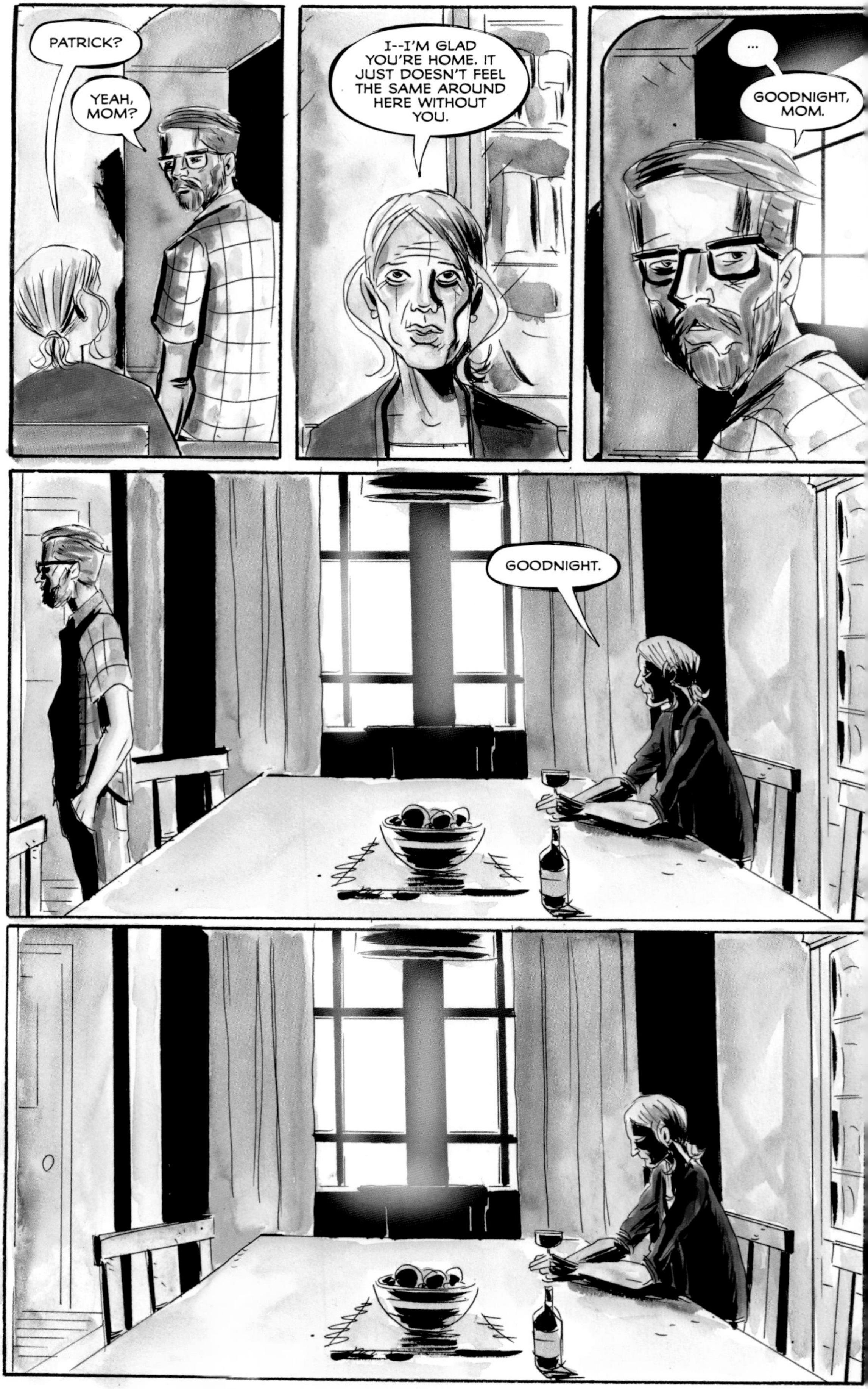
PATRICK?
YEAH, MOM?
I--I'M GLAD YOU'RE HOME. IT JUST DOESN'T FEEL THE SAME AROUND HERE WITHOUT YOU.
...
GOODNIGHT, MOM.
GOODNIGHT.

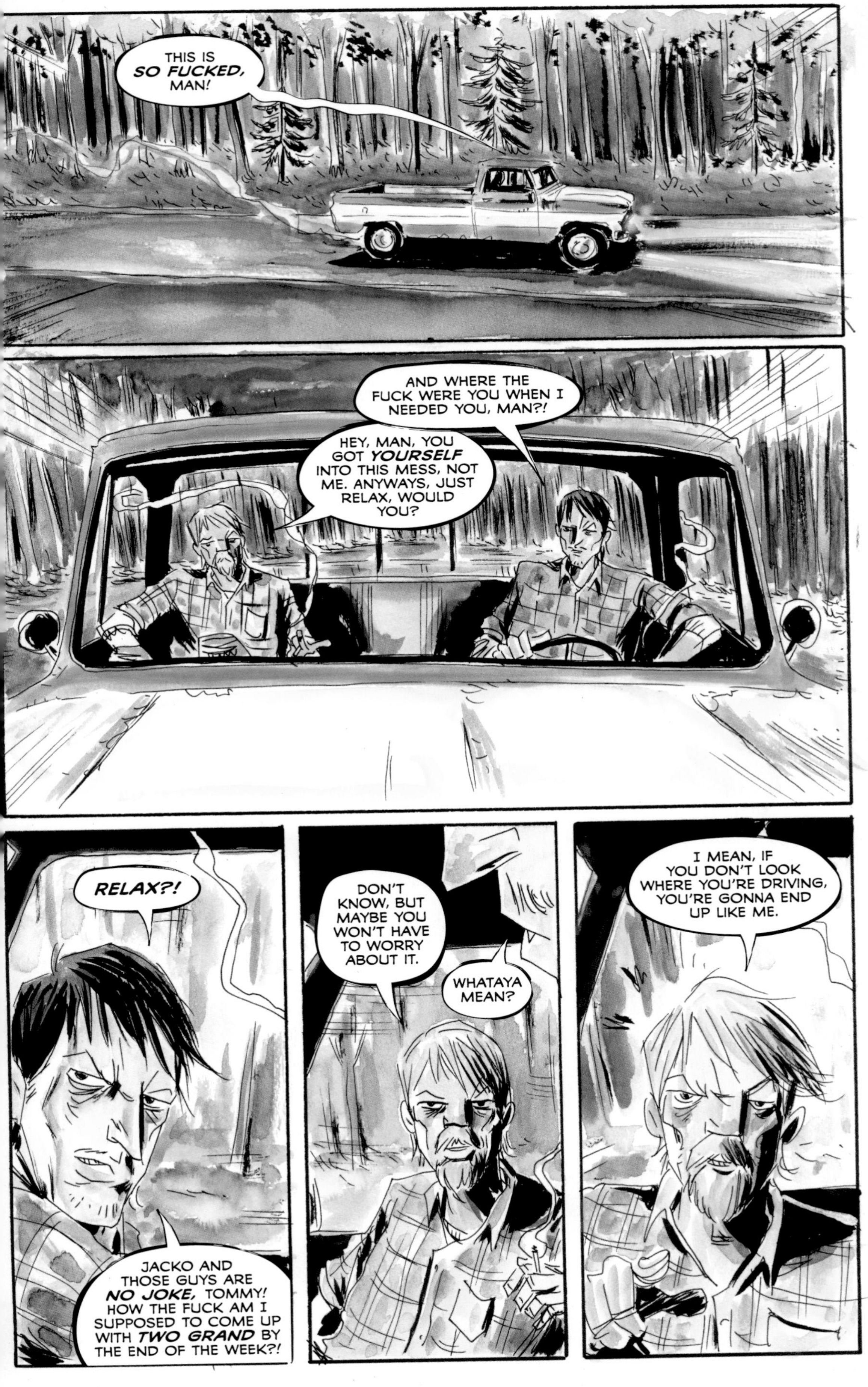

THIS IS **SO FUCKED,** MAN!
AND WHERE THE FUCK WERE YOU WHEN I NEEDED YOU, MAN?!
HEY, MAN, YOU GOT ***YOURSELF*** INTO THIS MESS, NOT ME. ANYWAYS, JUST RELAX, WOULD YOU?
RELAX?!
JACKO AND THOSE GUYS ARE ***NO JOKE,*** TOMMY! HOW THE FUCK AM I SUPPOSED TO COME UP WITH ***TWO GRAND*** BY THE END OF THE WEEK?!
DON'T KNOW, BUT MAYBE YOU WON'T HAVE TO WORRY ABOUT IT.
WHATAYA MEAN?
I MEAN, IF YOU DON'T LOOK WHERE YOU'RE DRIVING, YOU'RE GONNA END UP LIKE ME.

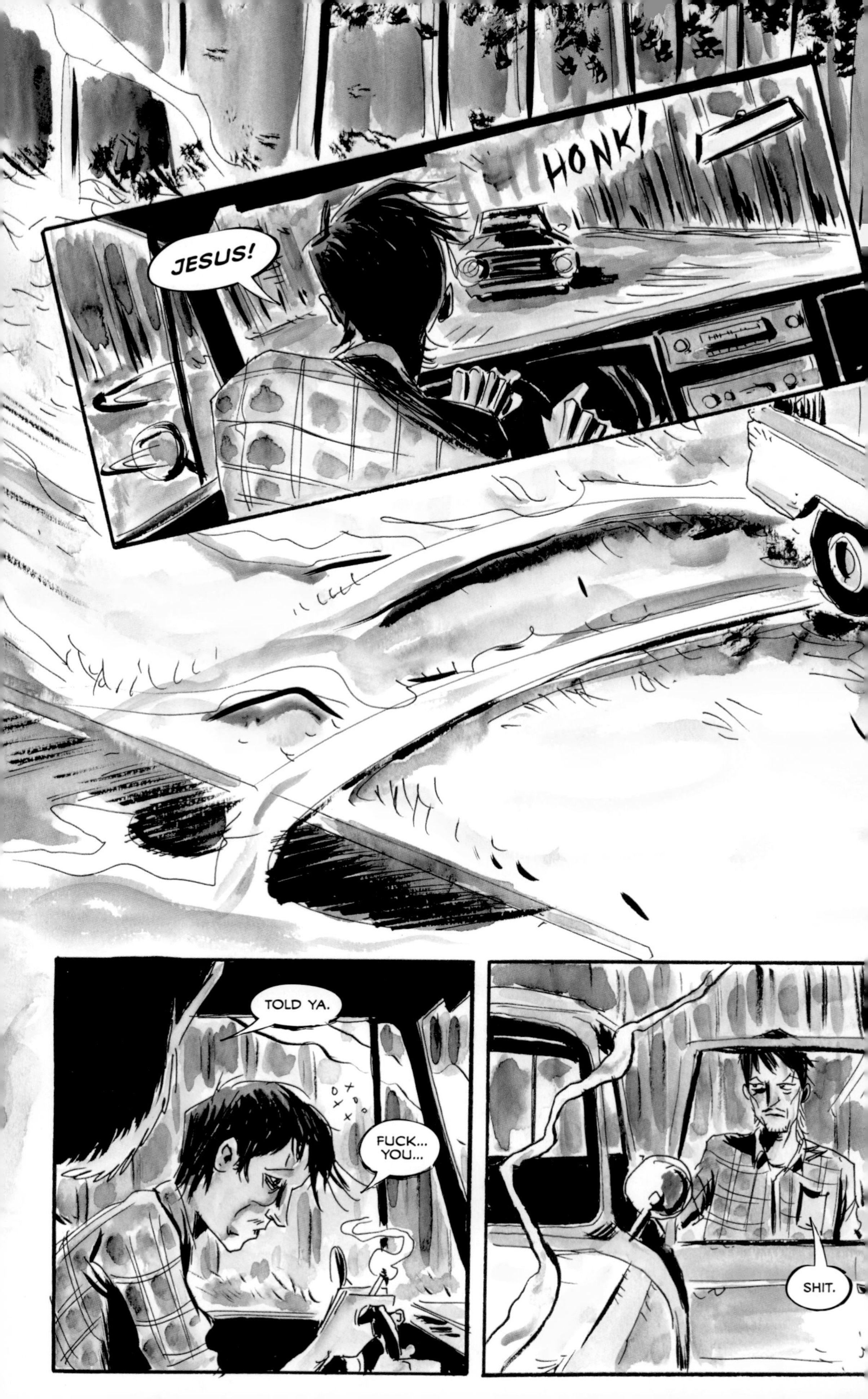
HONK!
JESUS!
TOLD YA.
FUCK... YOU...
SHIT.

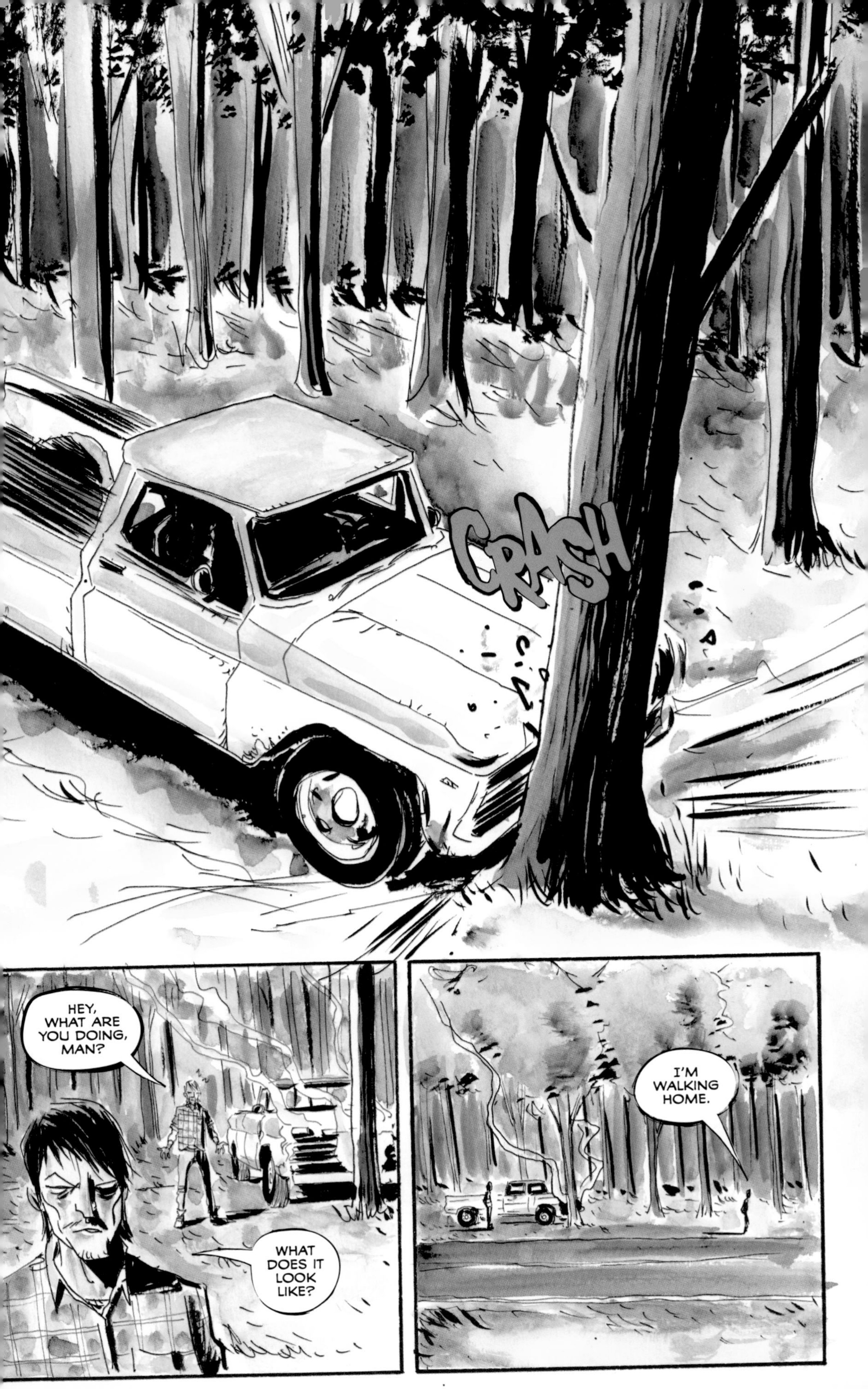
CRASH
HEY, WHAT ARE YOU DOING, MAN?
WHAT DOES IT LOOK LIKE?
I'M WALKING HOME.

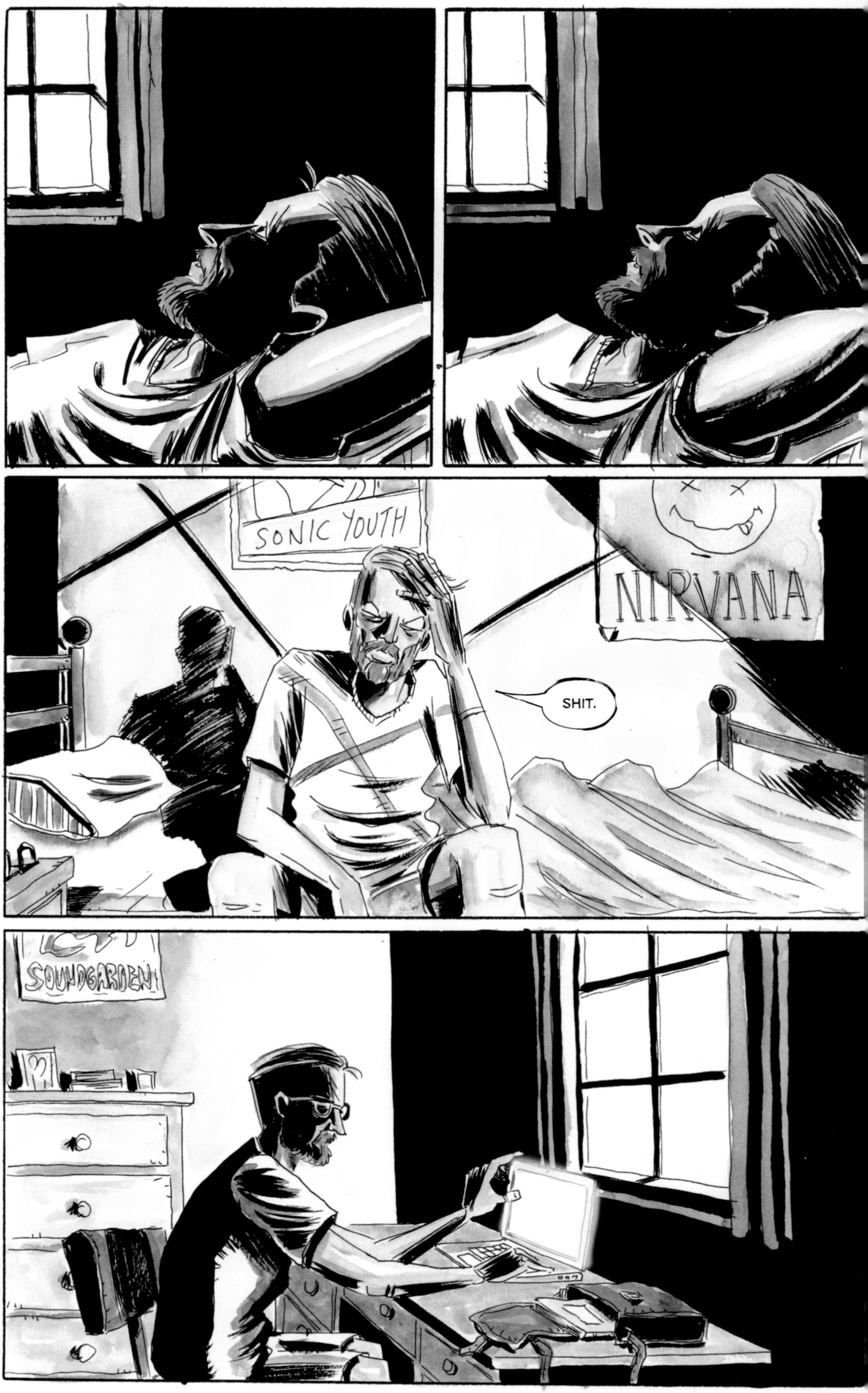
SONIC YOUTH
NIRVANA
SHIT.
SOUNDGARDEN

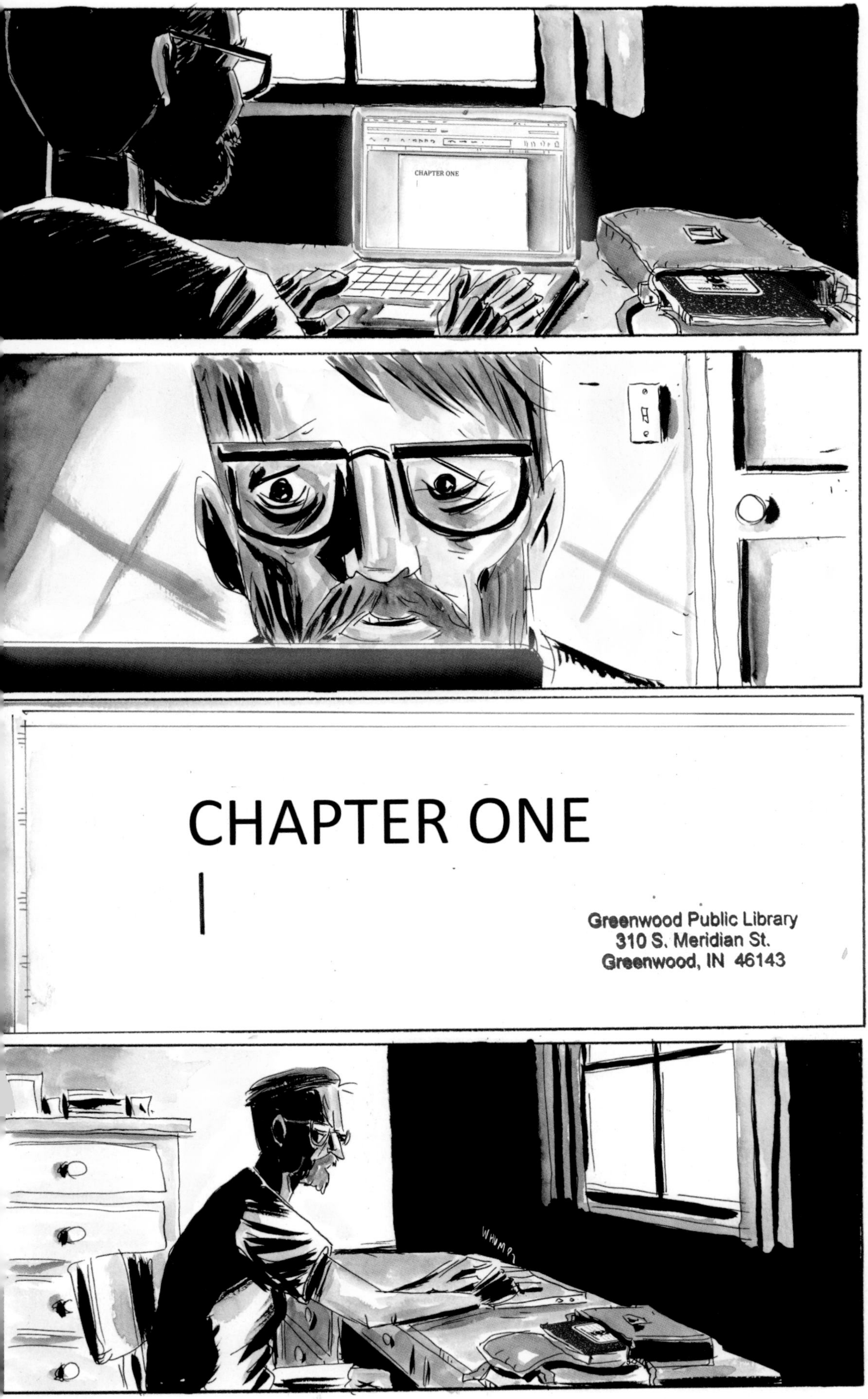
CHAPTER ONE
CHAPTER ONE
WHUMP

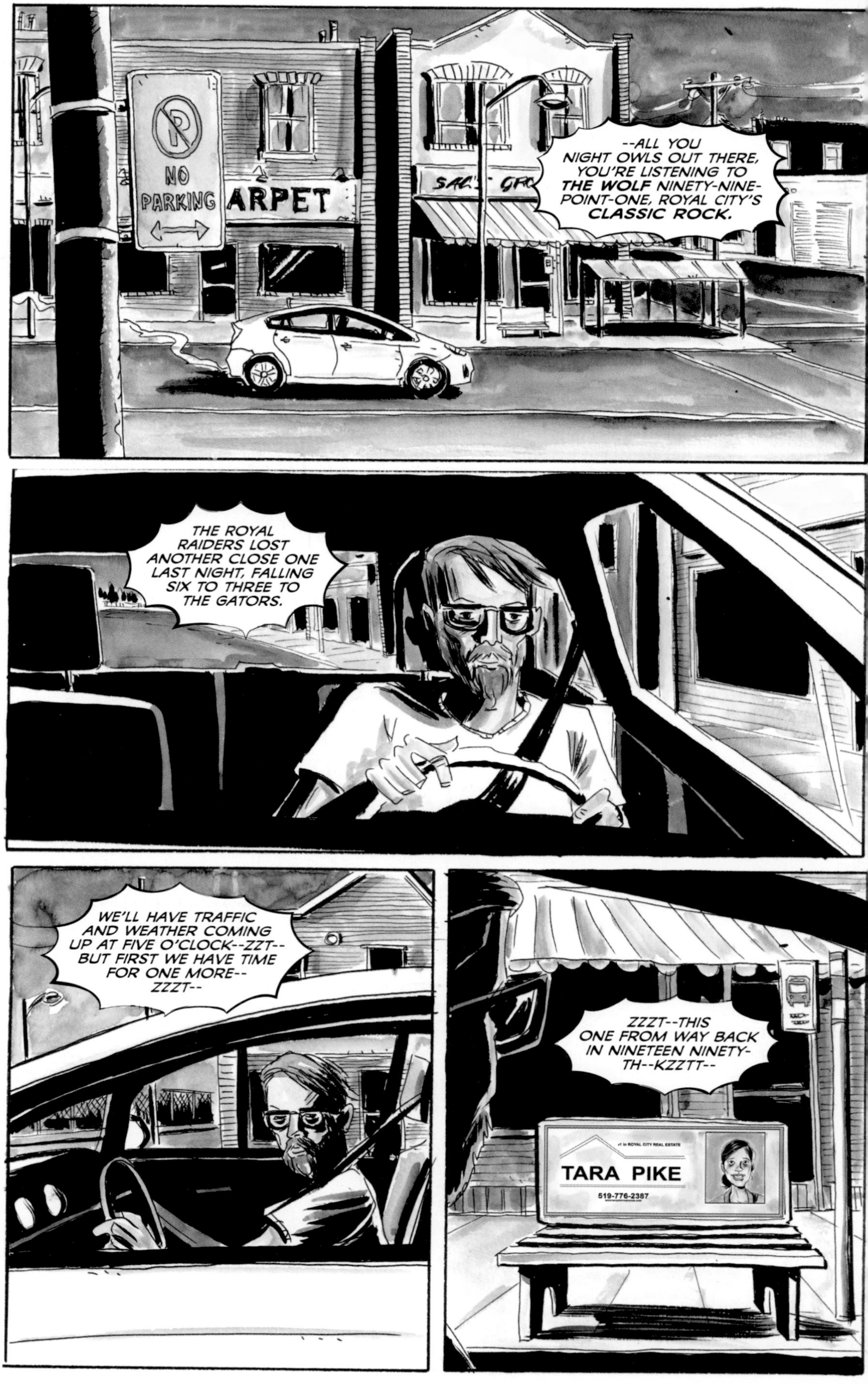

NO PARKING
ARPET
--ALL YOU NIGHT OWLS OUT THERE, YOU'RE LISTENING TO **THE WOLF** NINETY-NINE-POINT-ONE, ROYAL CITY'S **CLASSIC ROCK.**
THE ROYAL RAIDERS LOST ANOTHER CLOSE ONE LAST NIGHT, FALLING SIX TO THREE TO THE GATORS.
WE'LL HAVE TRAFFIC AND WEATHER COMING UP AT FIVE O'CLOCK--ZZT-- BUT FIRST WE HAVE TIME FOR ONE MORE-- ZZZT--
ZZZT--THIS ONE FROM WAY BACK IN NINETEEN NINETY-TH--KZZTT--
#1 in ROYAL CITY REAL ESTATE
TARA PIKE
519-776-2387

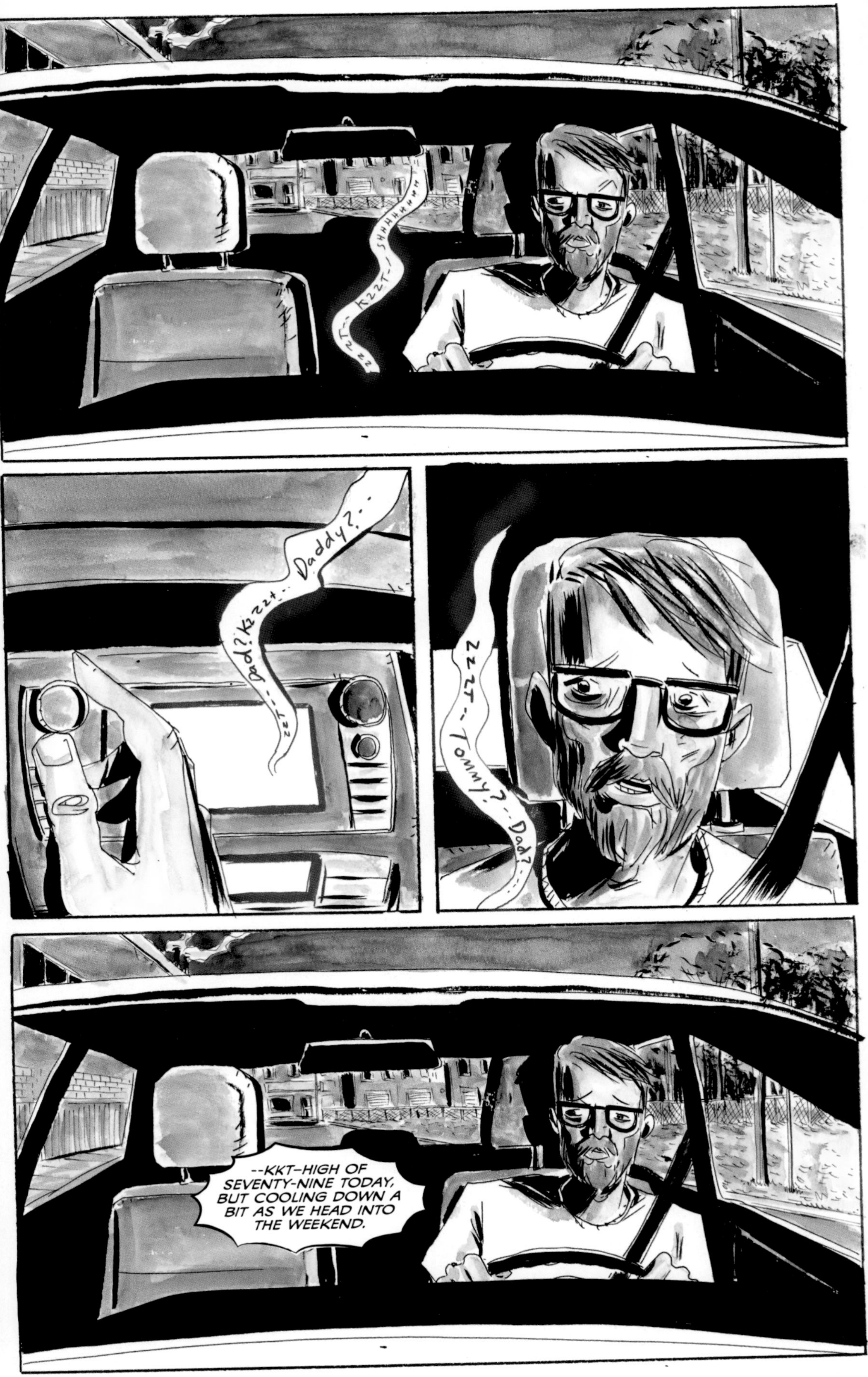
ZZZT-- KZZT-- SHHHHHHHHH
ZZZT-- Dad? KZZZT-- Daddy?--
ZZZT-- Tommy?-- Dad?--
--KKT-HIGH OF SEVENTY-NINE TODAY, BUT COOLING DOWN A BIT AS WE HEAD INTO THE WEEKEND.

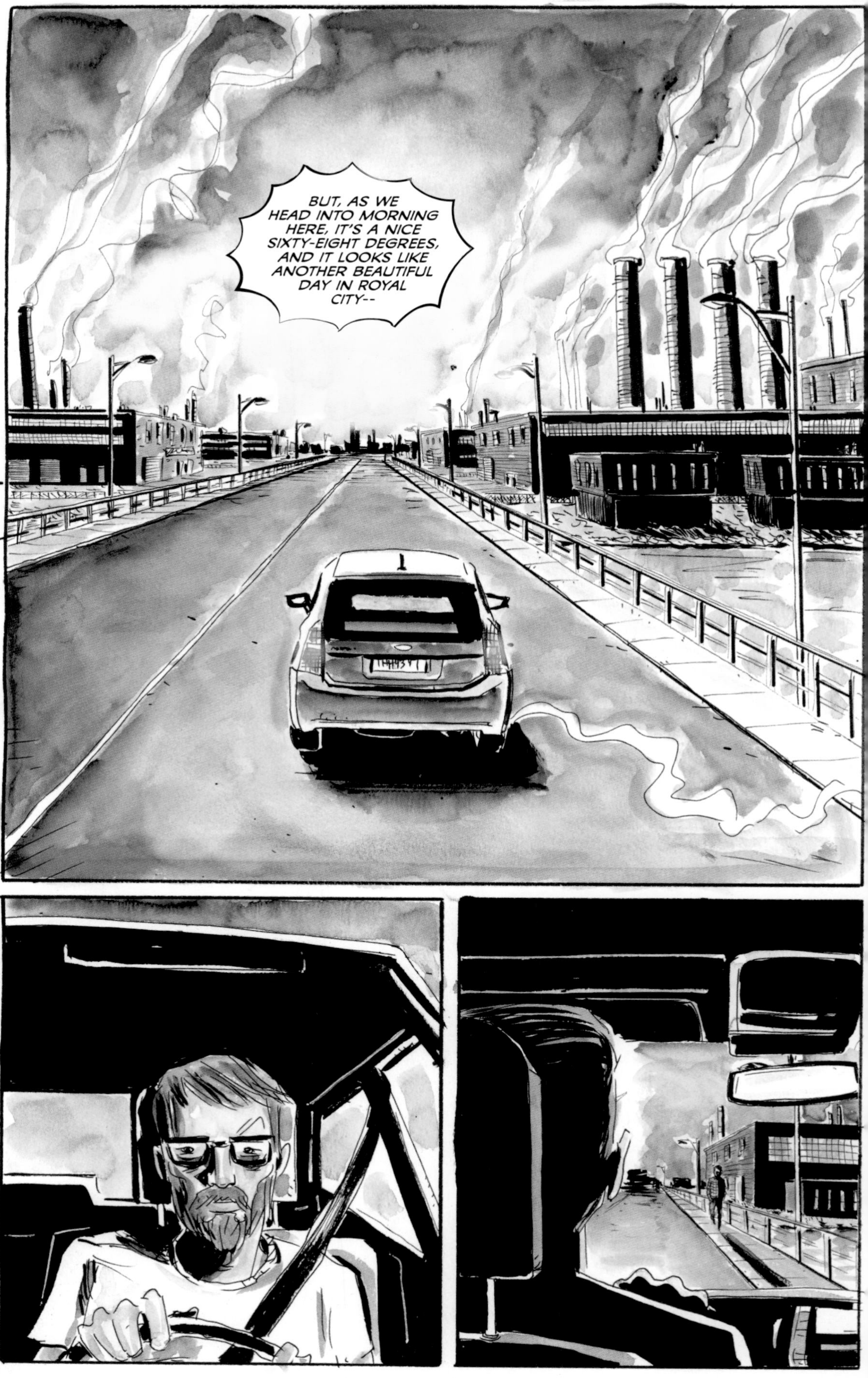
BUT, AS WE HEAD INTO MORNING HERE, IT'S A NICE SIXTY-EIGHT DEGREES, AND IT LOOKS LIKE ANOTHER BEAUTIFUL DAY IN ROYAL CITY--

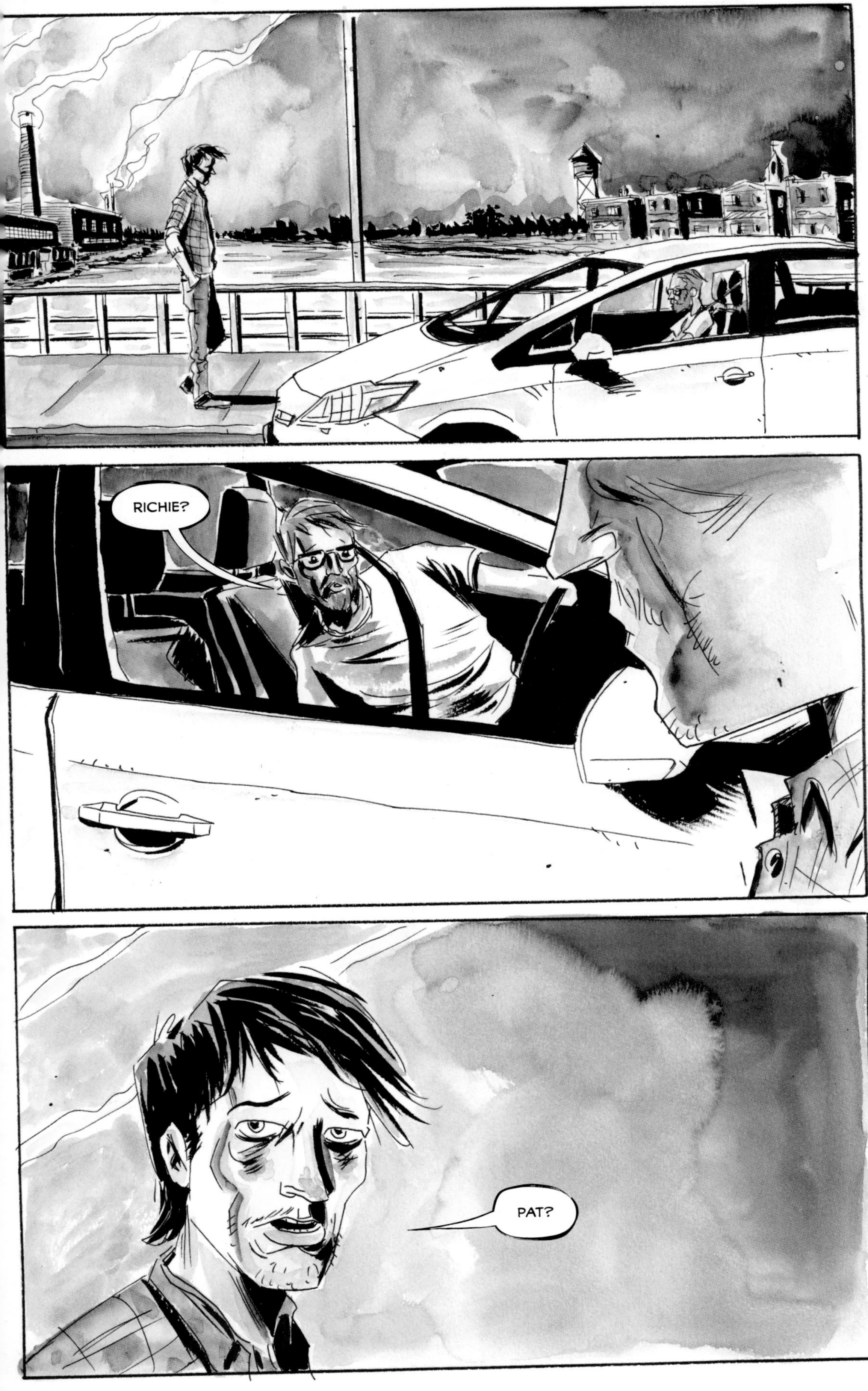
RICHIE?
PAT?

CHAPTER THREE

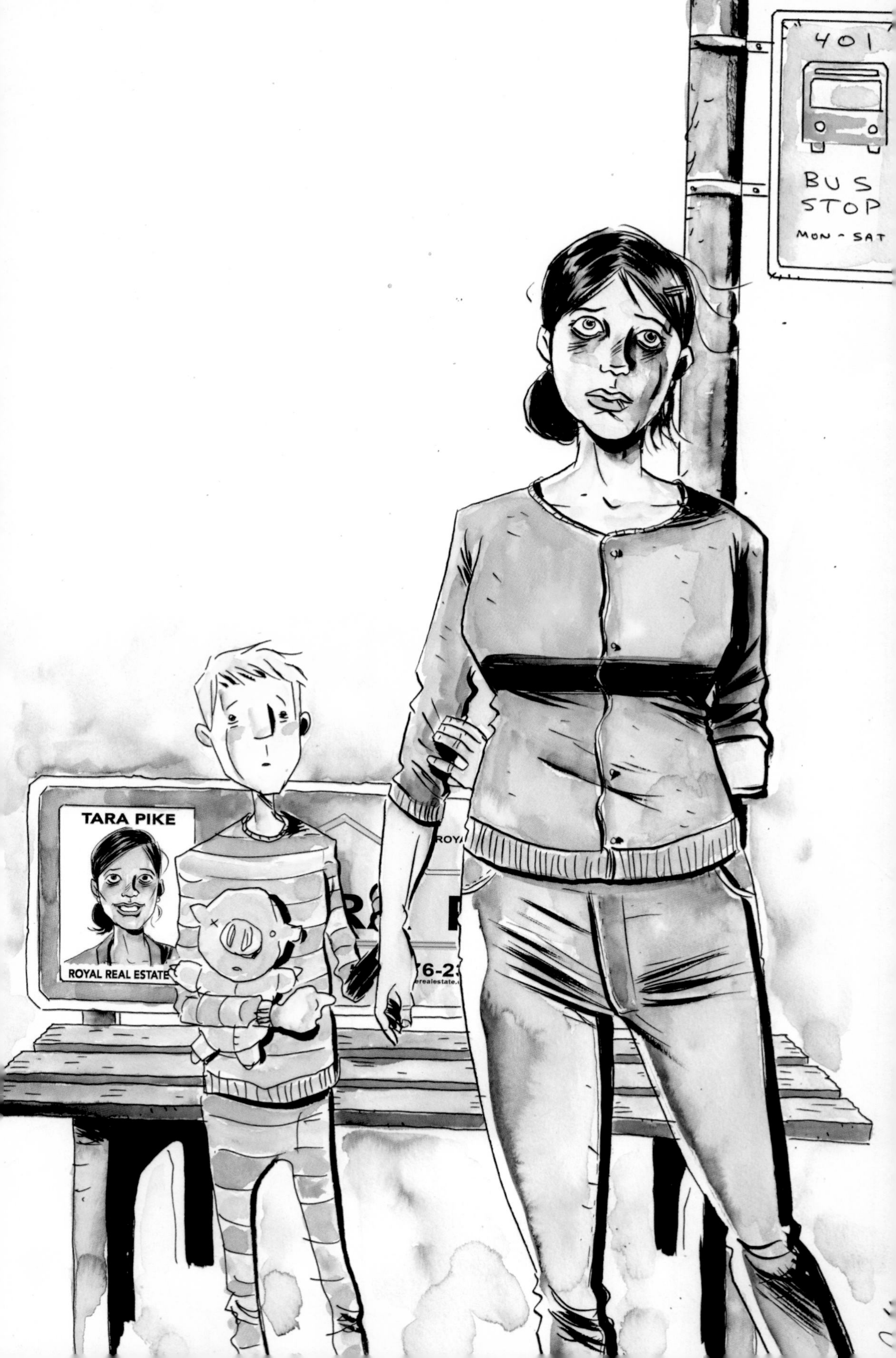
401
BUS STOP
MON - SAT
TARA PIKE
ROYAL REAL ESTATE

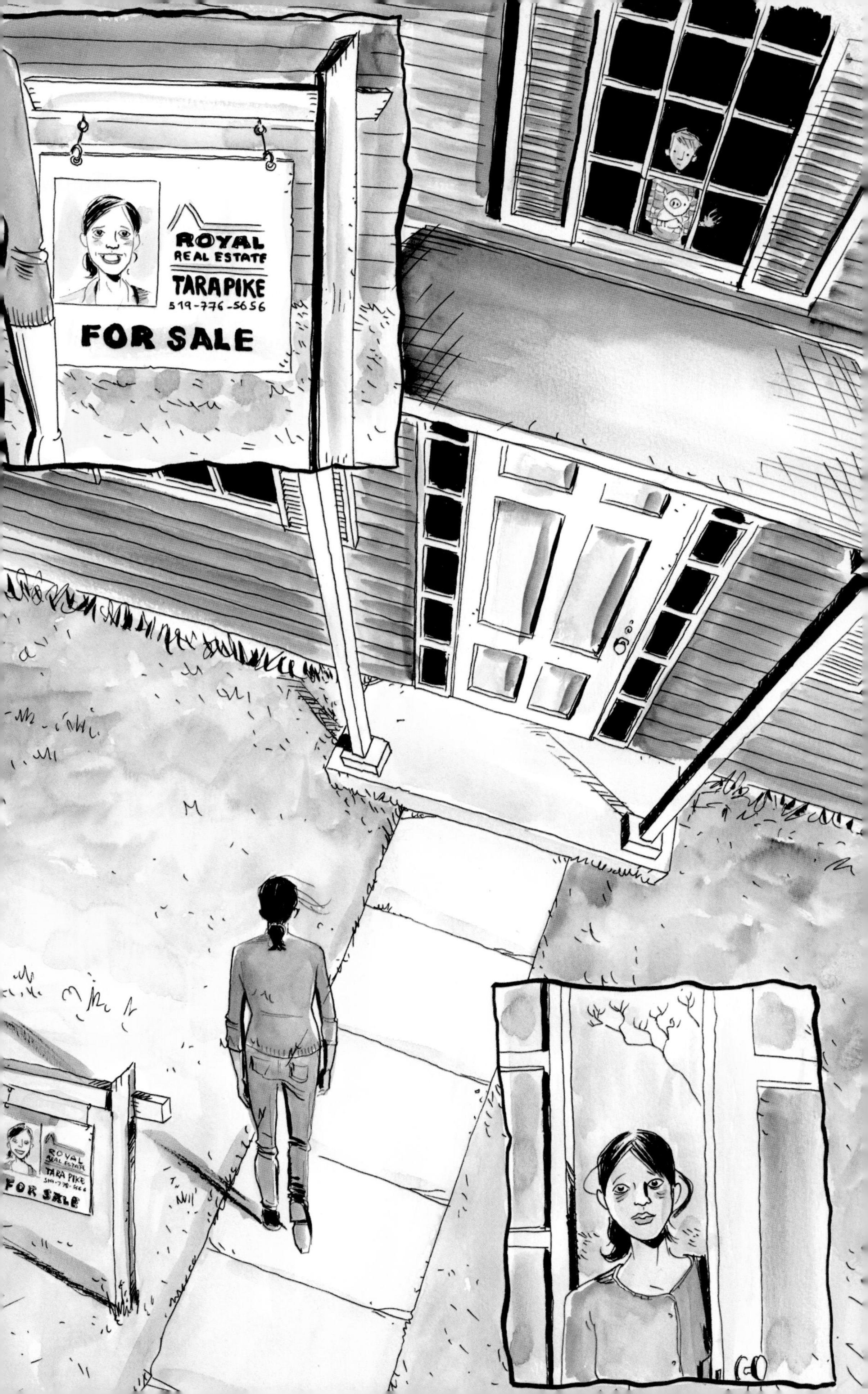
ROYAL
REAL ESTATE
TARA PIKE
519-776-5656
FOR SALE
ROYAL
REAL ESTATE
TARA PIKE
FOR SALE

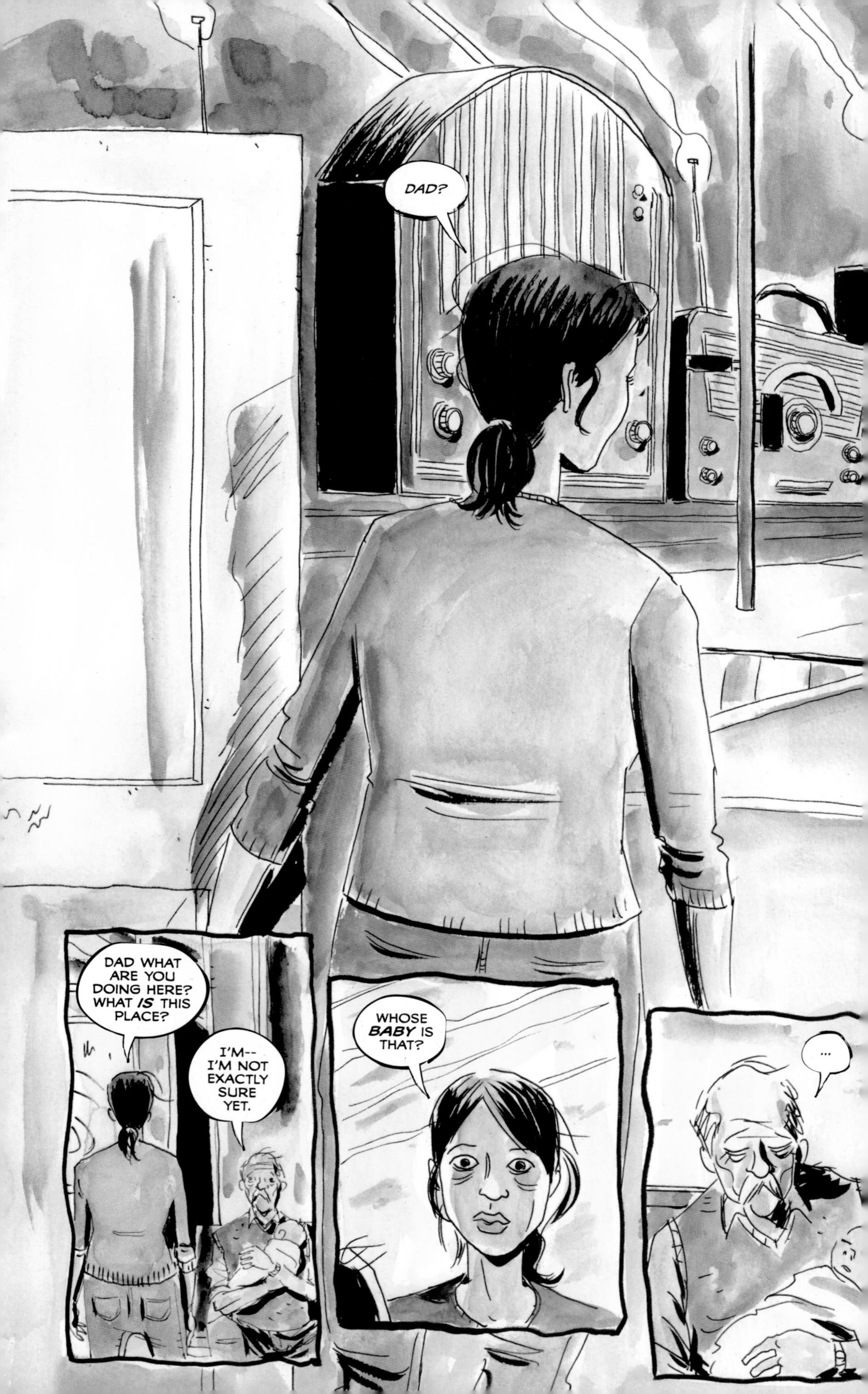
DAD?
DAD WHAT ARE YOU DOING HERE? WHAT *IS* THIS PLACE?
I'M-- I'M NOT EXACTLY SURE YET.
WHOSE *BABY* IS THAT?
...

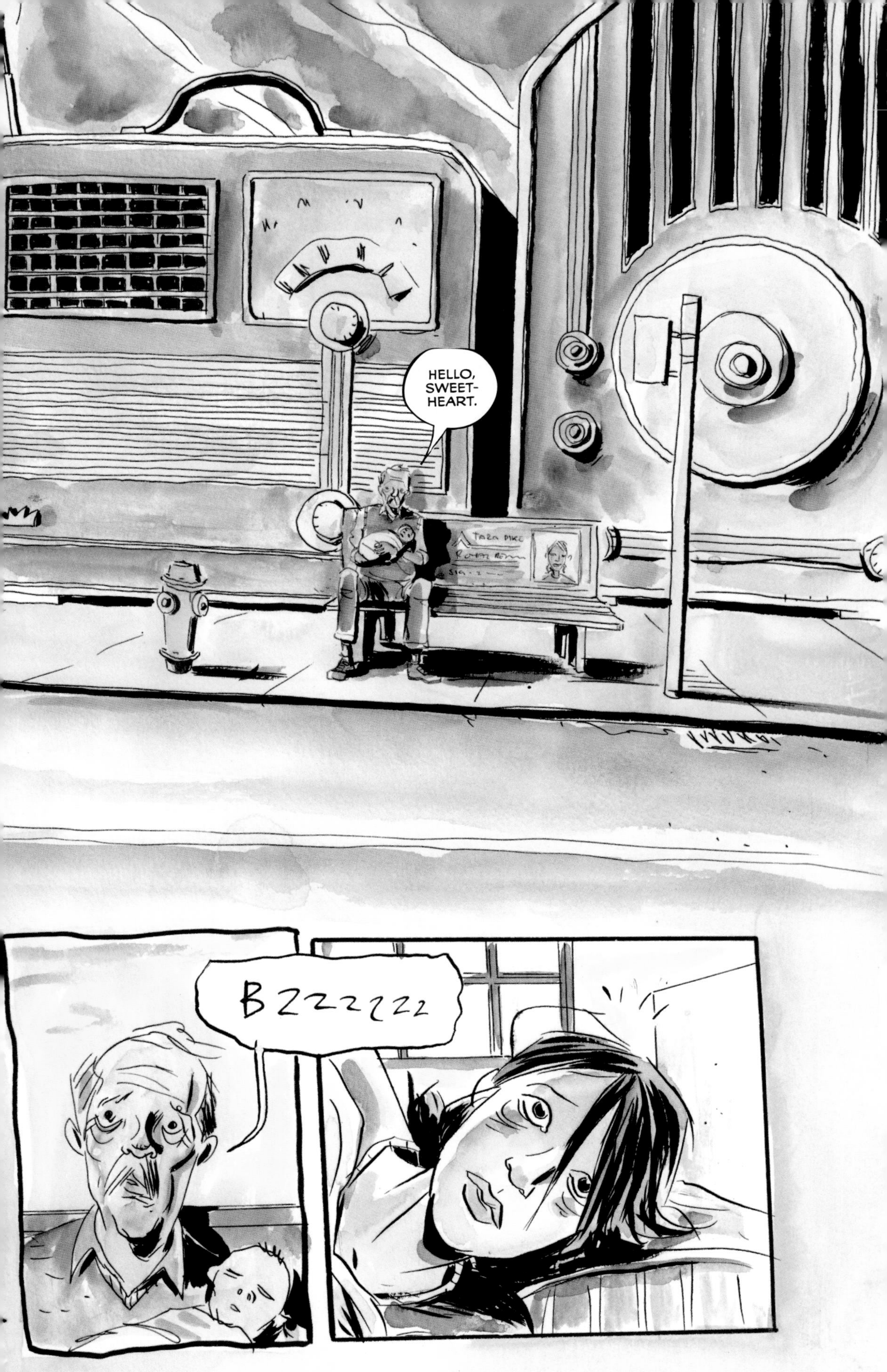
HELLO, SWEET-HEART.
Bzzzzzz

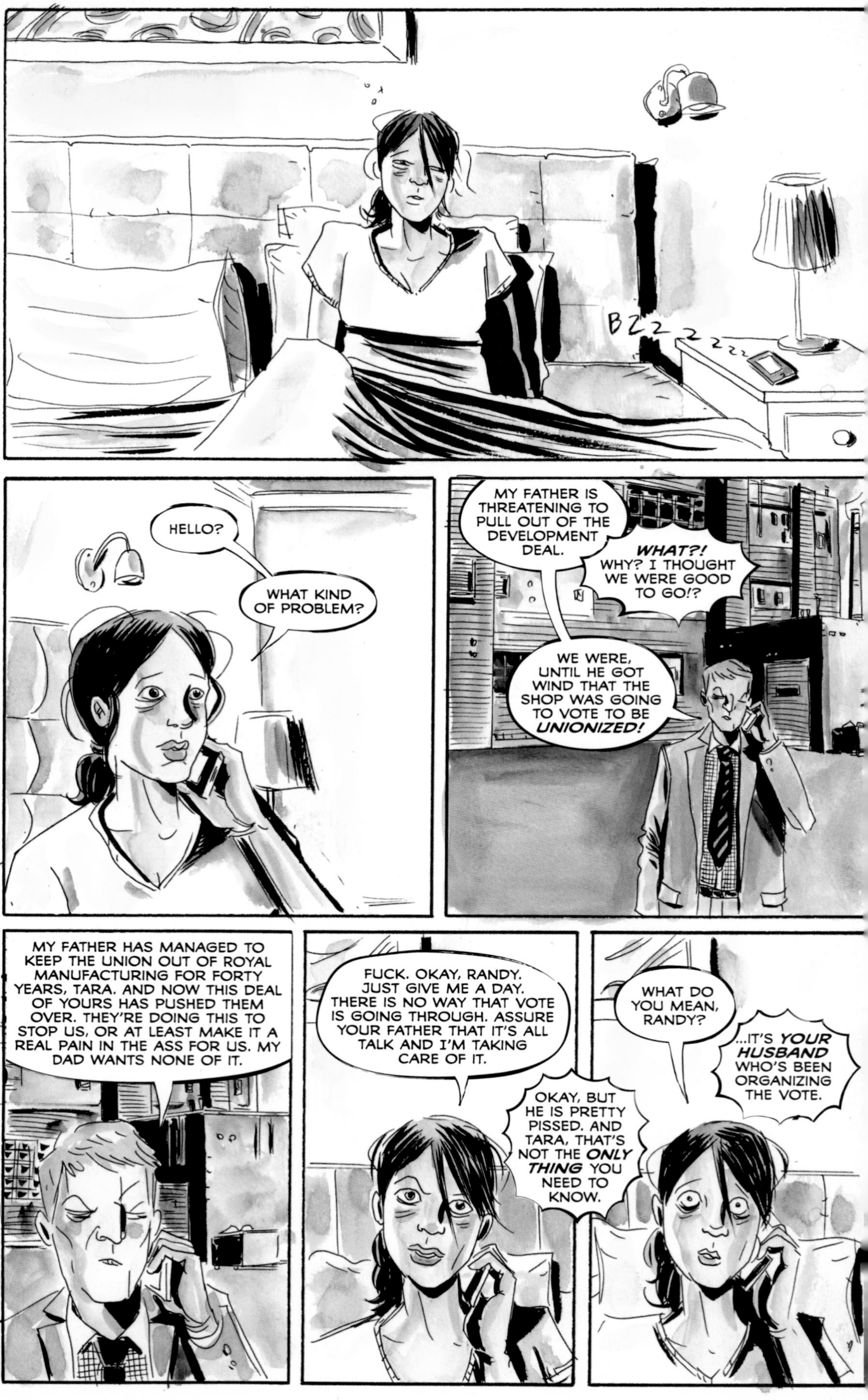
BZZZZZZZ
HELLO?
WHAT KIND OF PROBLEM?
MY FATHER IS THREATENING TO PULL OUT OF THE DEVELOPMENT DEAL.
WHAT?! WHY? I THOUGHT WE WERE GOOD TO GO!?
WE WERE, UNTIL HE GOT WIND THAT THE SHOP WAS GOING TO VOTE TO BE UNIONIZED!
MY FATHER HAS MANAGED TO KEEP THE UNION OUT OF ROYAL MANUFACTURING FOR FORTY YEARS, TARA. AND NOW THIS DEAL OF YOURS HAS PUSHED THEM OVER. THEY'RE DOING THIS TO STOP US, OR AT LEAST MAKE IT A REAL PAIN IN THE ASS FOR US. MY DAD WANTS NONE OF IT.
FUCK. OKAY, RANDY. JUST GIVE ME A DAY. THERE IS NO WAY THAT VOTE IS GOING THROUGH. ASSURE YOUR FATHER THAT IT'S ALL TALK AND I'M TAKING CARE OF IT.
OKAY, BUT HE IS PRETTY PISSED. AND TARA, THAT'S NOT THE ONLY THING YOU NEED TO KNOW.
WHAT DO YOU MEAN, RANDY?
...IT'S YOUR HUSBAND WHO'S BEEN ORGANIZING THE VOTE.

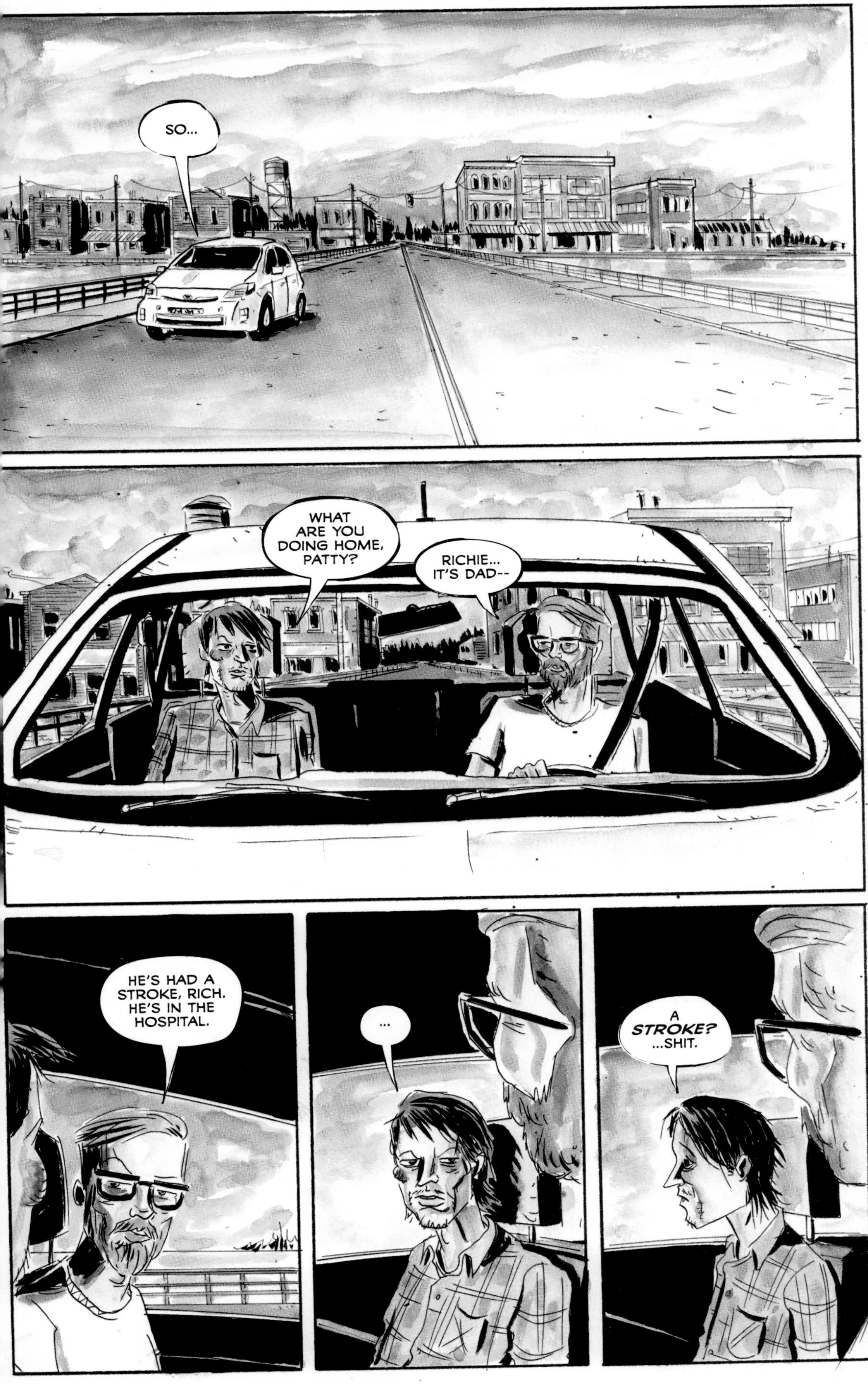
SO...
WHAT ARE YOU DOING HOME, PATTY?
RICHIE... IT'S DAD--
HE'S HAD A STROKE, RICH. HE'S IN THE HOSPITAL.
...
A *STROKE?* ...SHIT.

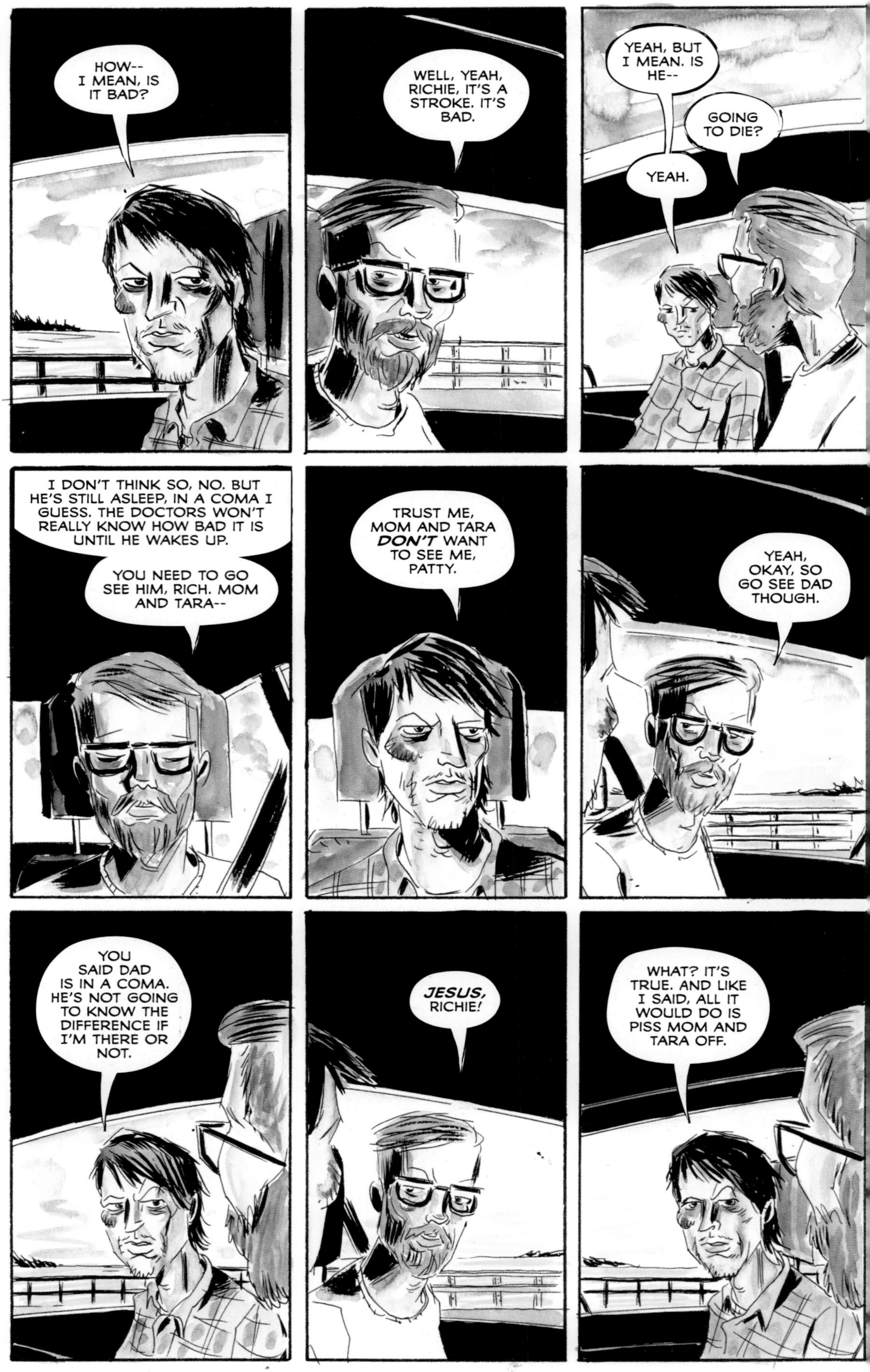
HOW-- I MEAN, IS IT BAD?
WELL, YEAH, RICHIE, IT'S A STROKE. IT'S BAD.
YEAH, BUT I MEAN. IS HE--
GOING TO DIE?
YEAH.
I DON'T THINK SO, NO. BUT HE'S STILL ASLEEP, IN A COMA I GUESS. THE DOCTORS WON'T REALLY KNOW HOW BAD IT IS UNTIL HE WAKES UP.
YOU NEED TO GO SEE HIM, RICH. MOM AND TARA--
TRUST ME, MOM AND TARA *DON'T* WANT TO SEE ME, PATTY.
YEAH, OKAY, SO GO SEE DAD THOUGH.
YOU SAID DAD IS IN A COMA. HE'S NOT GOING TO KNOW THE DIFFERENCE IF I'M THERE OR NOT.
JESUS, RICHIE!
WHAT? IT'S TRUE. AND LIKE I SAID, ALL IT WOULD DO IS PISS MOM AND TARA OFF.

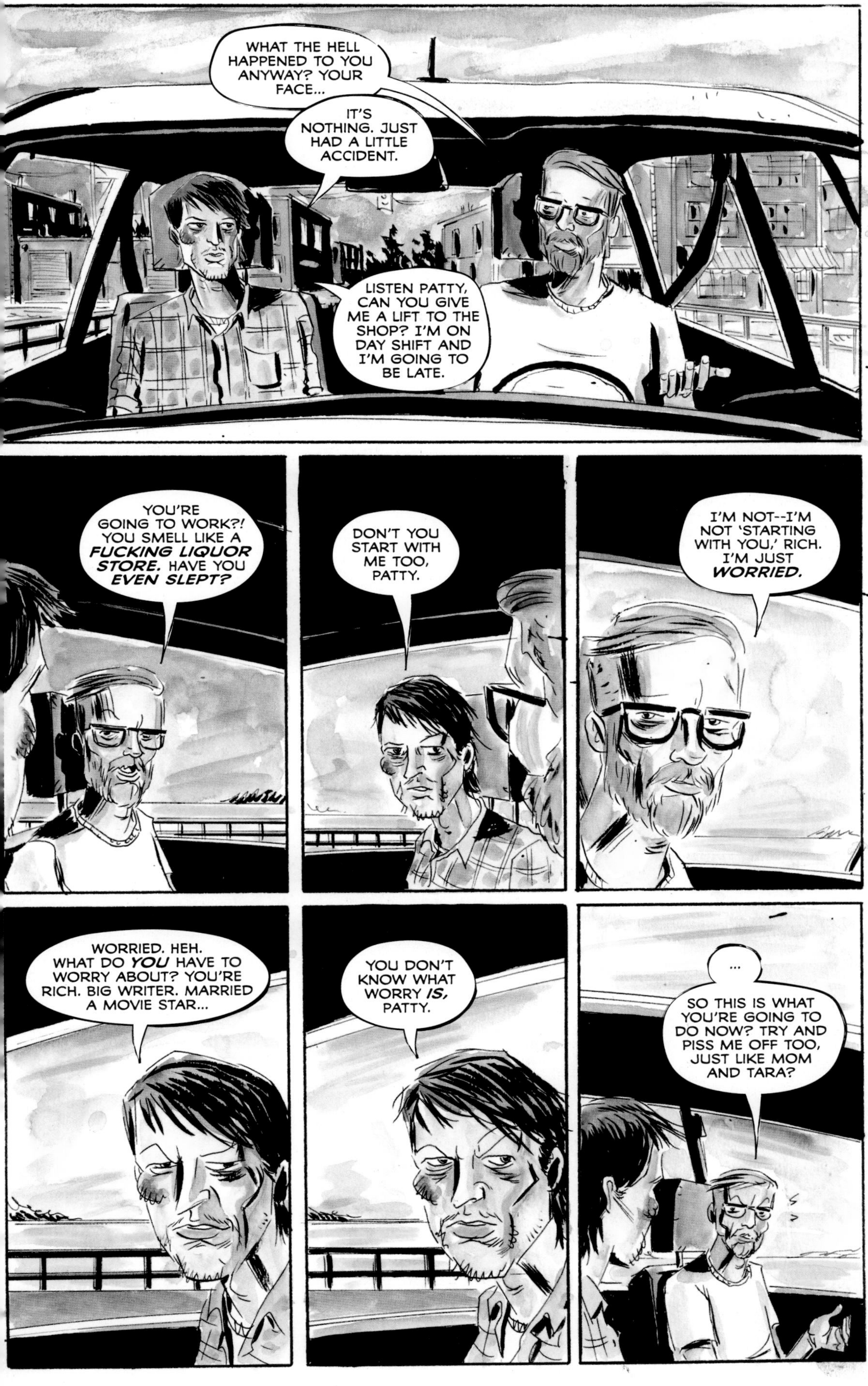
WHAT THE HELL HAPPENED TO YOU ANYWAY? YOUR FACE...
IT'S NOTHING. JUST HAD A LITTLE ACCIDENT.
LISTEN PATTY, CAN YOU GIVE ME A LIFT TO THE SHOP? I'M ON DAY SHIFT AND I'M GOING TO BE LATE.
YOU'RE GOING TO WORK?! YOU SMELL LIKE A FUCKING LIQUOR STORE. HAVE YOU EVEN SLEPT?
DON'T YOU START WITH ME TOO, PATTY.
I'M NOT--I'M NOT 'STARTING WITH YOU,' RICH. I'M JUST WORRIED.
WORRIED. HEH. WHAT DO YOU HAVE TO WORRY ABOUT? YOU'RE RICH. BIG WRITER. MARRIED A MOVIE STAR...
YOU DON'T KNOW WHAT WORRY IS, PATTY.
...
SO THIS IS WHAT YOU'RE GOING TO DO NOW? TRY AND PISS ME OFF TOO, JUST LIKE MOM AND TARA?

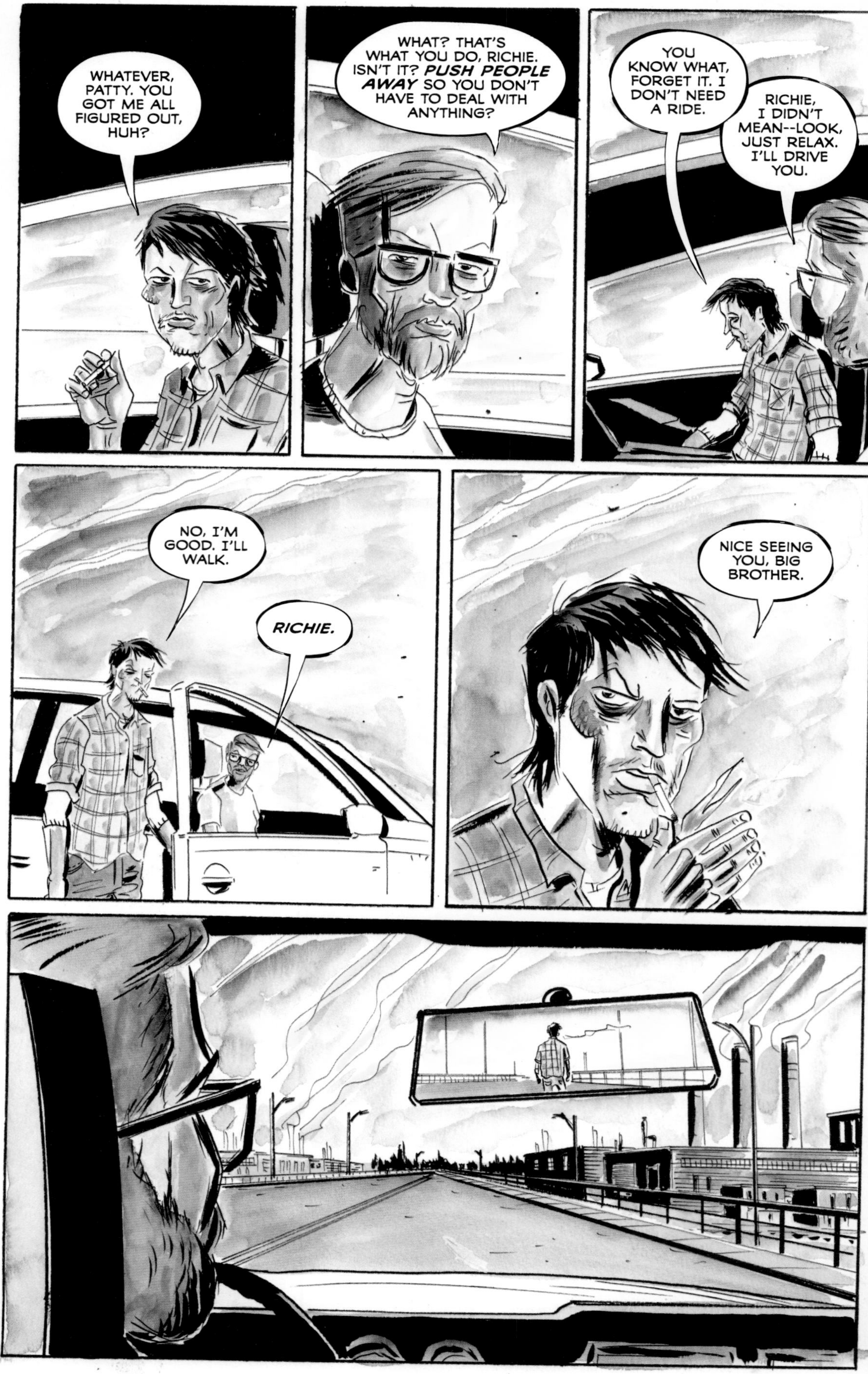
WHATEVER, PATTY. YOU GOT ME ALL FIGURED OUT, HUH?
WHAT? THAT'S WHAT YOU DO, RICHIE. ISN'T IT? PUSH PEOPLE AWAY SO YOU DON'T HAVE TO DEAL WITH ANYTHING?
YOU KNOW WHAT, FORGET IT. I DON'T NEED A RIDE.
RICHIE, I DIDN'T MEAN--LOOK, JUST RELAX. I'LL DRIVE YOU.
NO, I'M GOOD. I'LL WALK.
RICHIE.
NICE SEEING YOU, BIG BROTHER.

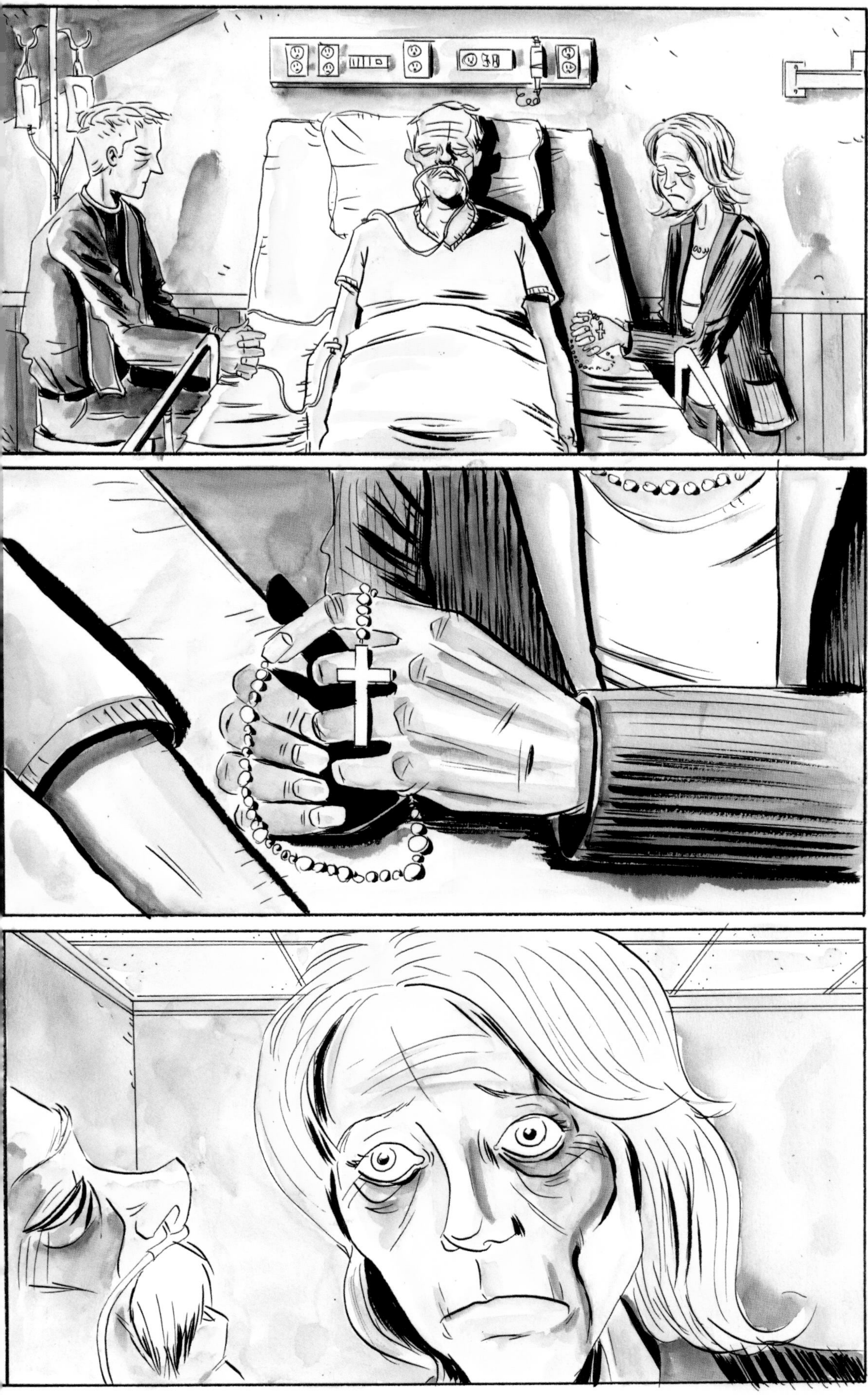

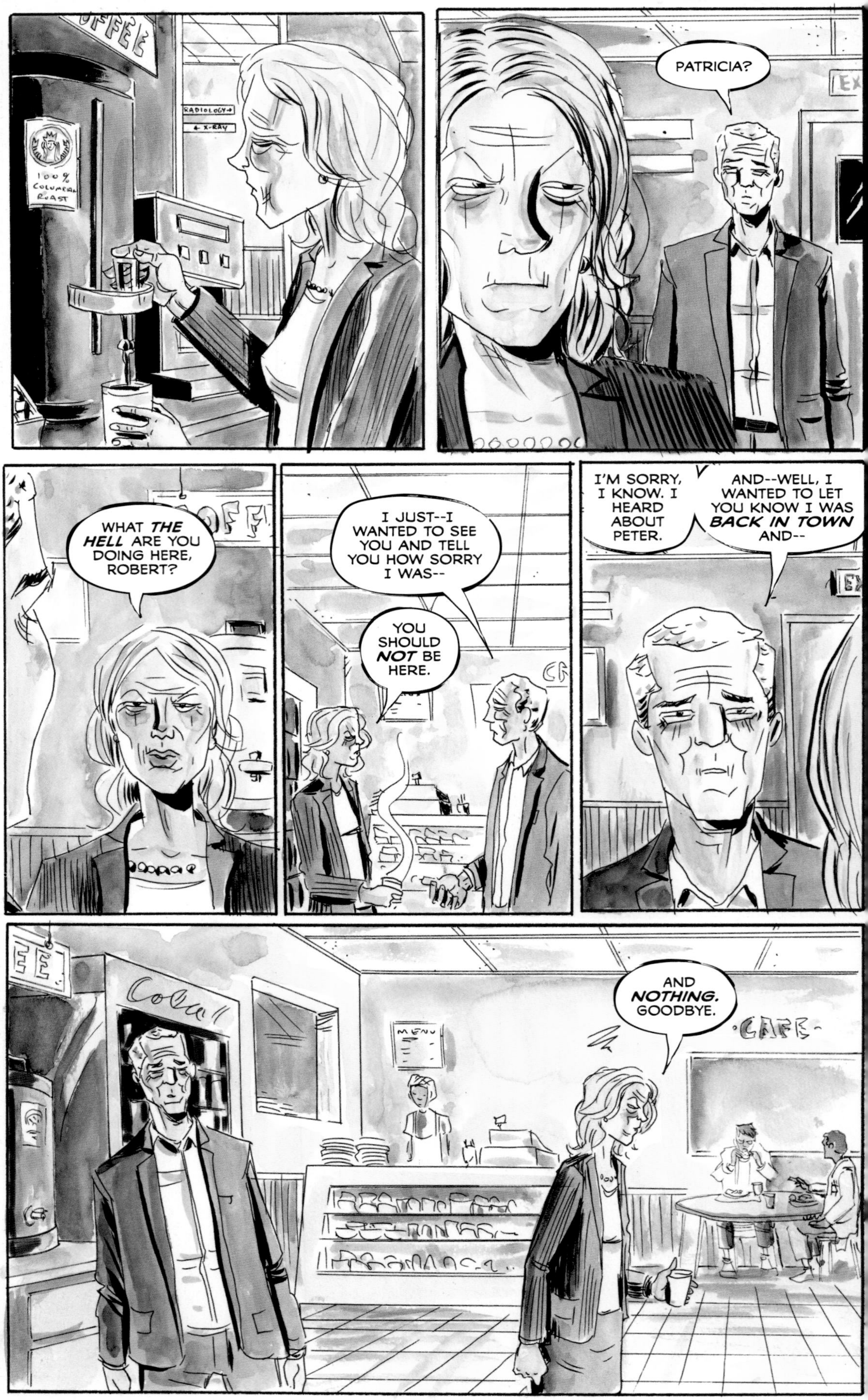
COFFEE
RADIOLOGY
X-RAY
100% COLUMBIAN ROAST
PATRICIA?
WHAT THE HELL ARE YOU DOING HERE, ROBERT?
I JUST--I WANTED TO SEE YOU AND TELL YOU HOW SORRY I WAS--
YOU SHOULD NOT BE HERE.
I'M SORRY, I KNOW. I HEARD ABOUT PETER.
AND--WELL, I WANTED TO LET YOU KNOW I WAS BACK IN TOWN AND--
MENU
CAFE
AND NOTHING. GOODBYE.

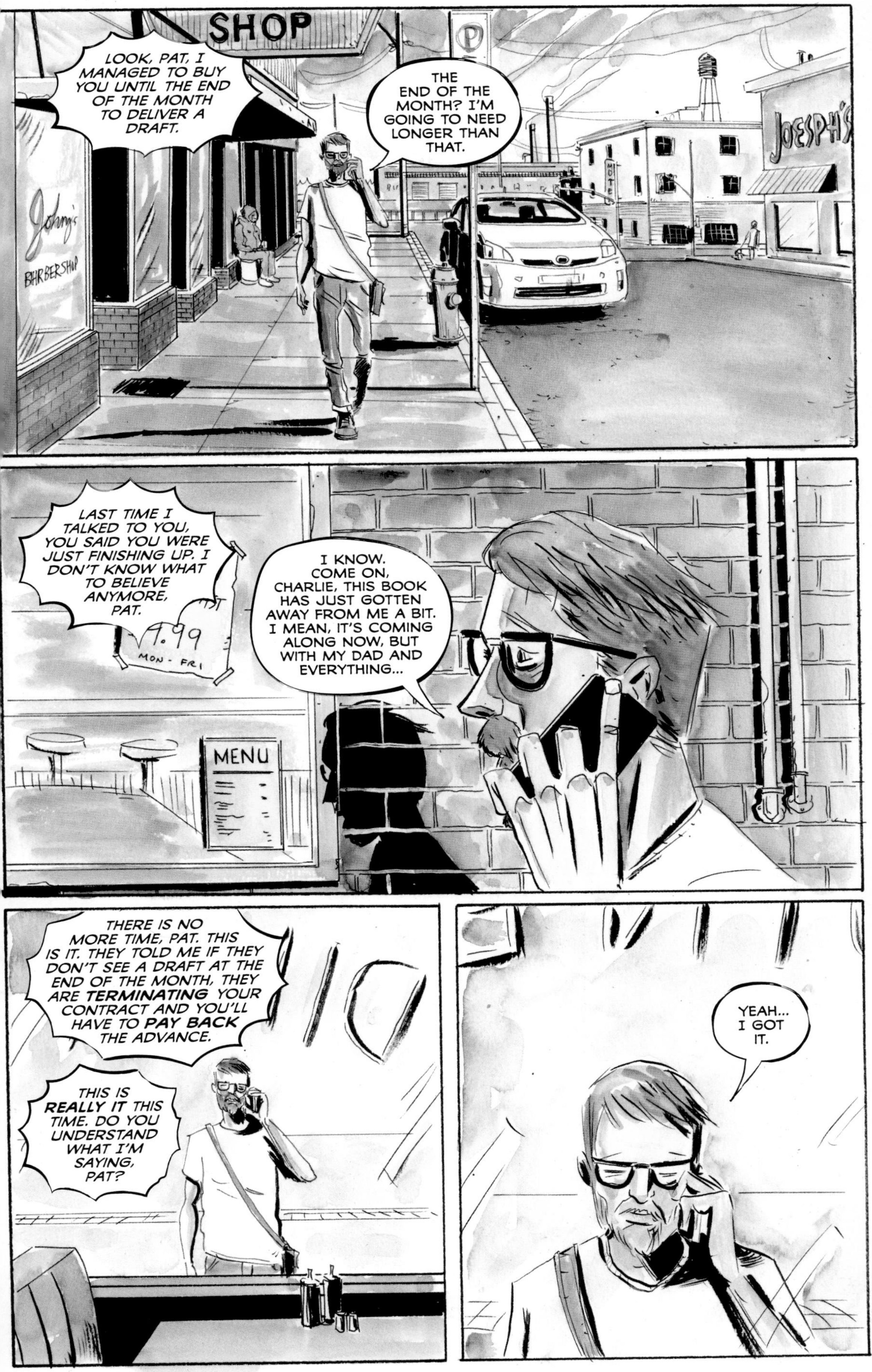
SHOP
LOOK, PAT, I MANAGED TO BUY YOU UNTIL THE END OF THE MONTH TO DELIVER A DRAFT.
THE END OF THE MONTH? I'M GOING TO NEED LONGER THAN THAT.
JOESPH'S
Johnny's BARBERSHOP
LAST TIME I TALKED TO YOU, YOU SAID YOU WERE JUST FINISHING UP. I DON'T KNOW WHAT TO BELIEVE ANYMORE, PAT.
I KNOW. COME ON, CHARLIE, THIS BOOK HAS JUST GOTTEN AWAY FROM ME A BIT. I MEAN, IT'S COMING ALONG NOW, BUT WITH MY DAD AND EVERYTHING...
MON - FRI
MENU
THERE IS NO MORE TIME, PAT. THIS IS IT. THEY TOLD ME IF THEY DON'T SEE A DRAFT AT THE END OF THE MONTH, THEY ARE TERMINATING YOUR CONTRACT AND YOU'LL HAVE TO PAY BACK THE ADVANCE.
THIS IS REALLY IT THIS TIME. DO YOU UNDERSTAND WHAT I'M SAYING, PAT?
YEAH... I GOT IT.

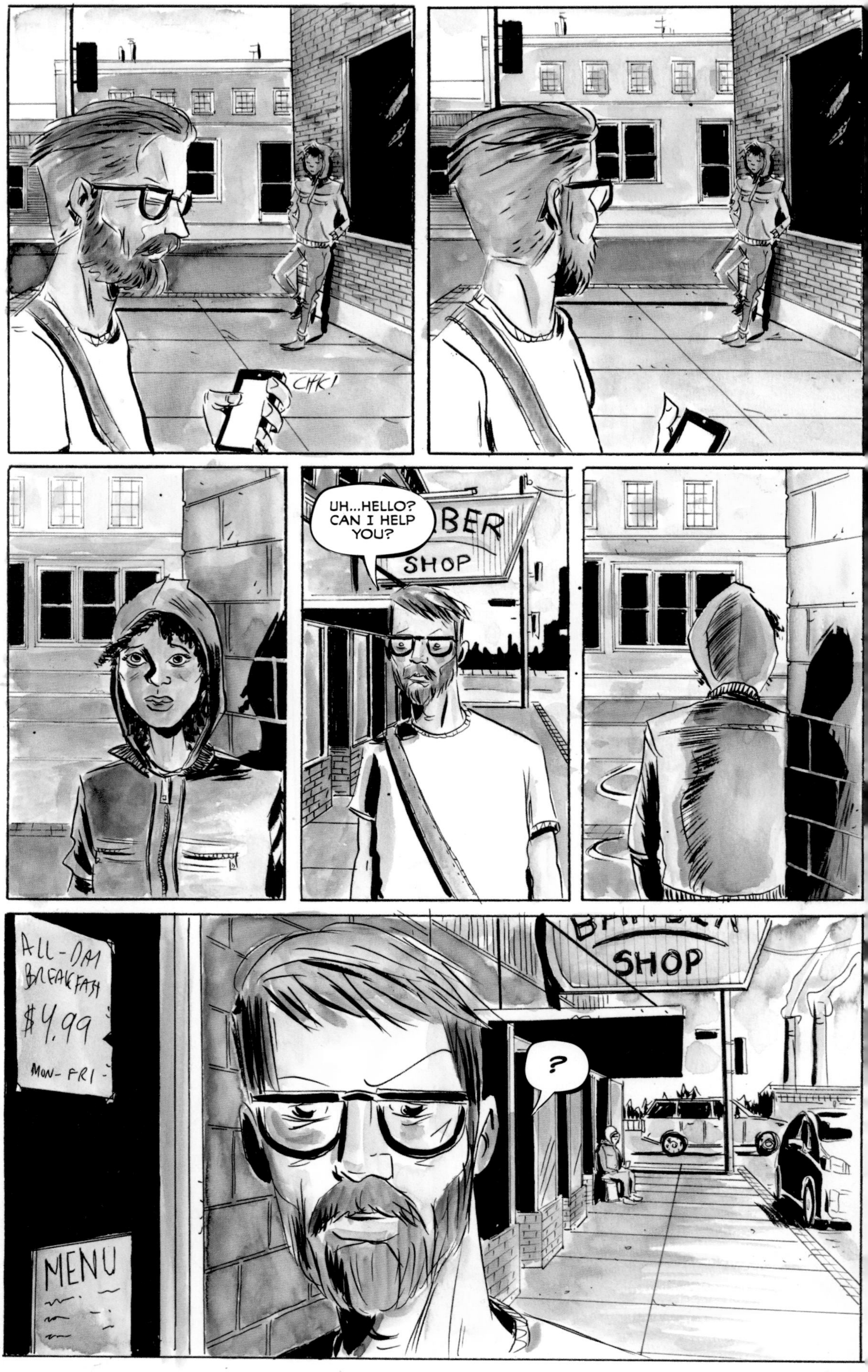
CHK!
UH...HELLO? CAN I HELP YOU?
BER
SHOP
ALL-DAY BREAKFAST $4.99 MON-FRI
MENU
SHOP
?

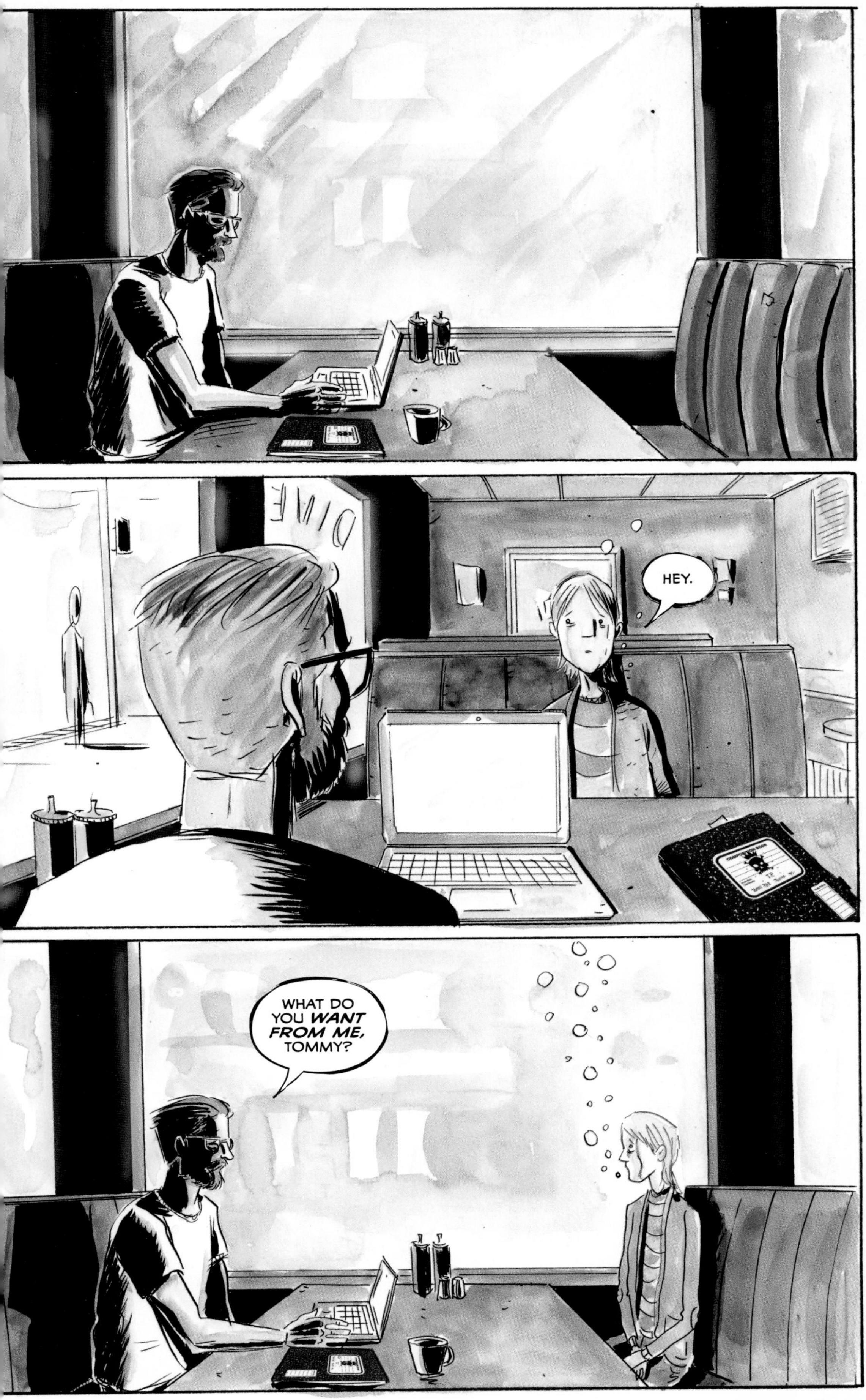
HEY.
WHAT DO YOU WANT FROM ME, TOMMY?

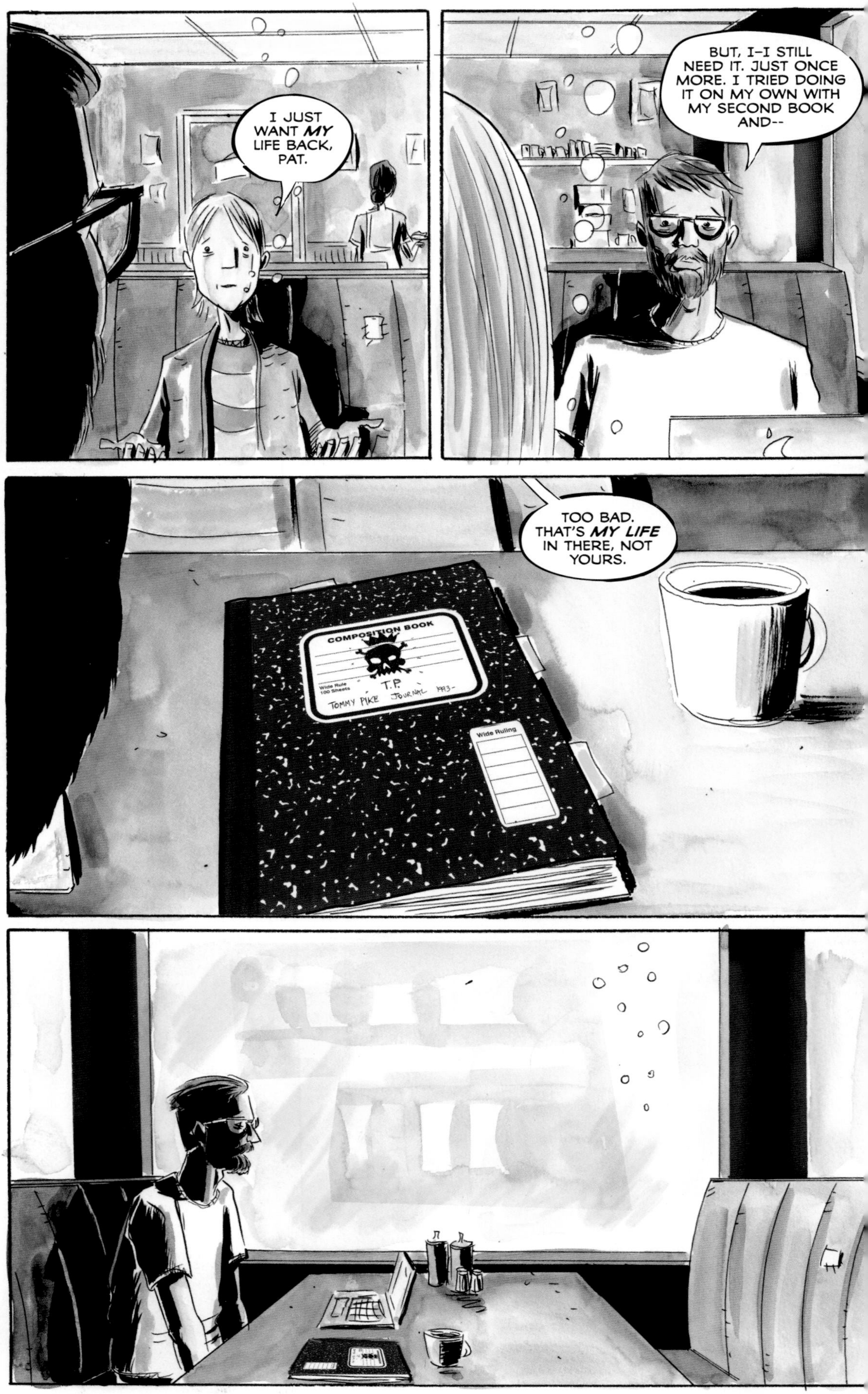
I JUST WANT *MY* LIFE BACK, PAT.
BUT, I--I STILL NEED IT. JUST ONCE MORE. I TRIED DOING IT ON MY OWN WITH MY SECOND BOOK AND--
TOO BAD. THAT'S *MY LIFE* IN THERE, NOT YOURS.
COMPOSITION BOOK
T.P.
Wide Rule 100 Sheets
TOMMY PIKE JOURNAL 1993-
Wide Ruling

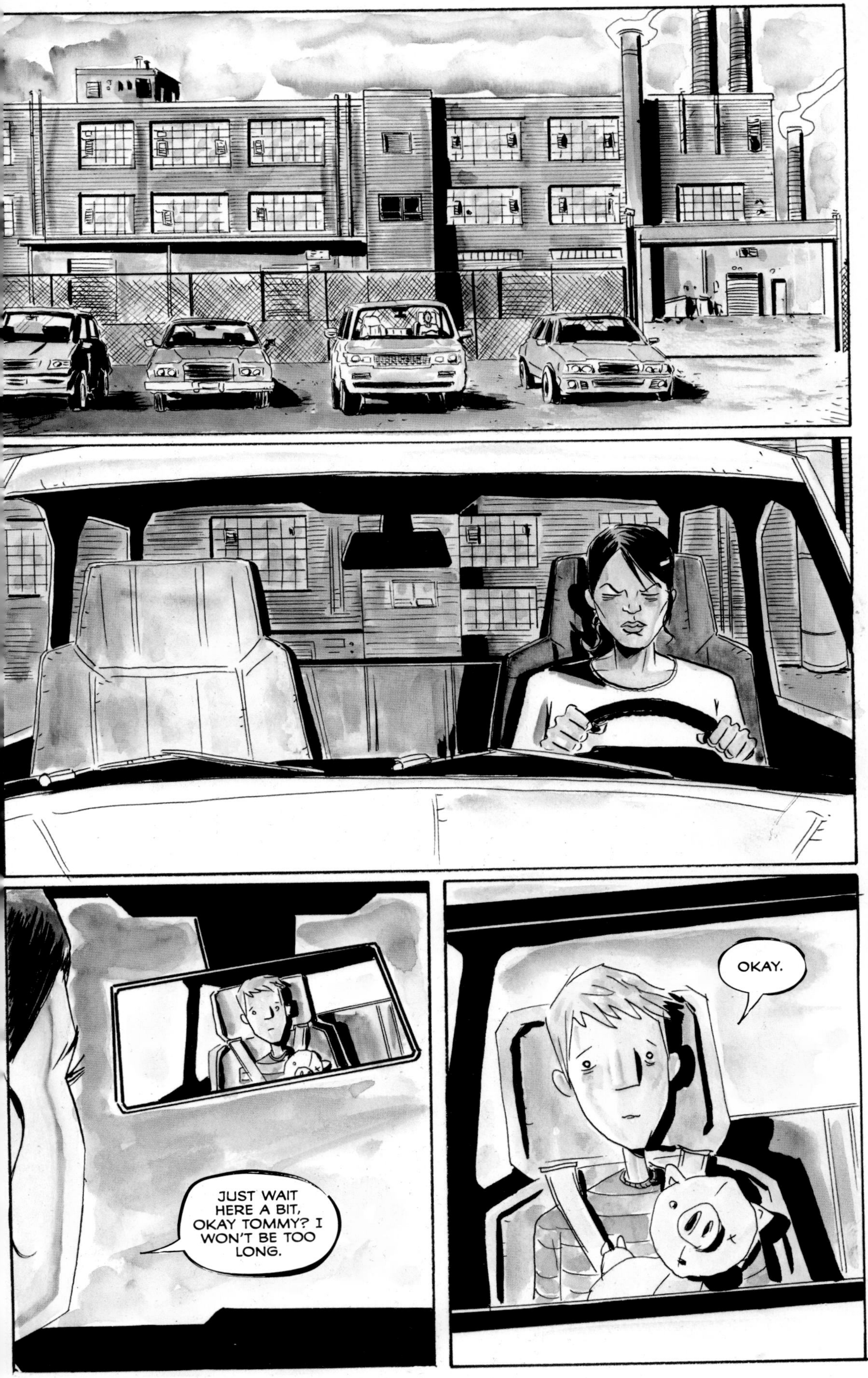
JUST WAIT HERE A BIT, OKAY TOMMY? I WON'T BE TOO LONG.
OKAY.

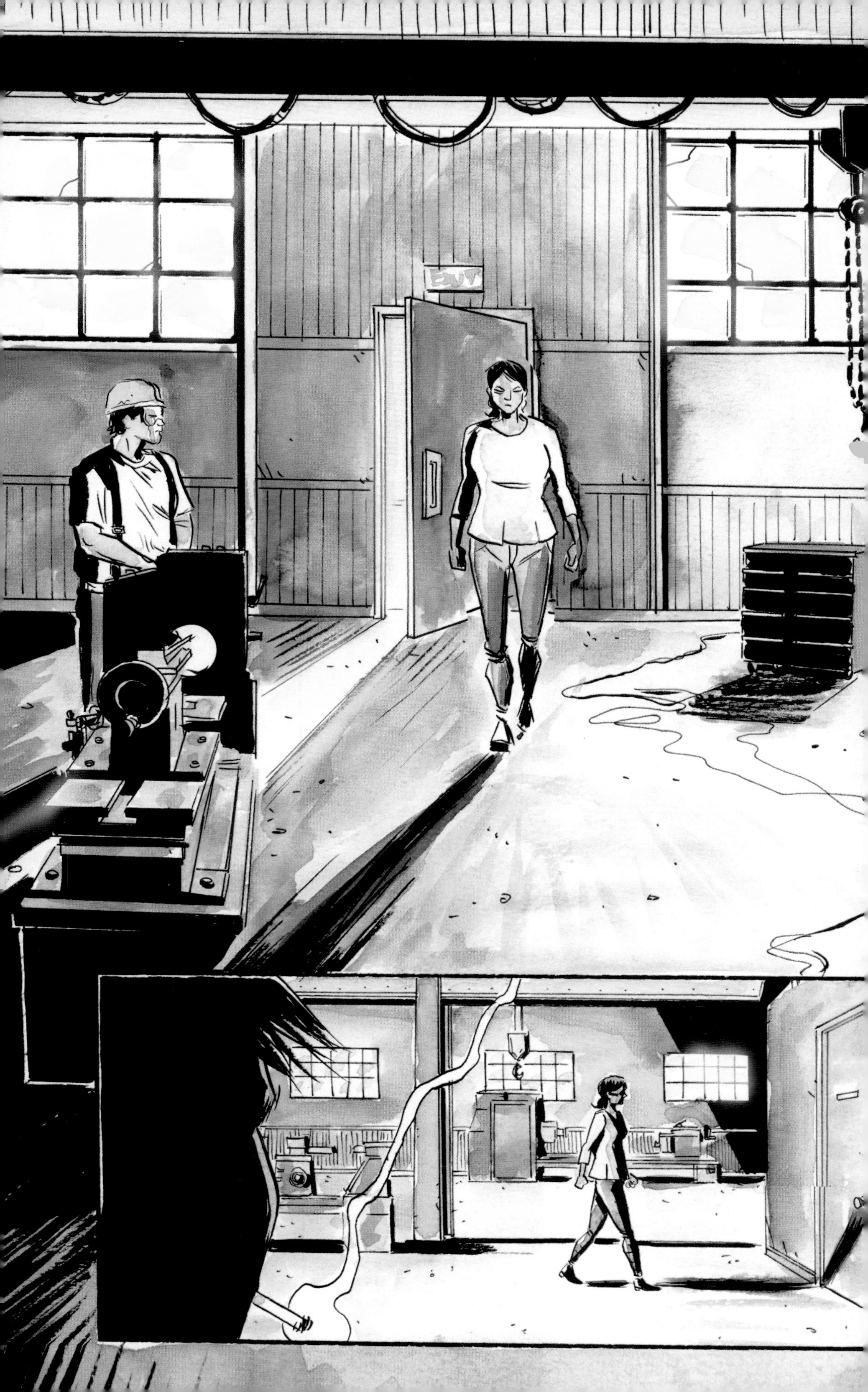

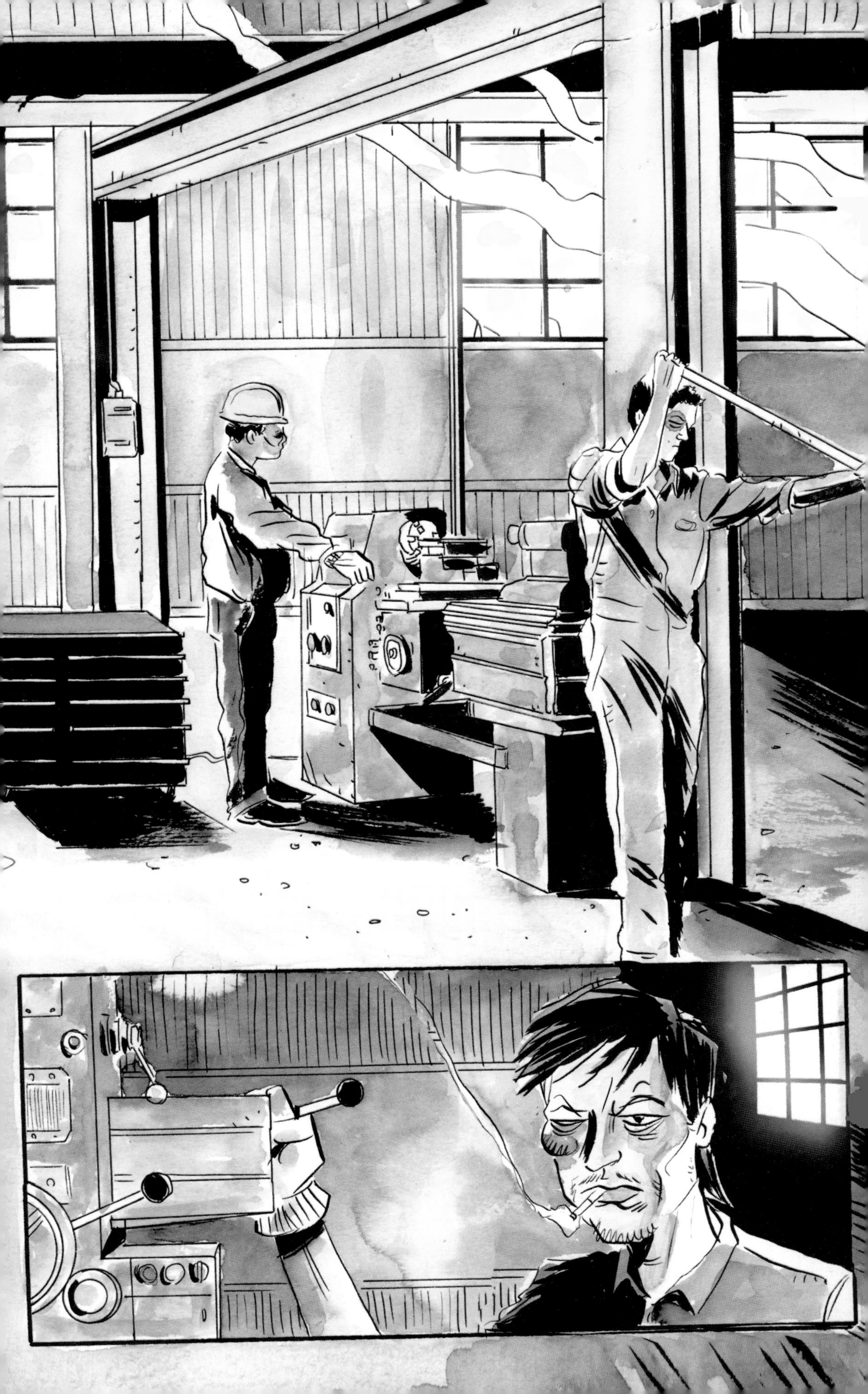

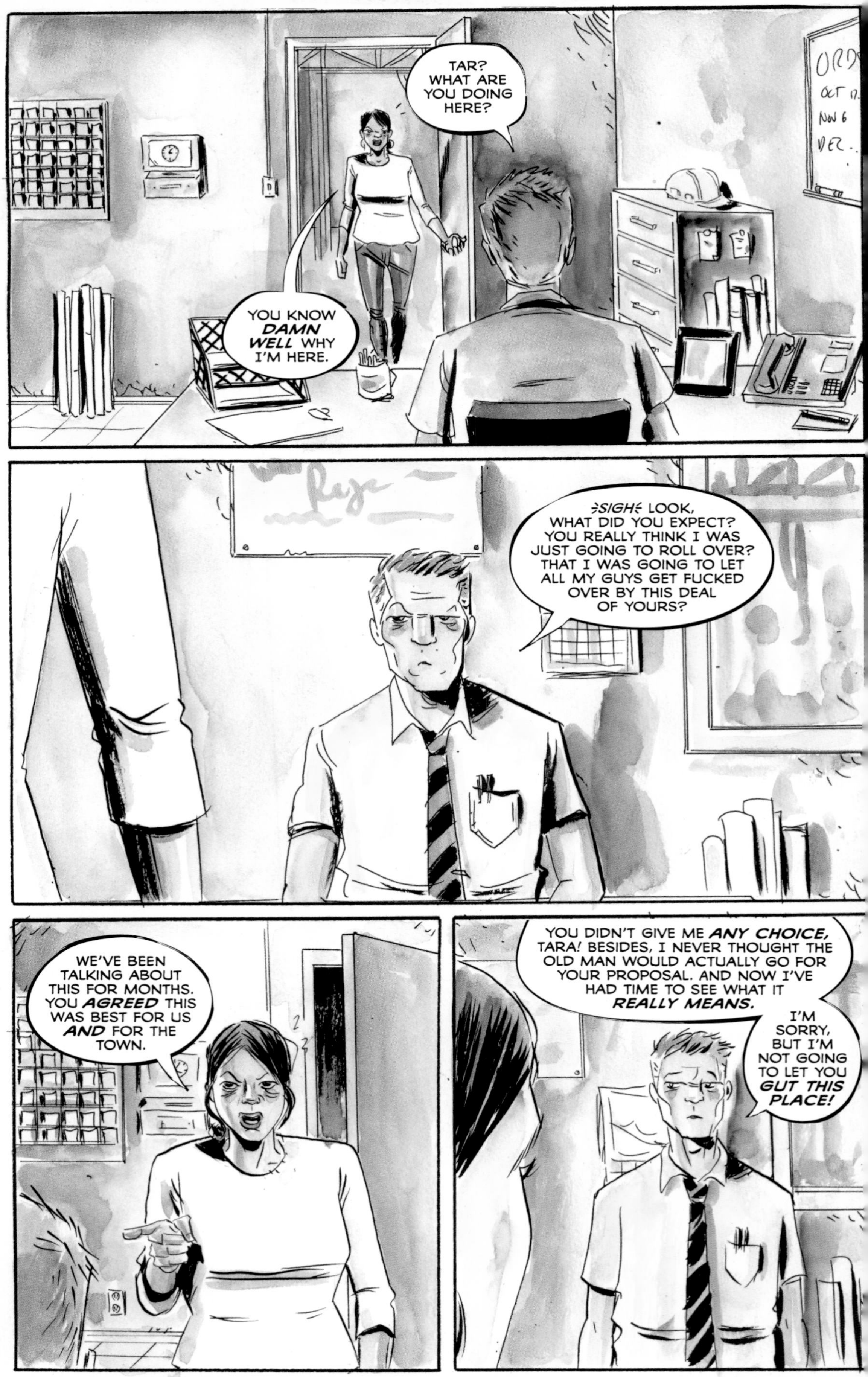
TAR? WHAT ARE YOU DOING HERE?
YOU KNOW DAMN WELL WHY I'M HERE.
SIGH LOOK, WHAT DID YOU EXPECT? YOU REALLY THINK I WAS JUST GOING TO ROLL OVER? THAT I WAS GOING TO LET ALL MY GUYS GET FUCKED OVER BY THIS DEAL OF YOURS?
WE'VE BEEN TALKING ABOUT THIS FOR MONTHS. YOU AGREED THIS WAS BEST FOR US AND FOR THE TOWN.
YOU DIDN'T GIVE ME ANY CHOICE, TARA! BESIDES, I NEVER THOUGHT THE OLD MAN WOULD ACTUALLY GO FOR YOUR PROPOSAL. AND NOW I'VE HAD TIME TO SEE WHAT IT REALLY MEANS.
I'M SORRY, BUT I'M NOT GOING TO LET YOU GUT THIS PLACE!

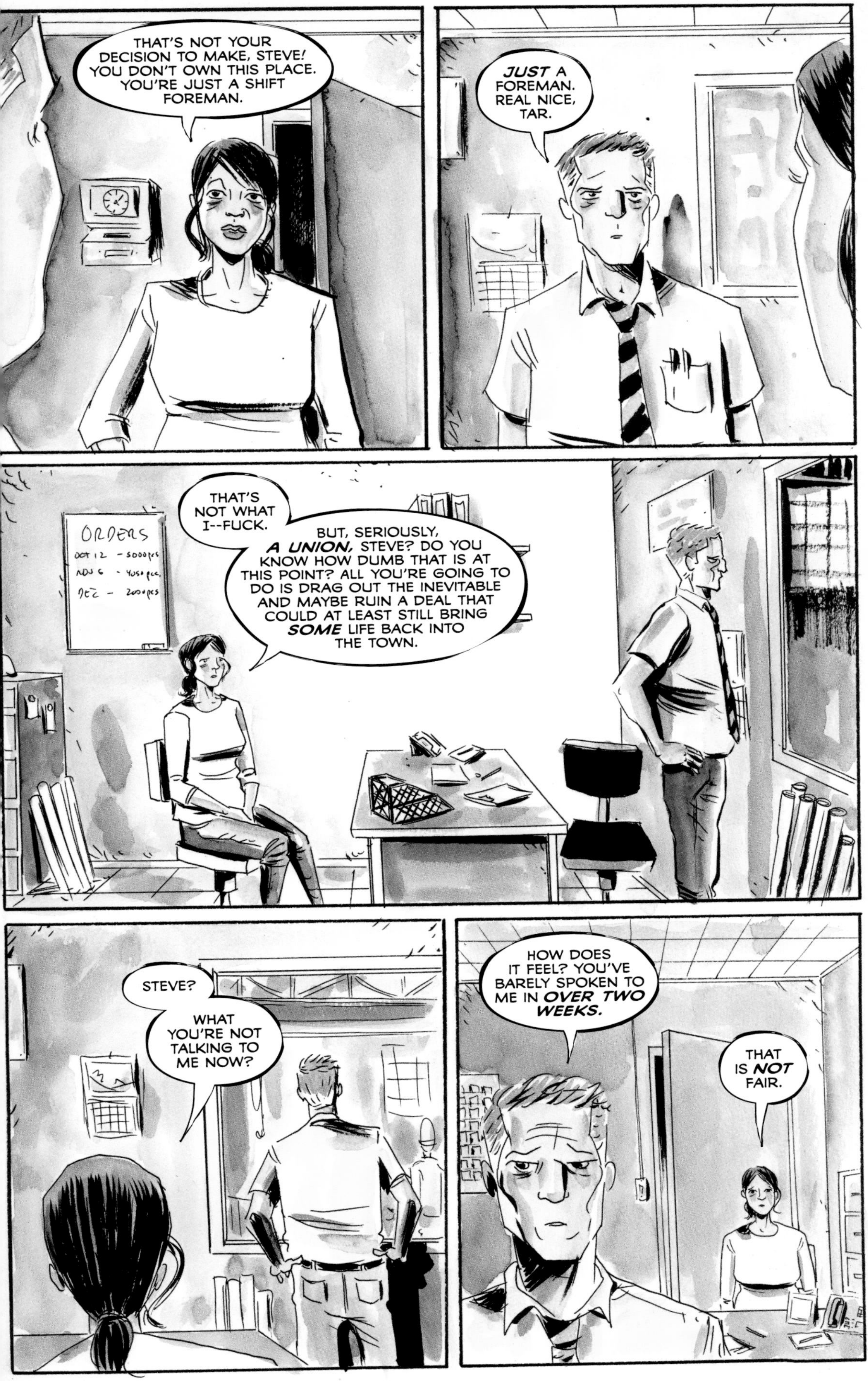
THAT'S NOT YOUR DECISION TO MAKE, STEVE! YOU DON'T OWN THIS PLACE. YOU'RE JUST A SHIFT FOREMAN.
JUST A FOREMAN. REAL NICE, TAR.
ORDERS
OCT 12 - 5000pcs
NOV 6 - 4050pcs
DEC - 2000pcs
THAT'S NOT WHAT I--FUCK.
BUT, SERIOUSLY, A UNION, STEVE? DO YOU KNOW HOW DUMB THAT IS AT THIS POINT? ALL YOU'RE GOING TO DO IS DRAG OUT THE INEVITABLE AND MAYBE RUIN A DEAL THAT COULD AT LEAST STILL BRING SOME LIFE BACK INTO THE TOWN.
STEVE?
WHAT YOU'RE NOT TALKING TO ME NOW?
HOW DOES IT FEEL? YOU'VE BARELY SPOKEN TO ME IN OVER TWO WEEKS.
THAT IS NOT FAIR.

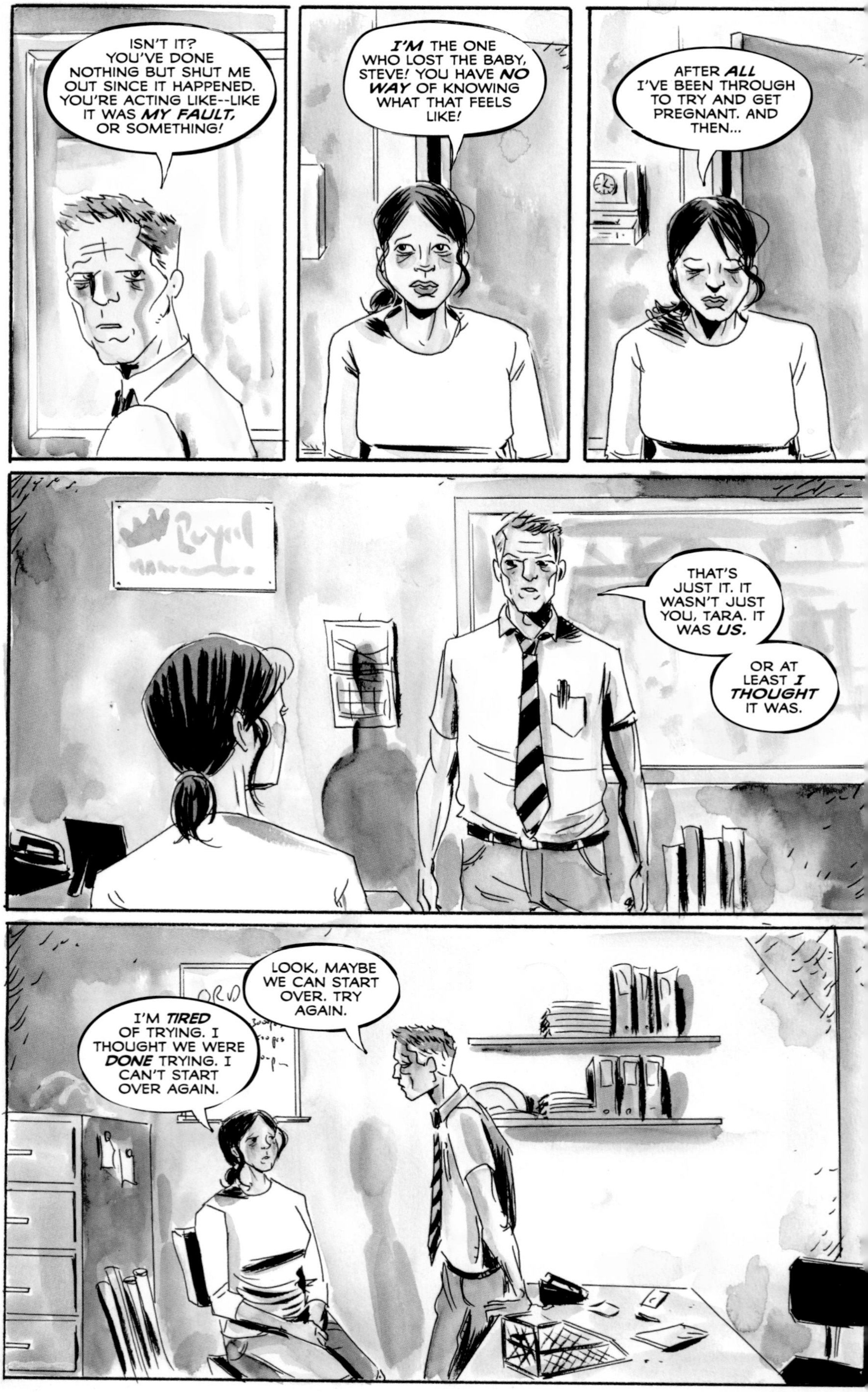
ISN'T IT? YOU'VE DONE NOTHING BUT SHUT ME OUT SINCE IT HAPPENED. YOU'RE ACTING LIKE--LIKE IT WAS MY FAULT, OR SOMETHING!
I'M THE ONE WHO LOST THE BABY, STEVE! YOU HAVE NO WAY OF KNOWING WHAT THAT FEELS LIKE!
AFTER ALL I'VE BEEN THROUGH TO TRY AND GET PREGNANT. AND THEN...
THAT'S JUST IT. IT WASN'T JUST YOU, TARA. IT WAS US.
OR AT LEAST I THOUGHT IT WAS.
LOOK, MAYBE WE CAN START OVER. TRY AGAIN.
I'M TIRED OF TRYING. I THOUGHT WE WERE DONE TRYING. I CAN'T START OVER AGAIN.

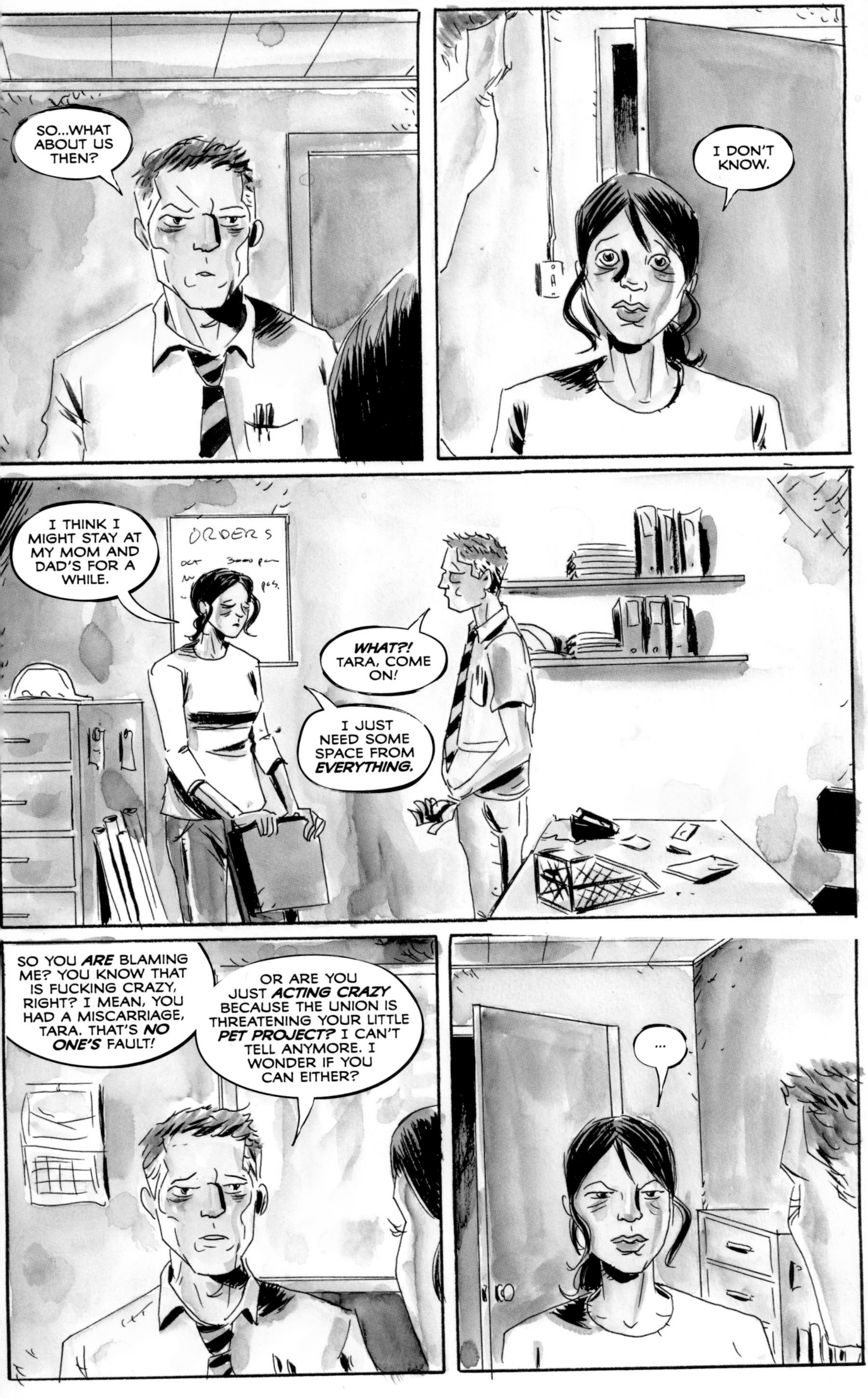
SO...WHAT ABOUT US THEN?
I DON'T KNOW.
I THINK I MIGHT STAY AT MY MOM AND DAD'S FOR A WHILE.
ORDERS
WHAT?! TARA, COME ON!
I JUST NEED SOME SPACE FROM *EVERYTHING.*
SO YOU *ARE* BLAMING ME? YOU KNOW THAT IS FUCKING CRAZY, RIGHT? I MEAN, YOU HAD A MISCARRIAGE, TARA. THAT'S *NO ONE'S* FAULT!
OR ARE YOU JUST *ACTING CRAZY* BECAUSE THE UNION IS THREATENING YOUR LITTLE *PET PROJECT?* I CAN'T TELL ANYMORE. I WONDER IF YOU CAN EITHER?
...

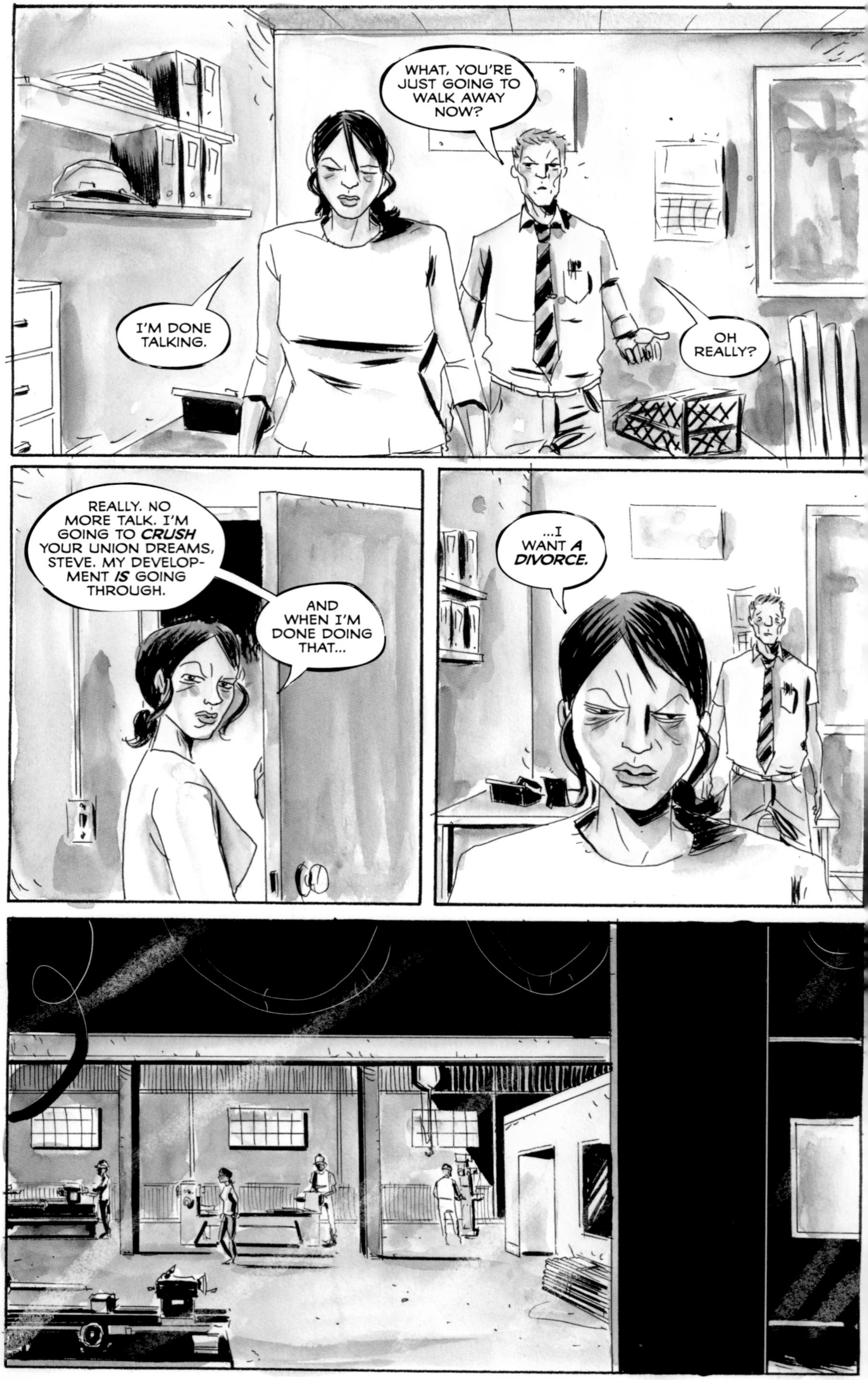
WHAT, YOU'RE JUST GOING TO WALK AWAY NOW?
I'M DONE TALKING.
OH REALLY?
REALLY. NO MORE TALK. I'M GOING TO *CRUSH* YOUR UNION DREAMS, STEVE. MY DEVELOPMENT *IS* GOING THROUGH.
AND WHEN I'M DONE DOING THAT...
...I WANT *A DIVORCE.*

PIKE, PETER

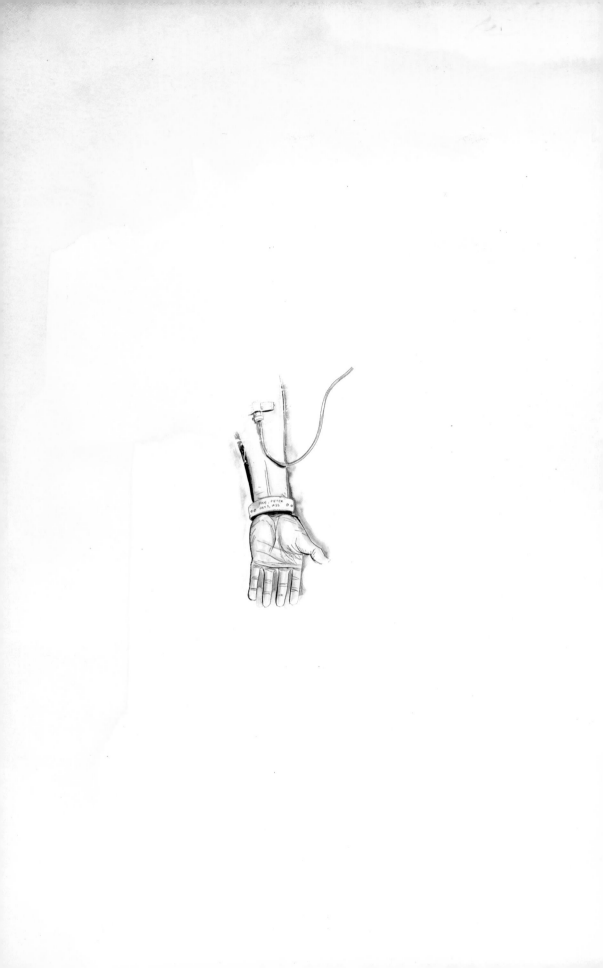

CHAPTER FOUR

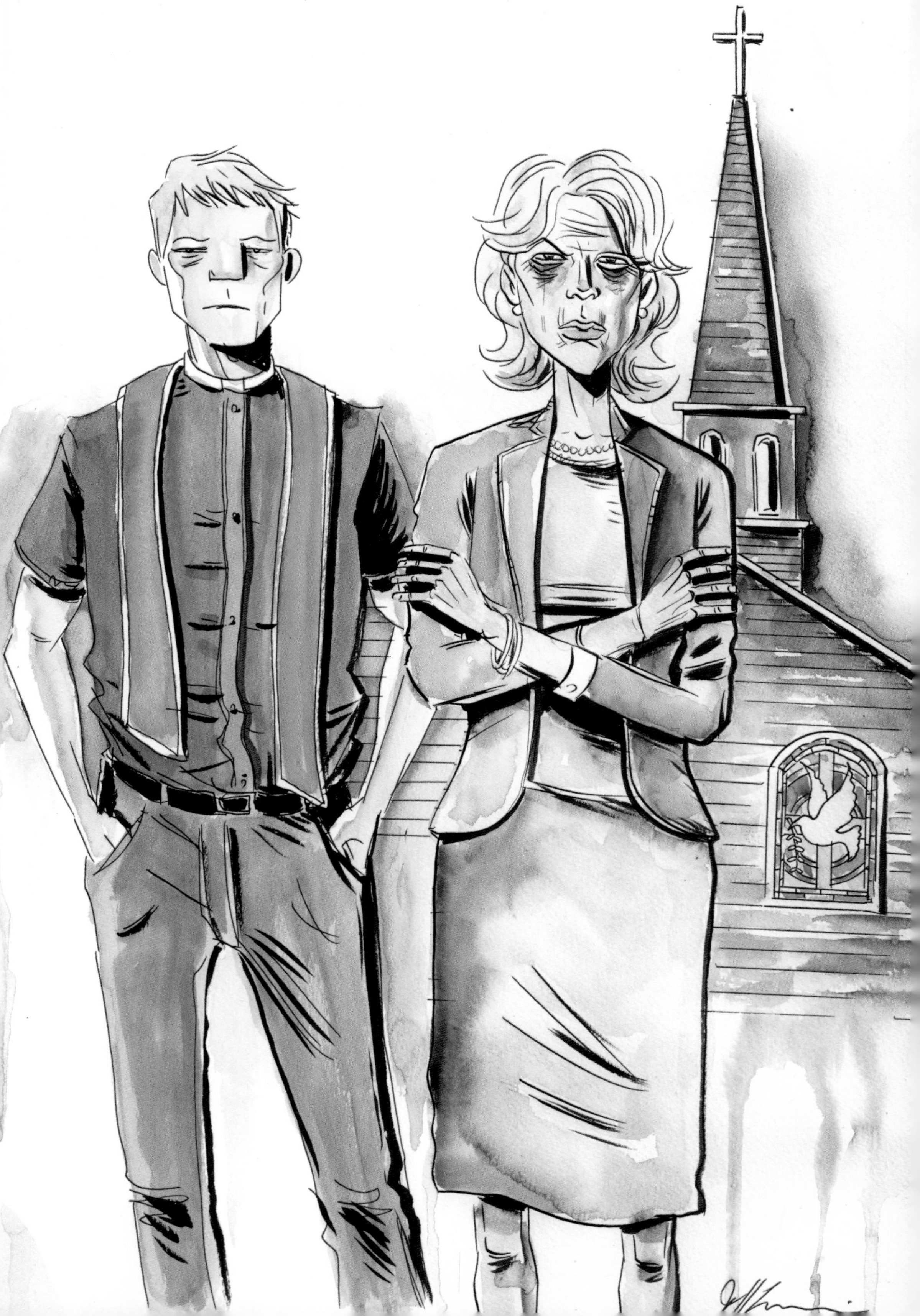

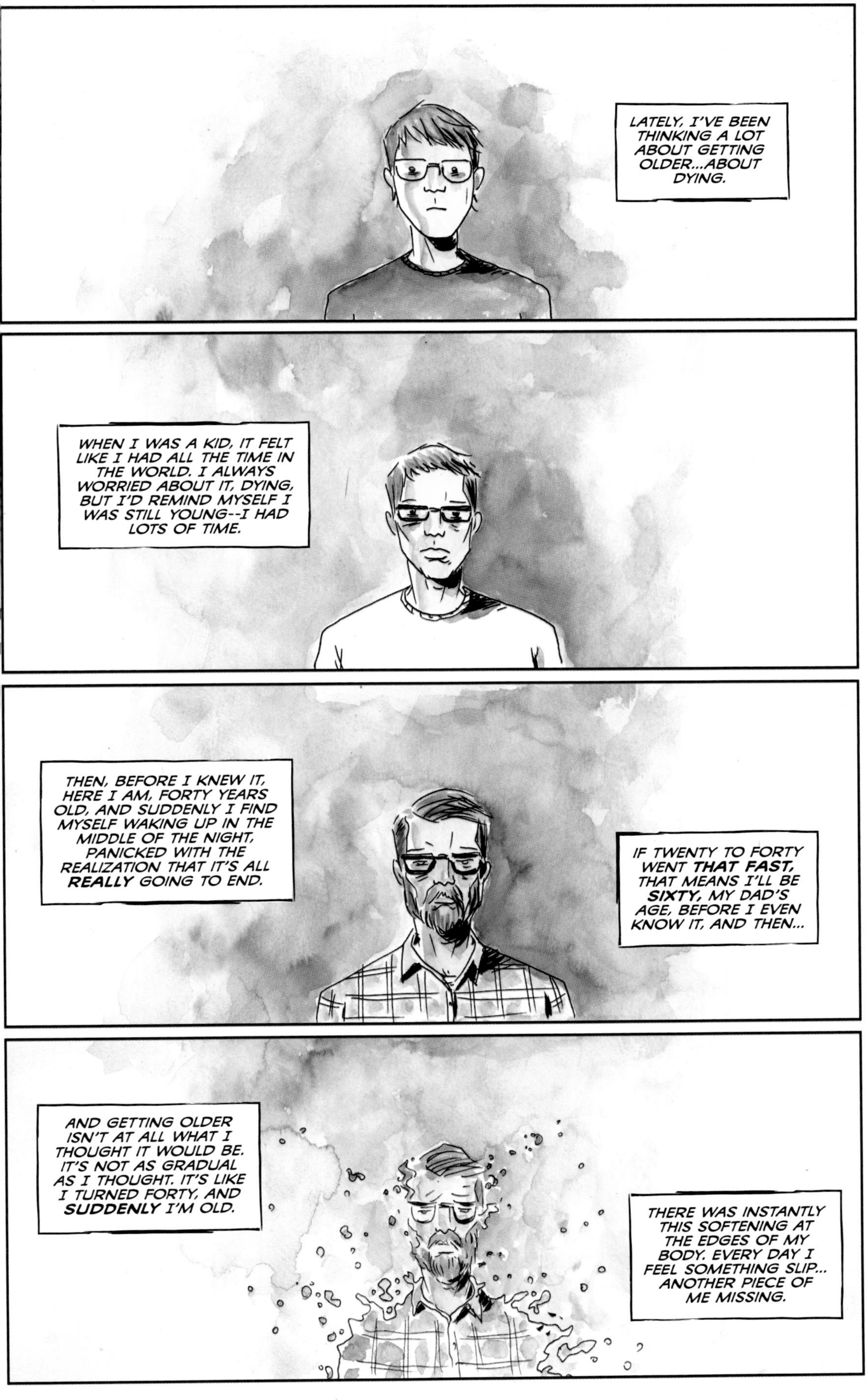

LATELY, I'VE BEEN THINKING A LOT ABOUT GETTING OLDER...ABOUT DYING.
WHEN I WAS A KID, IT FELT LIKE I HAD ALL THE TIME IN THE WORLD. I ALWAYS WORRIED ABOUT IT, DYING, BUT I'D REMIND MYSELF I WAS STILL YOUNG--I HAD LOTS OF TIME.
THEN, BEFORE I KNEW IT, HERE I AM, FORTY YEARS OLD, AND SUDDENLY I FIND MYSELF WAKING UP IN THE MIDDLE OF THE NIGHT, PANICKED WITH THE REALIZATION THAT IT'S ALL **REALLY** GOING TO END.
IF TWENTY TO FORTY WENT **THAT FAST,** THAT MEANS I'LL BE **SIXTY,** MY DAD'S AGE, BEFORE I EVEN KNOW IT, AND THEN...
AND GETTING OLDER ISN'T AT ALL WHAT I THOUGHT IT WOULD BE. IT'S NOT AS GRADUAL AS I THOUGHT. IT'S LIKE I TURNED FORTY, AND **SUDDENLY** I'M OLD.
THERE WAS INSTANTLY THIS SOFTENING AT THE EDGES OF MY BODY. EVERY DAY I FEEL SOMETHING SLIP... ANOTHER PIECE OF ME MISSING.

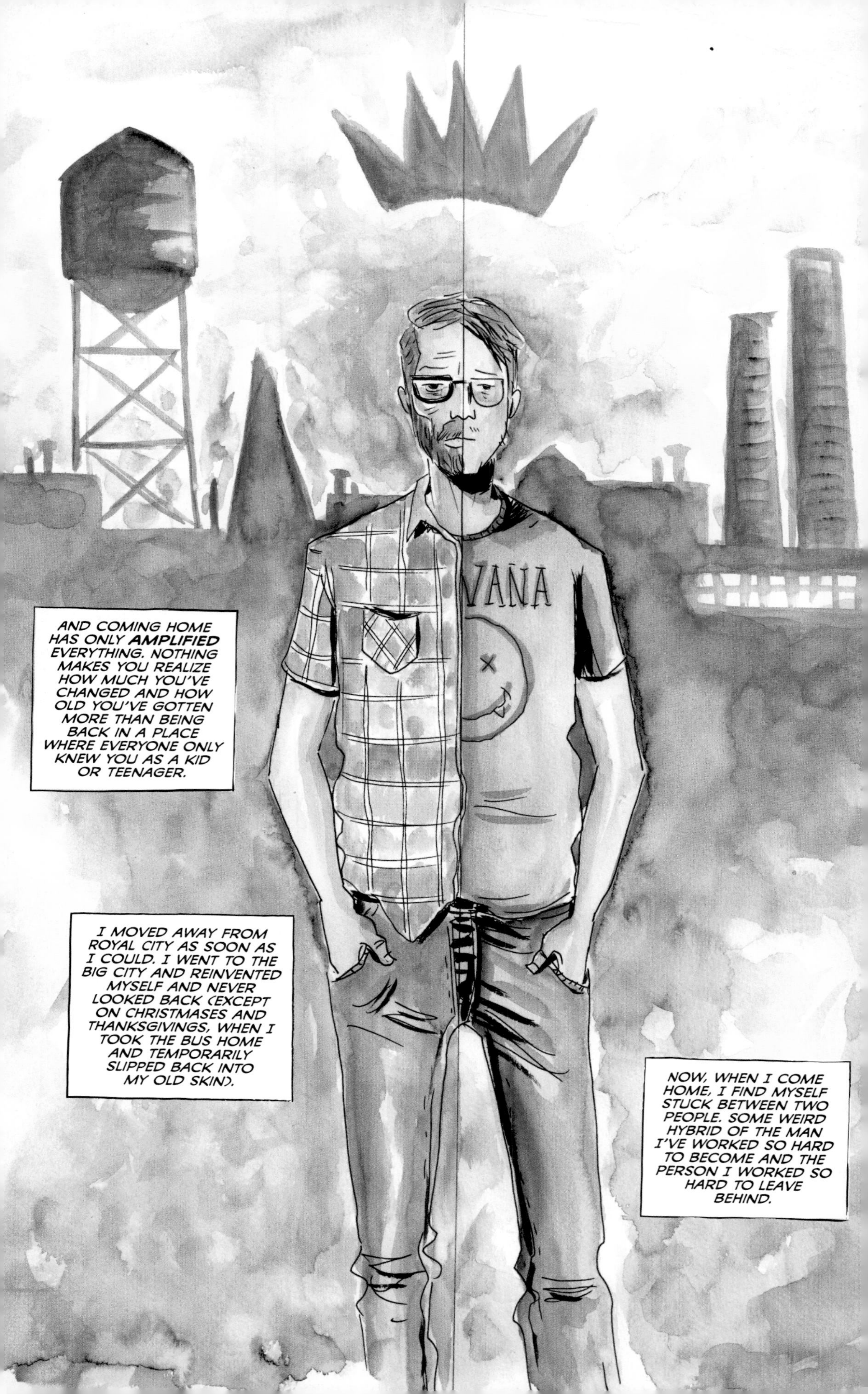
AND COMING HOME HAS ONLY **AMPLIFIED** EVERYTHING. NOTHING MAKES YOU REALIZE HOW MUCH YOU'VE CHANGED AND HOW OLD YOU'VE GOTTEN MORE THAN BEING BACK IN A PLACE WHERE EVERYONE ONLY KNEW YOU AS A KID OR TEENAGER.
VANA
I MOVED AWAY FROM ROYAL CITY AS SOON AS I COULD. I WENT TO THE BIG CITY AND REINVENTED MYSELF AND NEVER LOOKED BACK (EXCEPT ON CHRISTMASES AND THANKSGIVINGS, WHEN I TOOK THE BUS HOME AND TEMPORARILY SLIPPED BACK INTO MY OLD SKIN).
NOW, WHEN I COME HOME, I FIND MYSELF STUCK BETWEEN TWO PEOPLE. SOME WEIRD HYBRID OF THE MAN I'VE WORKED SO HARD TO BECOME AND THE PERSON I WORKED SO HARD TO LEAVE BEHIND.

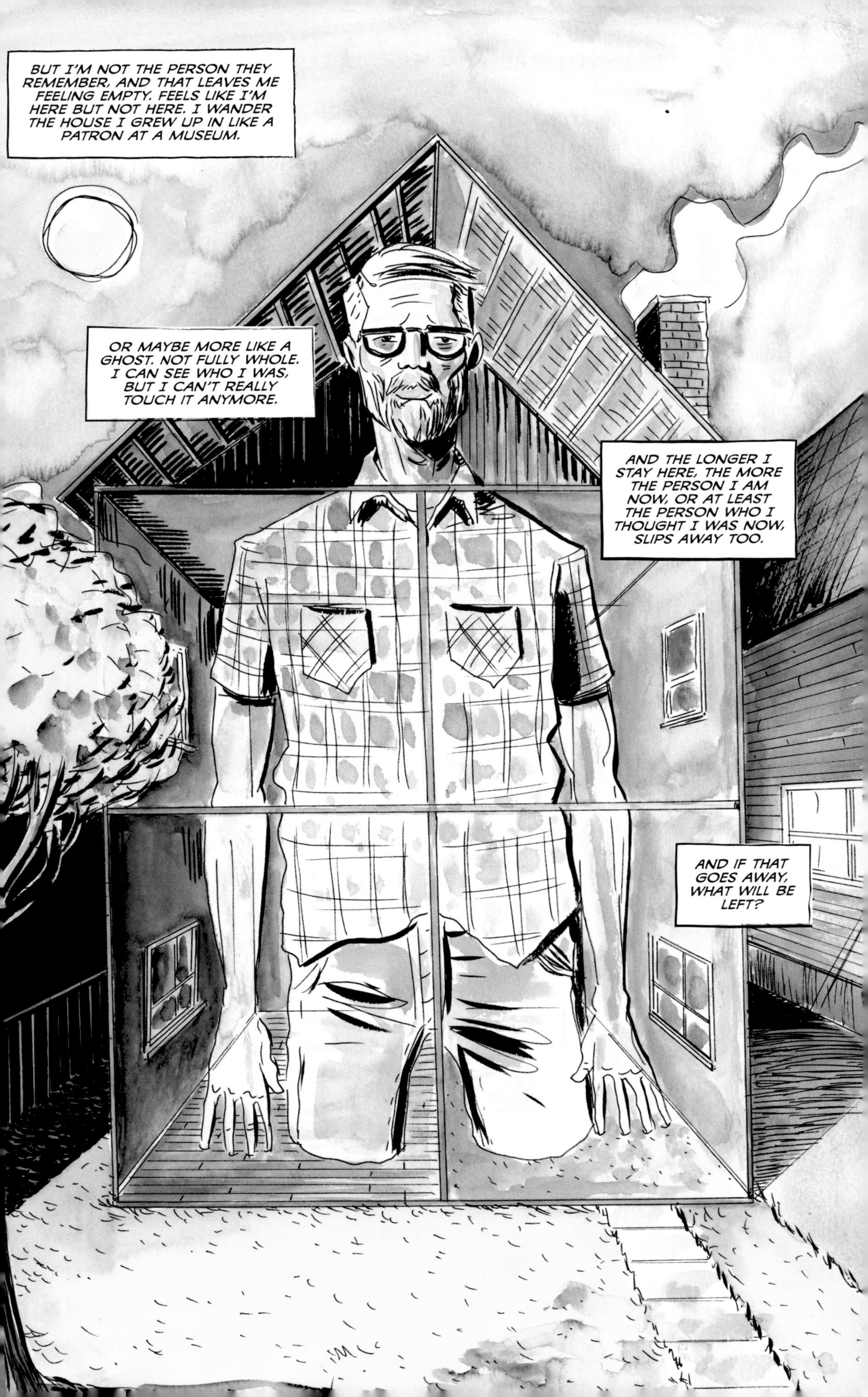
BUT I'M NOT THE PERSON THEY REMEMBER, AND THAT LEAVES ME FEELING EMPTY. FEELS LIKE I'M HERE BUT NOT HERE. I WANDER THE HOUSE I GREW UP IN LIKE A PATRON AT A MUSEUM.
OR MAYBE MORE LIKE A GHOST. NOT FULLY WHOLE. I CAN SEE WHO I WAS, BUT I CAN'T REALLY TOUCH IT ANYMORE.
AND THE LONGER I STAY HERE, THE MORE THE PERSON I AM NOW, OR AT LEAST THE PERSON WHO I THOUGHT I WAS NOW, SLIPS AWAY TOO.
AND IF THAT GOES AWAY, WHAT WILL BE LEFT?

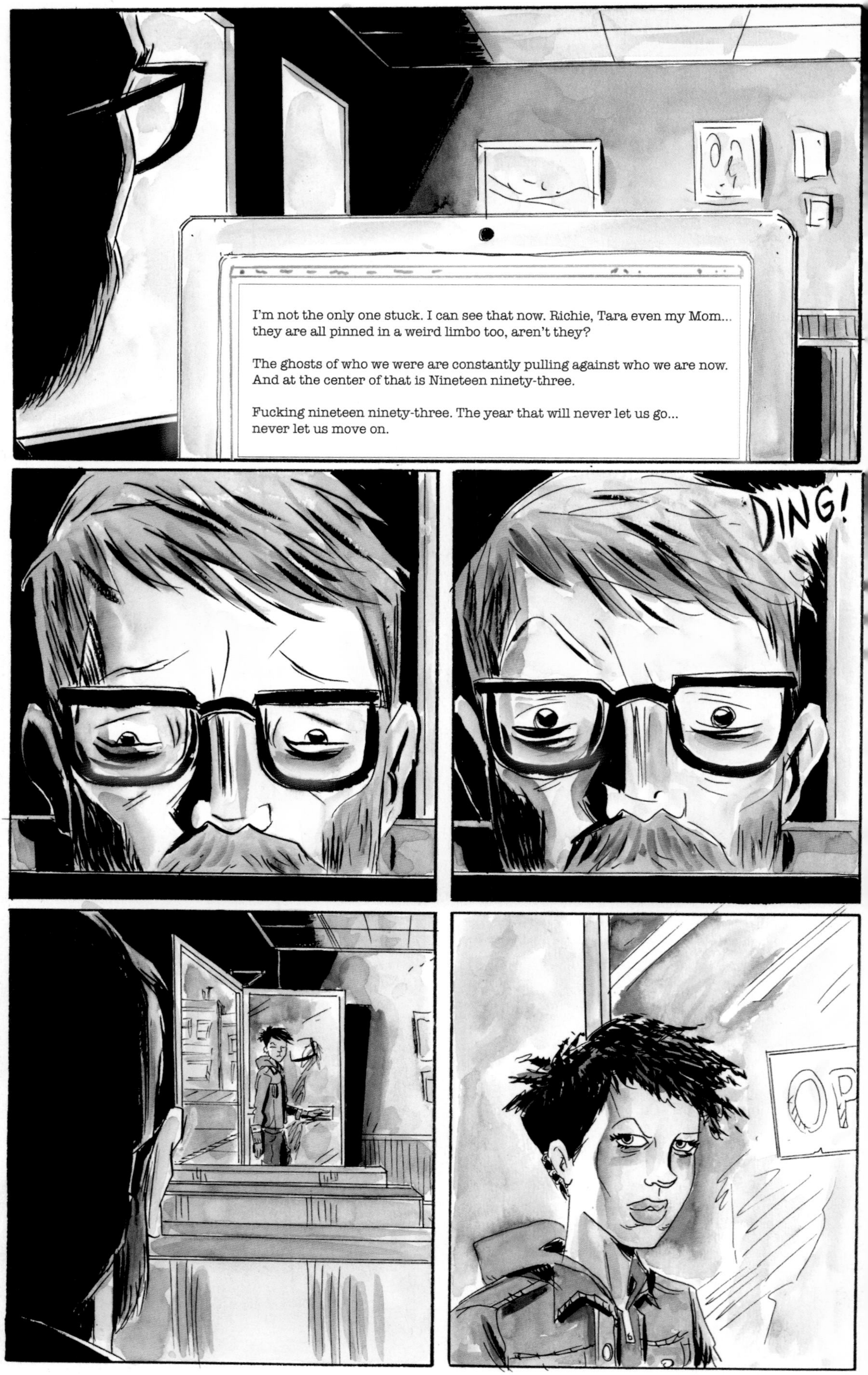
I'm not the only one stuck. I can see that now. Richie, Tara even my Mom... they are all pinned in a weird limbo too, aren't they?
The ghosts of who we were are constantly pulling against who we are now. And at the center of that is Nineteen ninety-three.
Fucking nineteen ninety-three. The year that will never let us go... never let us move on.
DING!

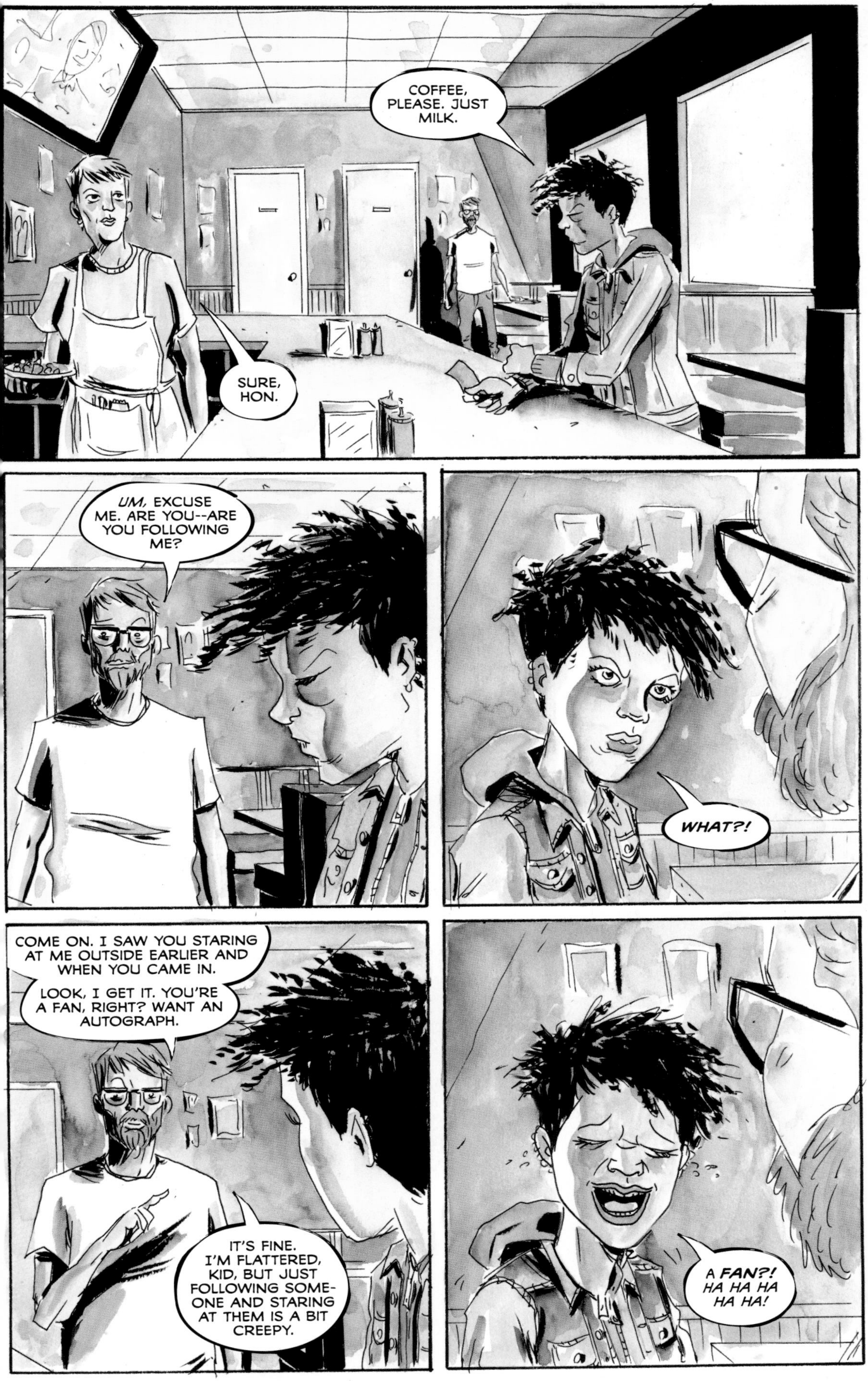
COFFEE, PLEASE. JUST MILK.
SURE, HON.
UM, EXCUSE ME. ARE YOU--ARE YOU FOLLOWING ME?
WHAT?!
COME ON. I SAW YOU STARING AT ME OUTSIDE EARLIER AND WHEN YOU CAME IN.
LOOK, I GET IT. YOU'RE A FAN, RIGHT? WANT AN AUTOGRAPH.
IT'S FINE. I'M FLATTERED, KID, BUT JUST FOLLOWING SOME-ONE AND STARING AT THEM IS A BIT CREEPY.
A FAN?! HA HA HA HA HA!

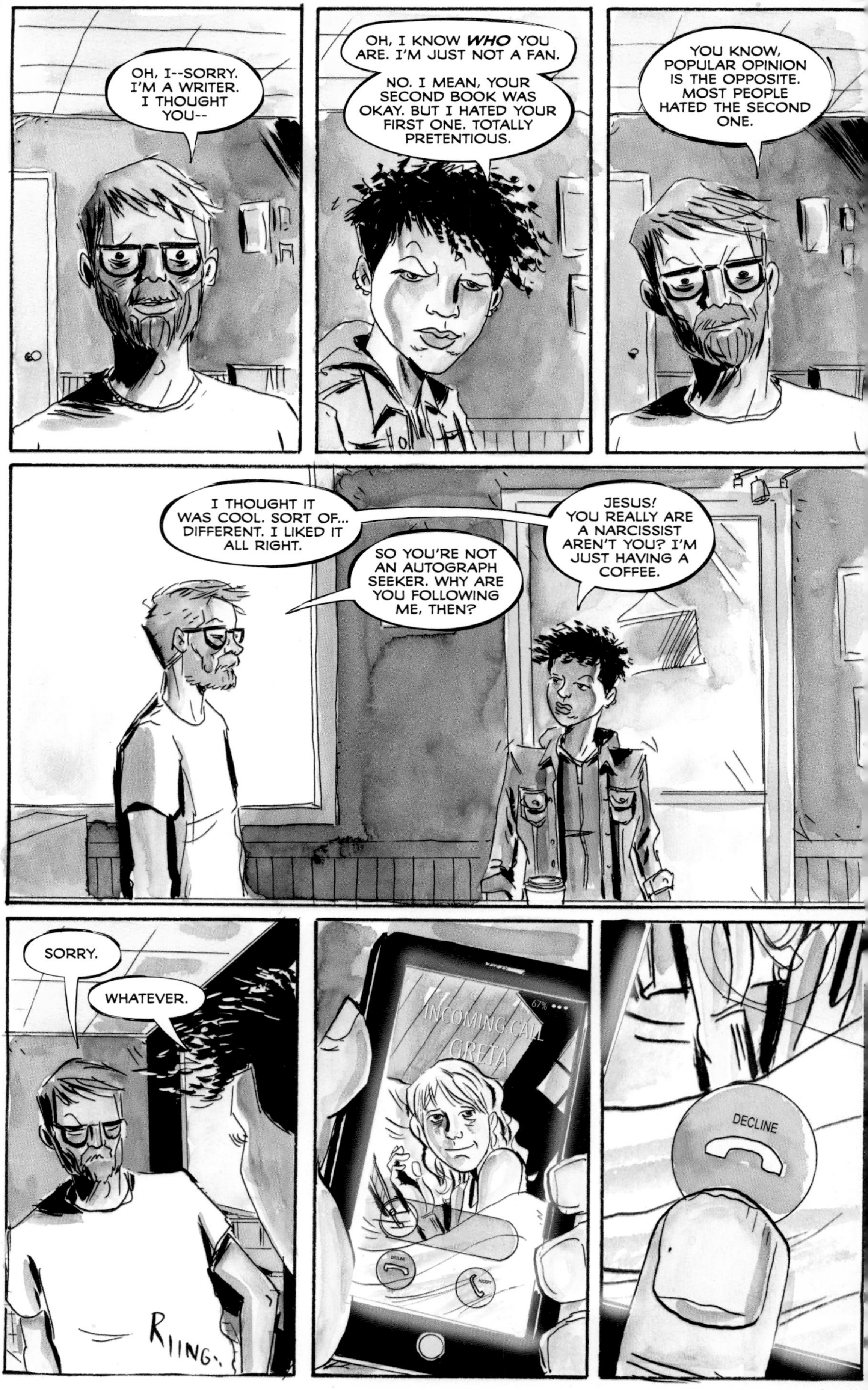
OH, I--SORRY. I'M A WRITER. I THOUGHT YOU--
OH, I KNOW *WHO* YOU ARE. I'M JUST NOT A FAN.
NO. I MEAN, YOUR SECOND BOOK WAS OKAY. BUT I HATED YOUR FIRST ONE. TOTALLY PRETENTIOUS.
YOU KNOW, POPULAR OPINION IS THE OPPOSITE. MOST PEOPLE HATED THE SECOND ONE.
I THOUGHT IT WAS COOL. SORT OF... DIFFERENT. I LIKED IT ALL RIGHT.
JESUS! YOU REALLY ARE A NARCISSIST AREN'T YOU? I'M JUST HAVING A COFFEE.
SO YOU'RE NOT AN AUTOGRAPH SEEKER. WHY ARE YOU FOLLOWING ME, THEN?
SORRY.
WHATEVER.
RIING.
INCOMING CALL
GRETA
67%
DECLINE
ACCEPT
DECLINE

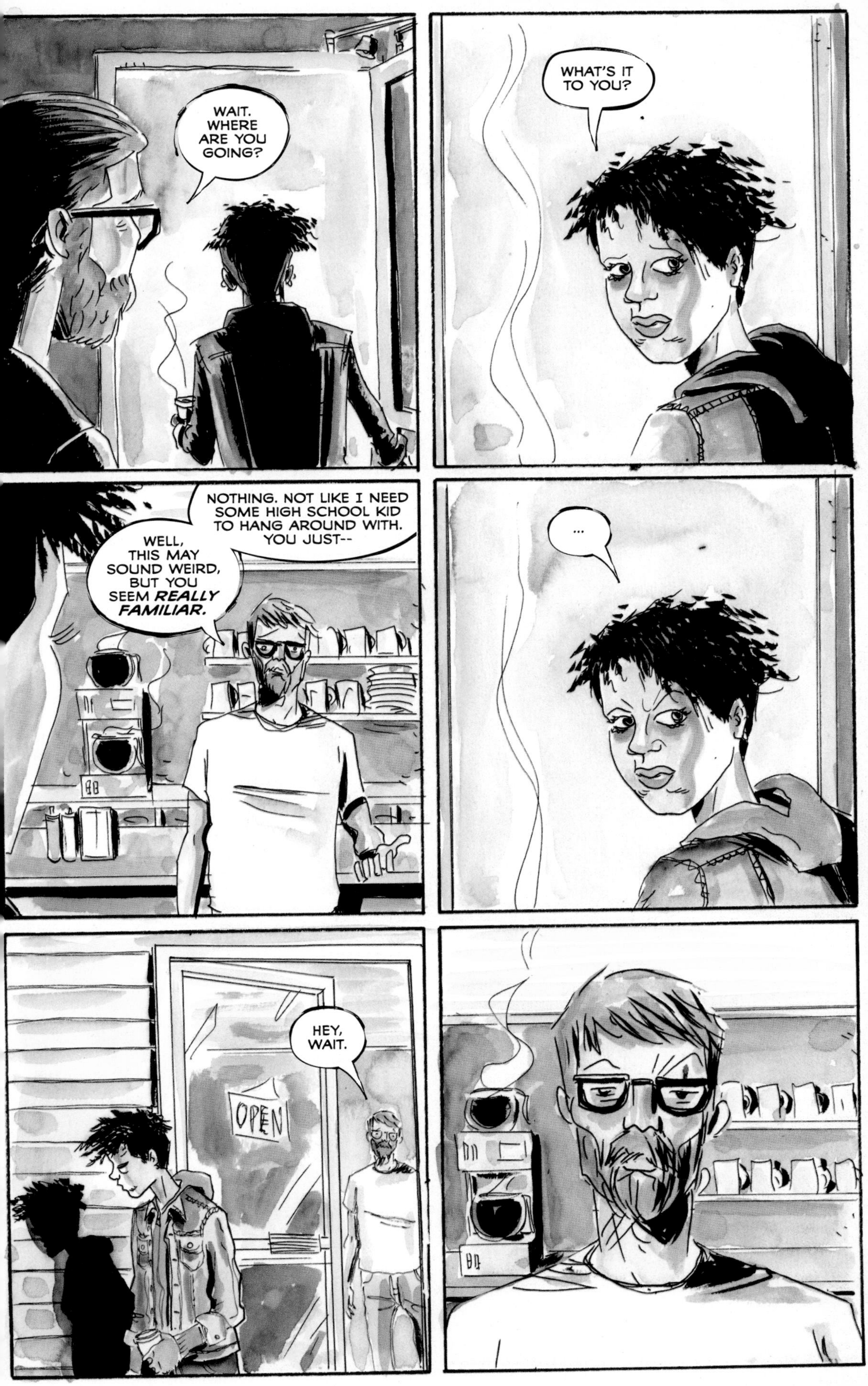
WAIT. WHERE ARE YOU GOING?
WHAT'S IT TO YOU?
WELL, THIS MAY SOUND WEIRD, BUT YOU SEEM REALLY FAMILIAR.
NOTHING. NOT LIKE I NEED SOME HIGH SCHOOL KID TO HANG AROUND WITH. YOU JUST--
...
OPEN
HEY, WAIT.

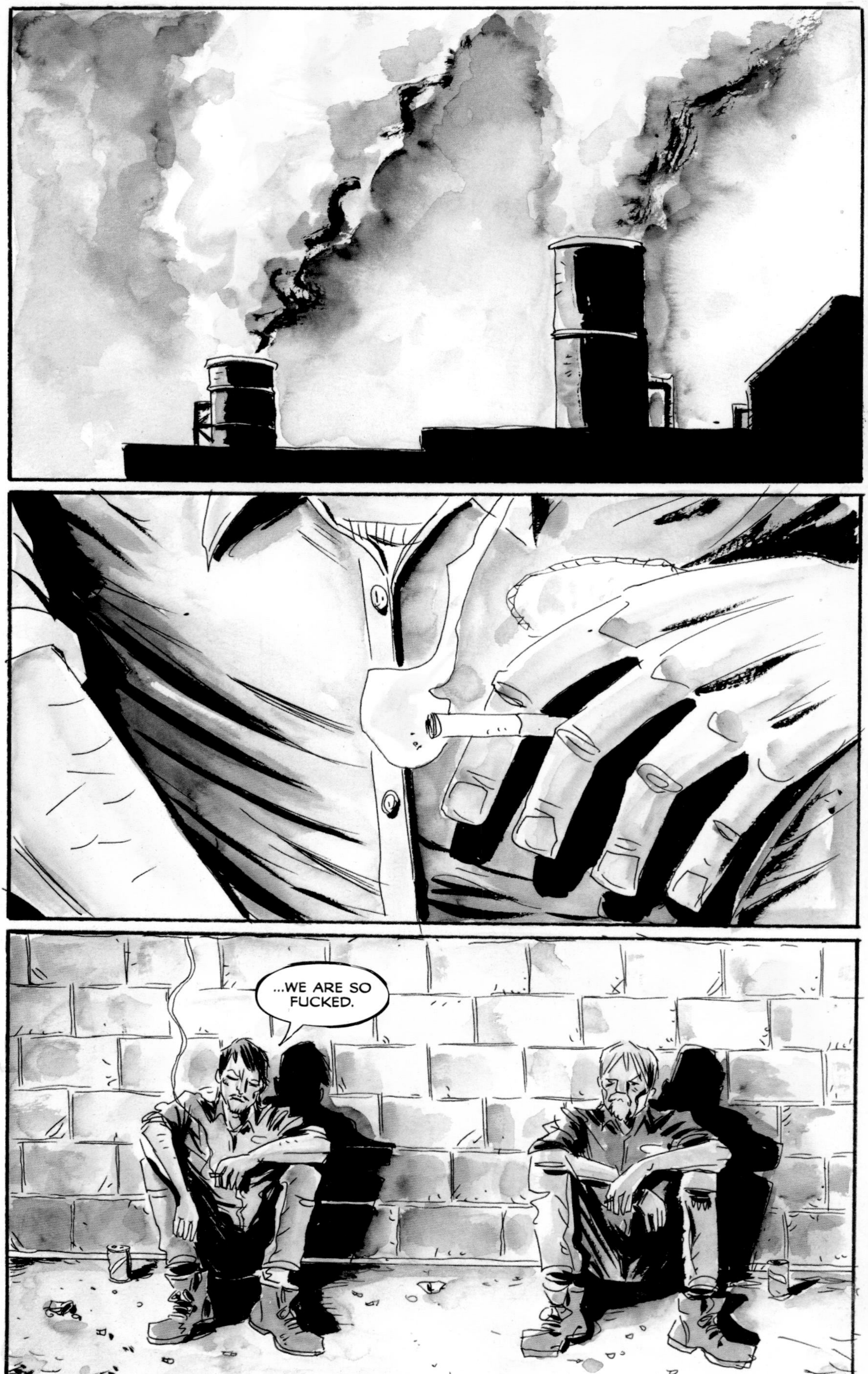
...WE ARE SO FUCKED.

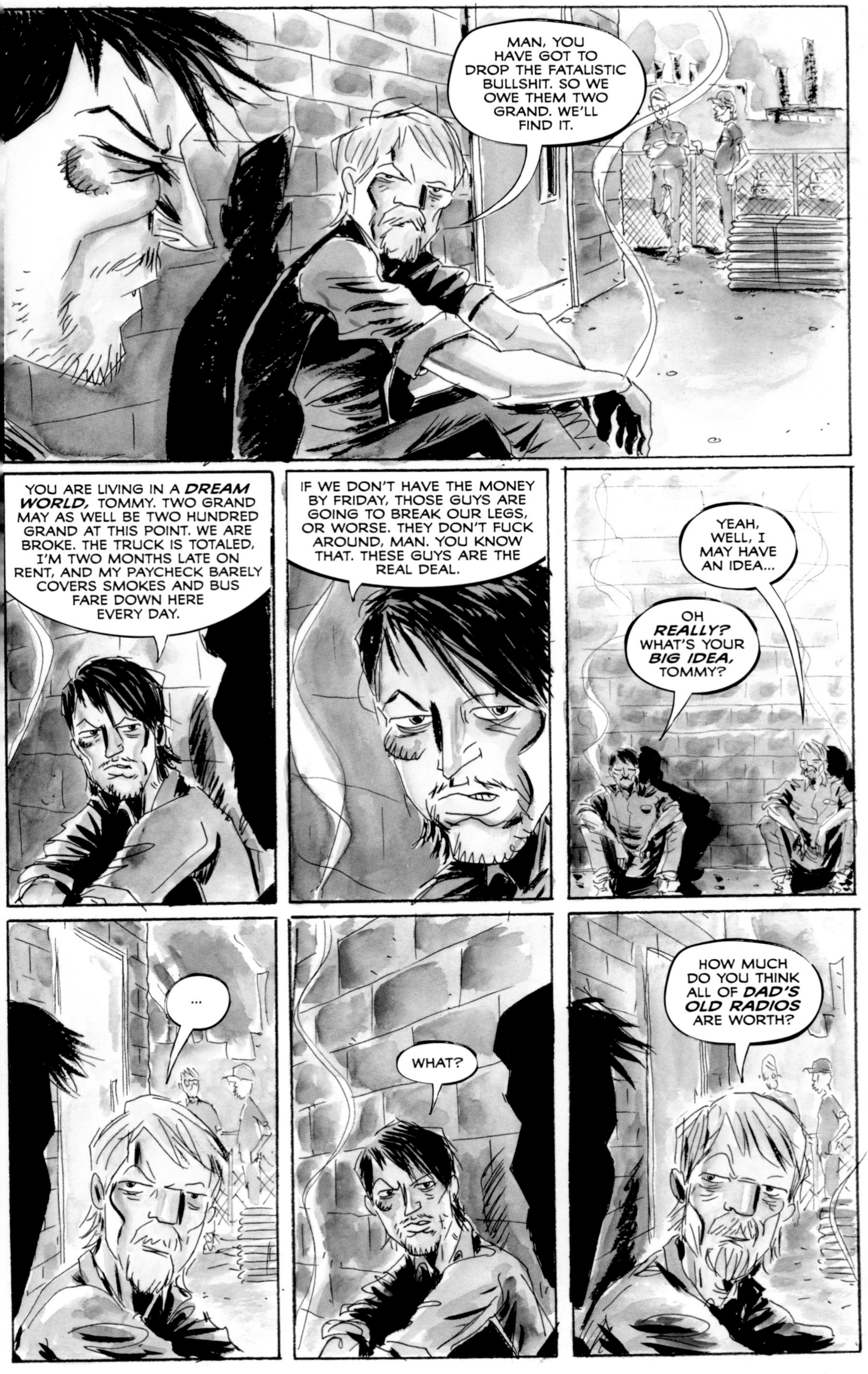
MAN, YOU HAVE GOT TO DROP THE FATALISTIC BULLSHIT. SO WE OWE THEM TWO GRAND. WE'LL FIND IT.
YOU ARE LIVING IN A *DREAM WORLD,* TOMMY. TWO GRAND MAY AS WELL BE TWO HUNDRED GRAND AT THIS POINT. WE ARE BROKE. THE TRUCK IS TOTALED, I'M TWO MONTHS LATE ON RENT, AND MY PAYCHECK BARELY COVERS SMOKES AND BUS FARE DOWN HERE EVERY DAY.
IF WE DON'T HAVE THE MONEY BY FRIDAY, THOSE GUYS ARE GOING TO BREAK OUR LEGS, OR WORSE. THEY DON'T FUCK AROUND, MAN. YOU KNOW THAT. THESE GUYS ARE THE REAL DEAL.
YEAH, WELL, I MAY HAVE AN IDEA...
OH *REALLY?* WHAT'S YOUR *BIG IDEA,* TOMMY?
...
WHAT?
HOW MUCH DO YOU THINK ALL OF *DAD'S OLD RADIOS* ARE WORTH?

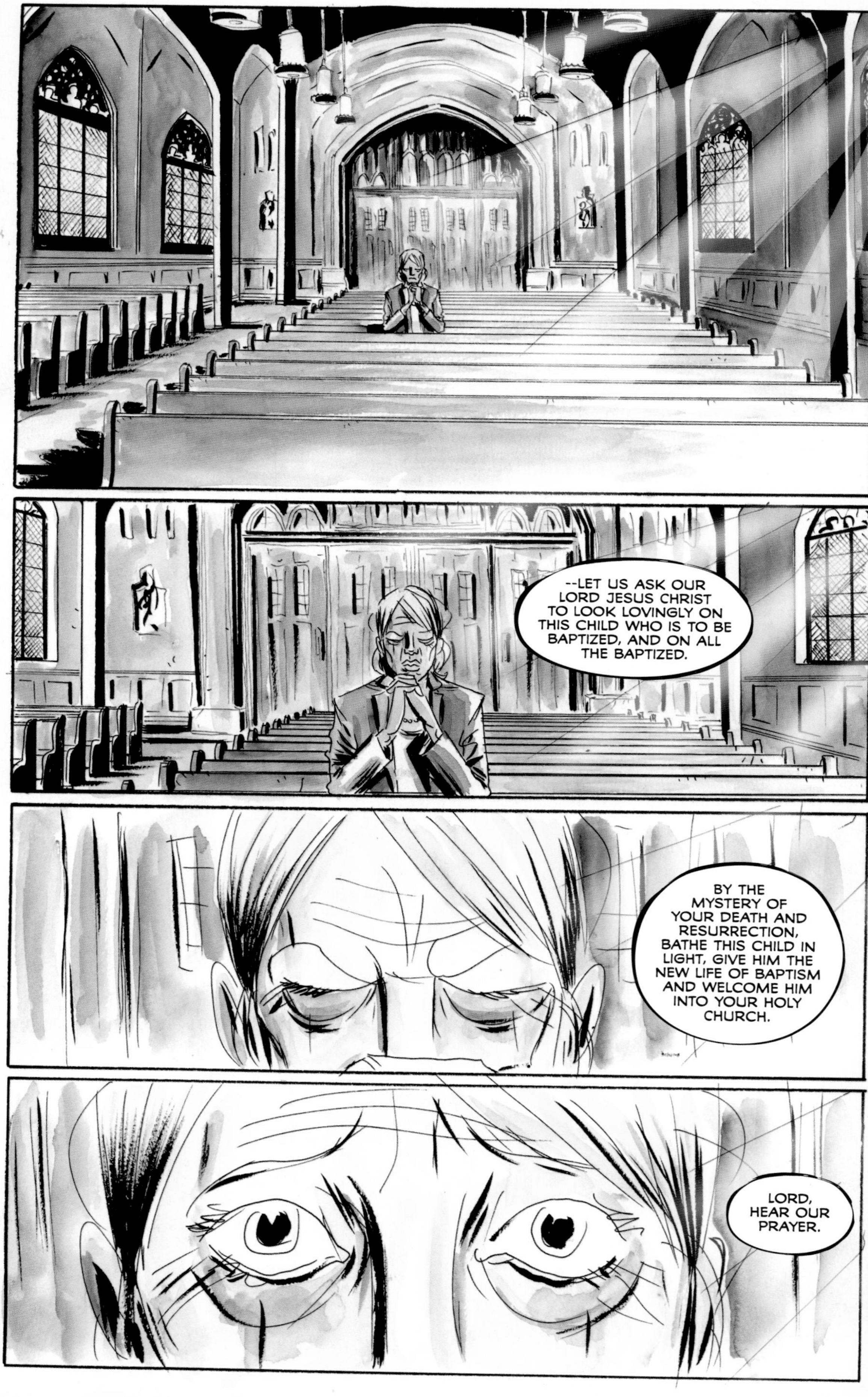
--LET US ASK OUR LORD JESUS CHRIST TO LOOK LOVINGLY ON THIS CHILD WHO IS TO BE BAPTIZED, AND ON ALL THE BAPTIZED.
BY THE MYSTERY OF YOUR DEATH AND RESURRECTION, BATHE THIS CHILD IN LIGHT, GIVE HIM THE NEW LIFE OF BAPTISM AND WELCOME HIM INTO YOUR HOLY CHURCH.
LORD, HEAR OUR PRAYER.

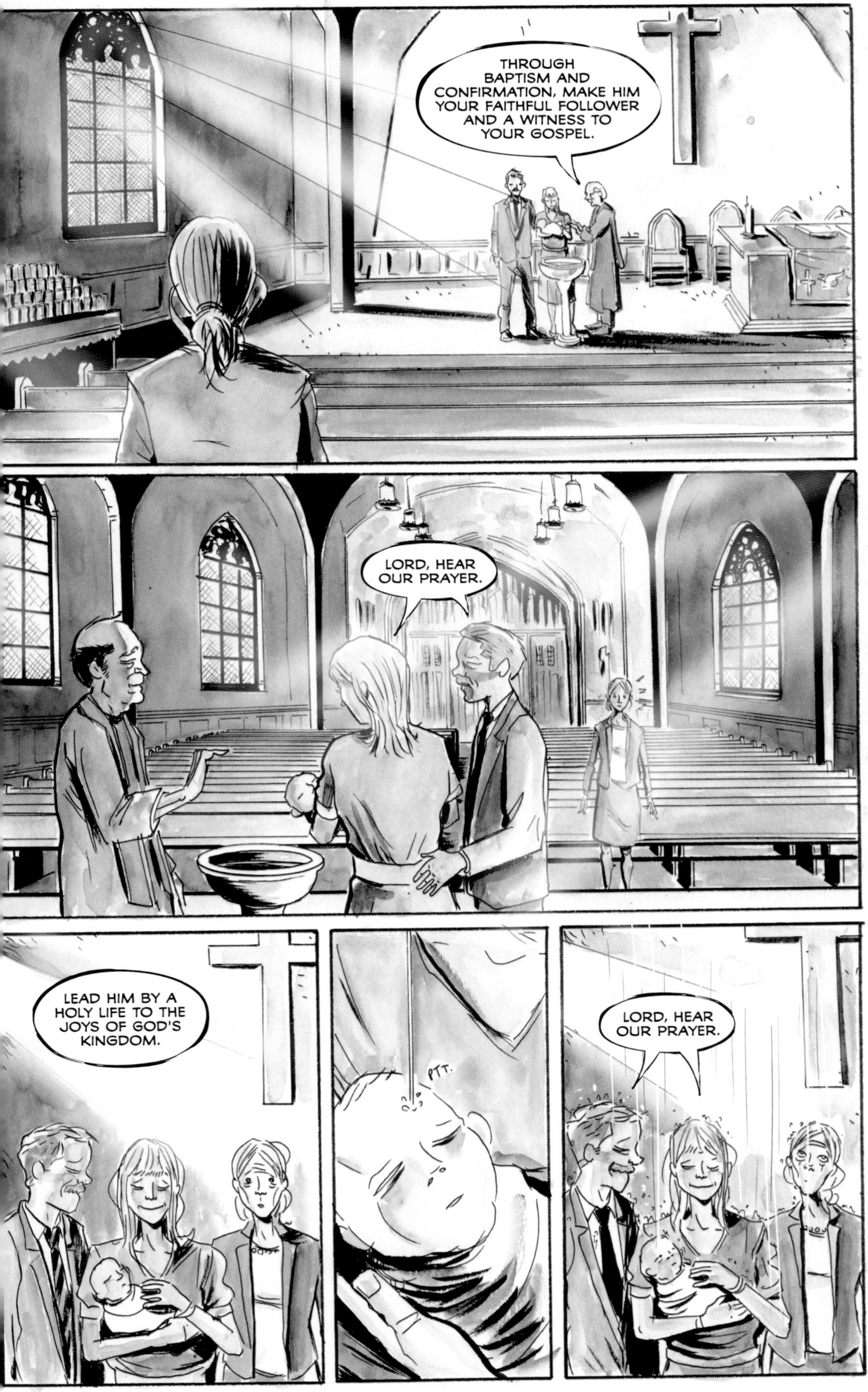
THROUGH BAPTISM AND CONFIRMATION, MAKE HIM YOUR FAITHFUL FOLLOWER AND A WITNESS TO YOUR GOSPEL.
LORD, HEAR OUR PRAYER.
LEAD HIM BY A HOLY LIFE TO THE JOYS OF GOD'S KINGDOM.
PTT.
LORD, HEAR OUR PRAYER.

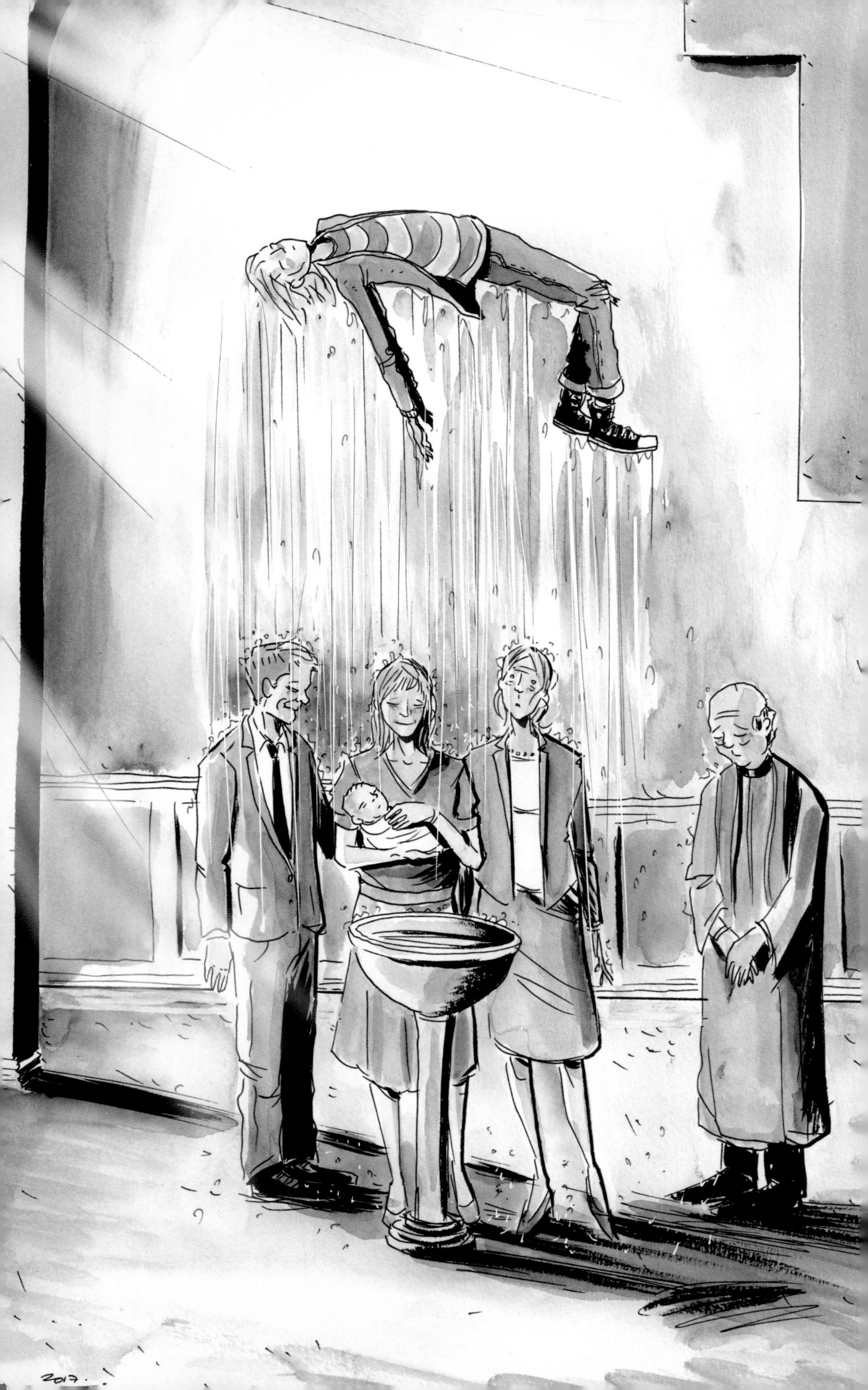
2017.

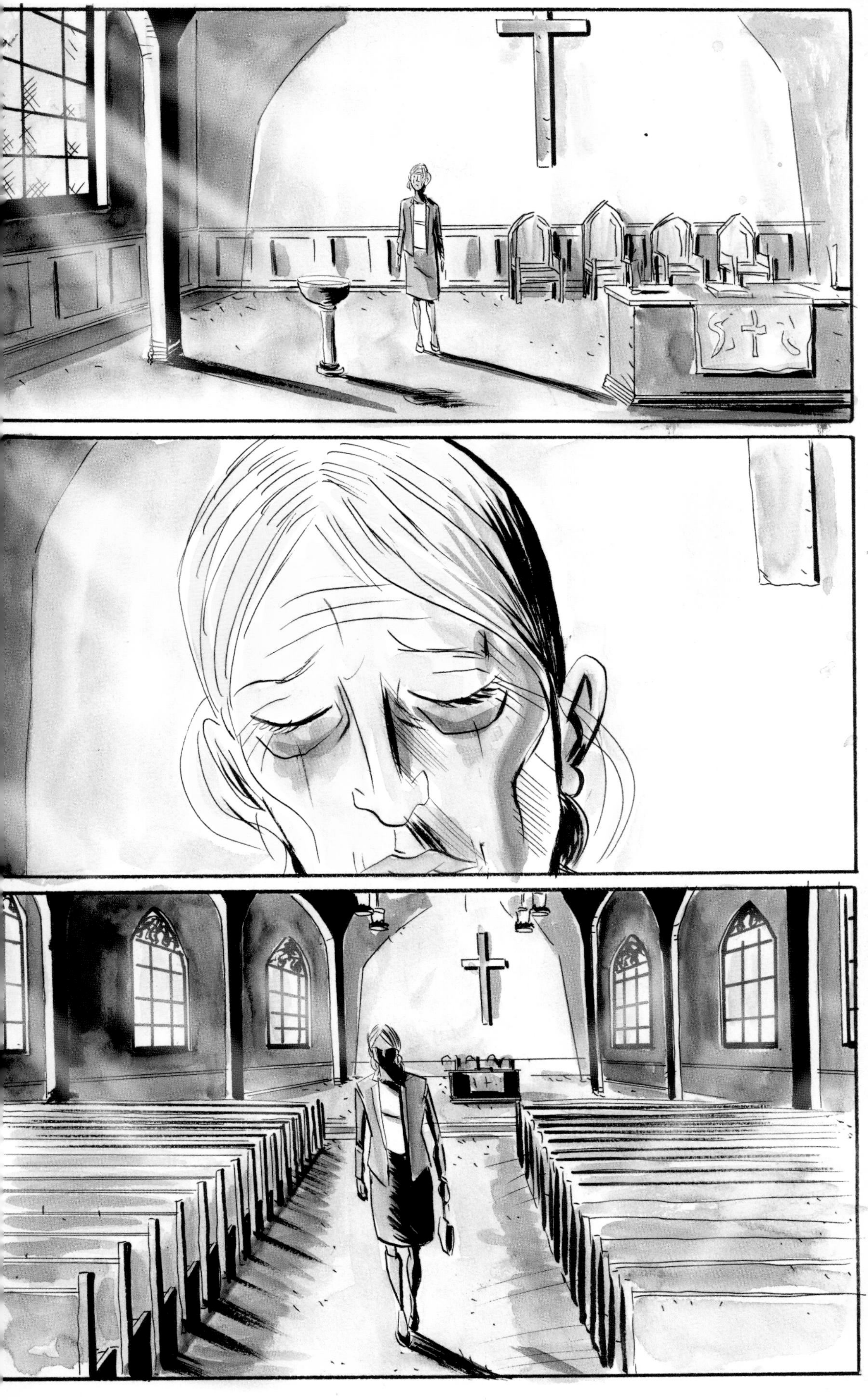

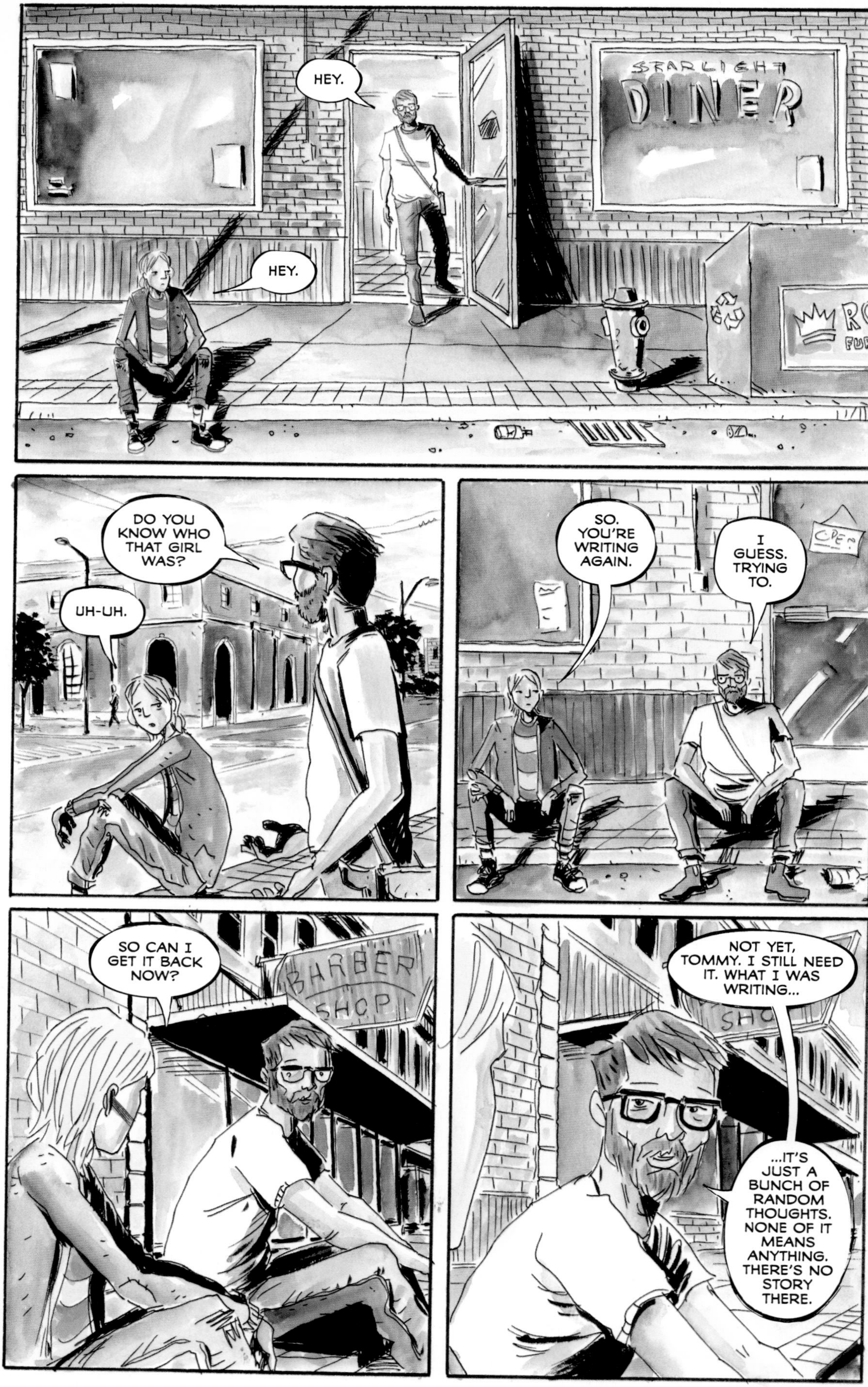

STARLIGHT DINER
HEY.
HEY.
RO
FUR
DO YOU KNOW WHO THAT GIRL WAS?
UH-UH.
SO. YOU'RE WRITING AGAIN.
I GUESS. TRYING TO.
SO CAN I GET IT BACK NOW?
BARBER SHOP
NOT YET, TOMMY. I STILL NEED IT. WHAT I WAS WRITING...
...IT'S JUST A BUNCH OF RANDOM THOUGHTS. NONE OF IT MEANS ANYTHING. THERE'S NO STORY THERE.

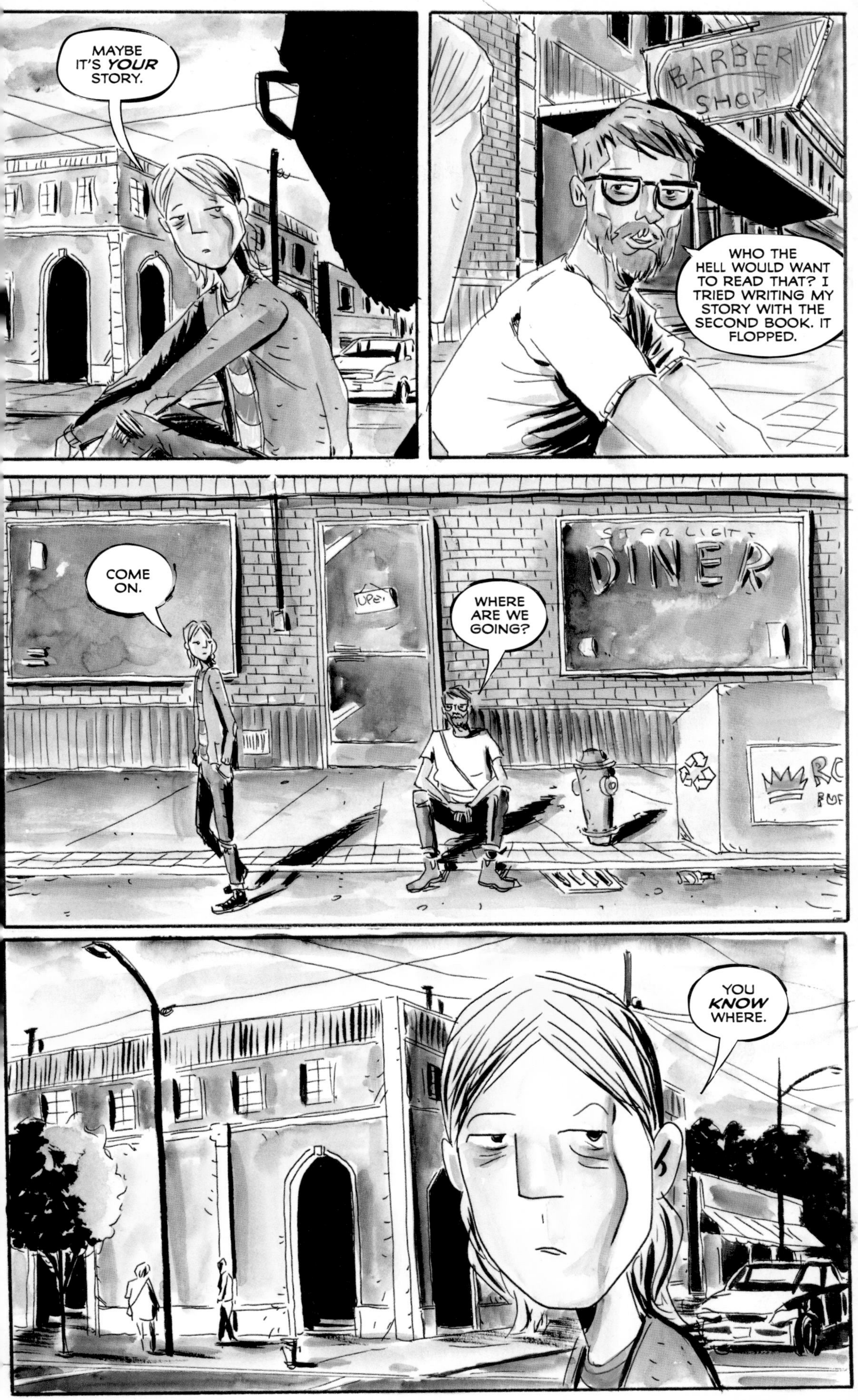
MAYBE IT'S *YOUR* STORY.
BARBER SHOP
WHO THE HELL WOULD WANT TO READ THAT? I TRIED WRITING MY STORY WITH THE SECOND BOOK. IT FLOPPED.
DINER
COME ON.
WHERE ARE WE GOING?
YOU *KNOW* WHERE.

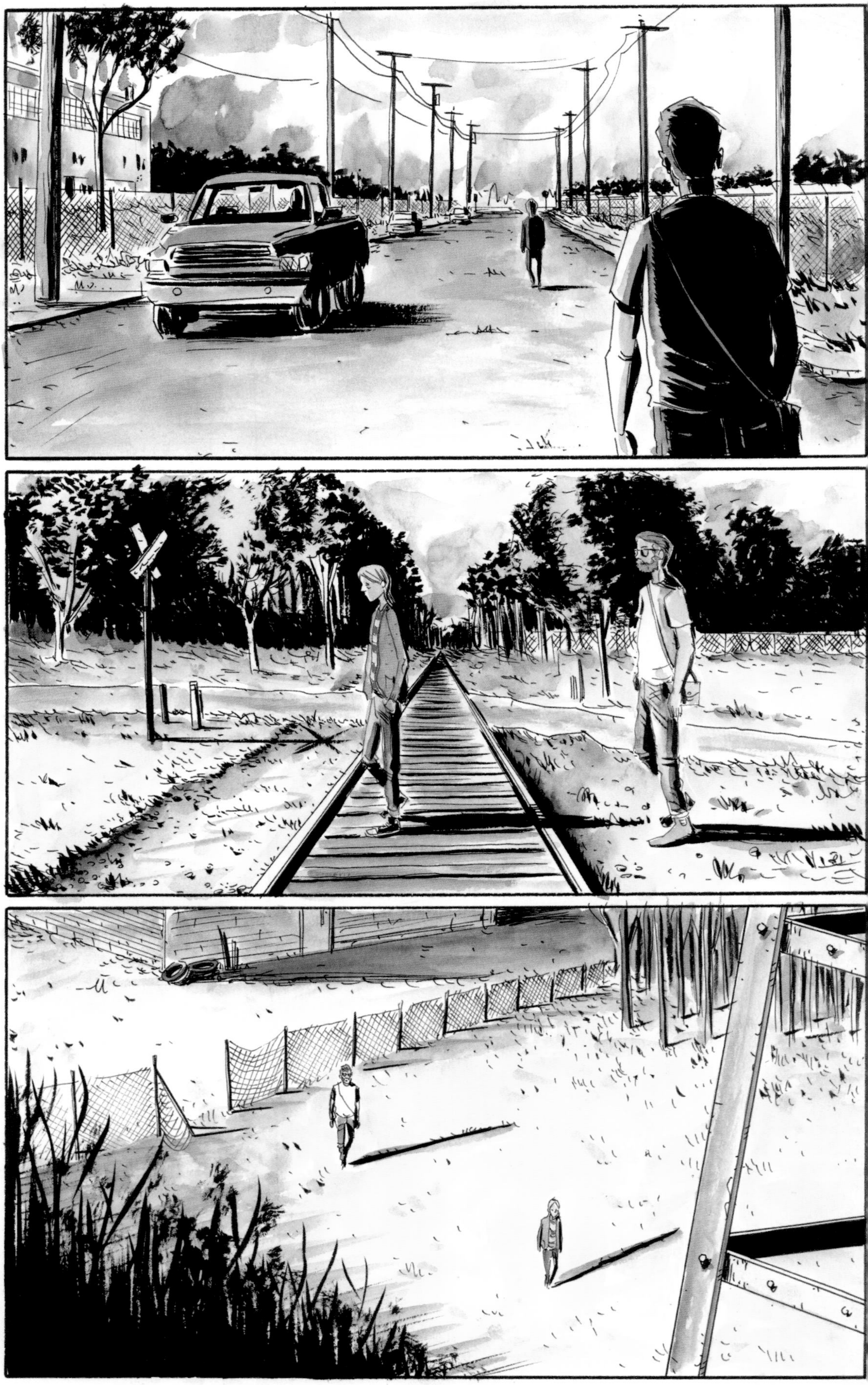

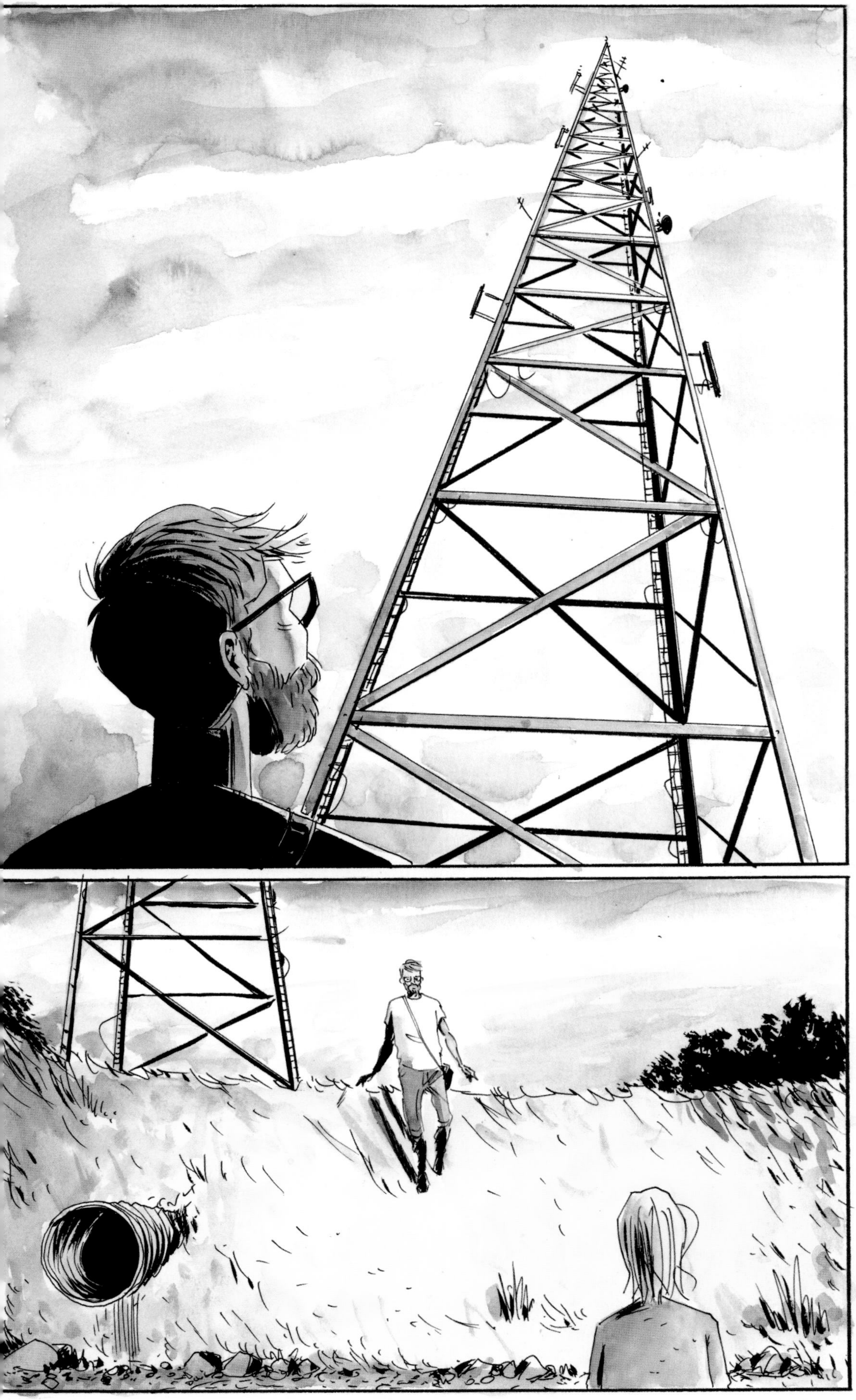

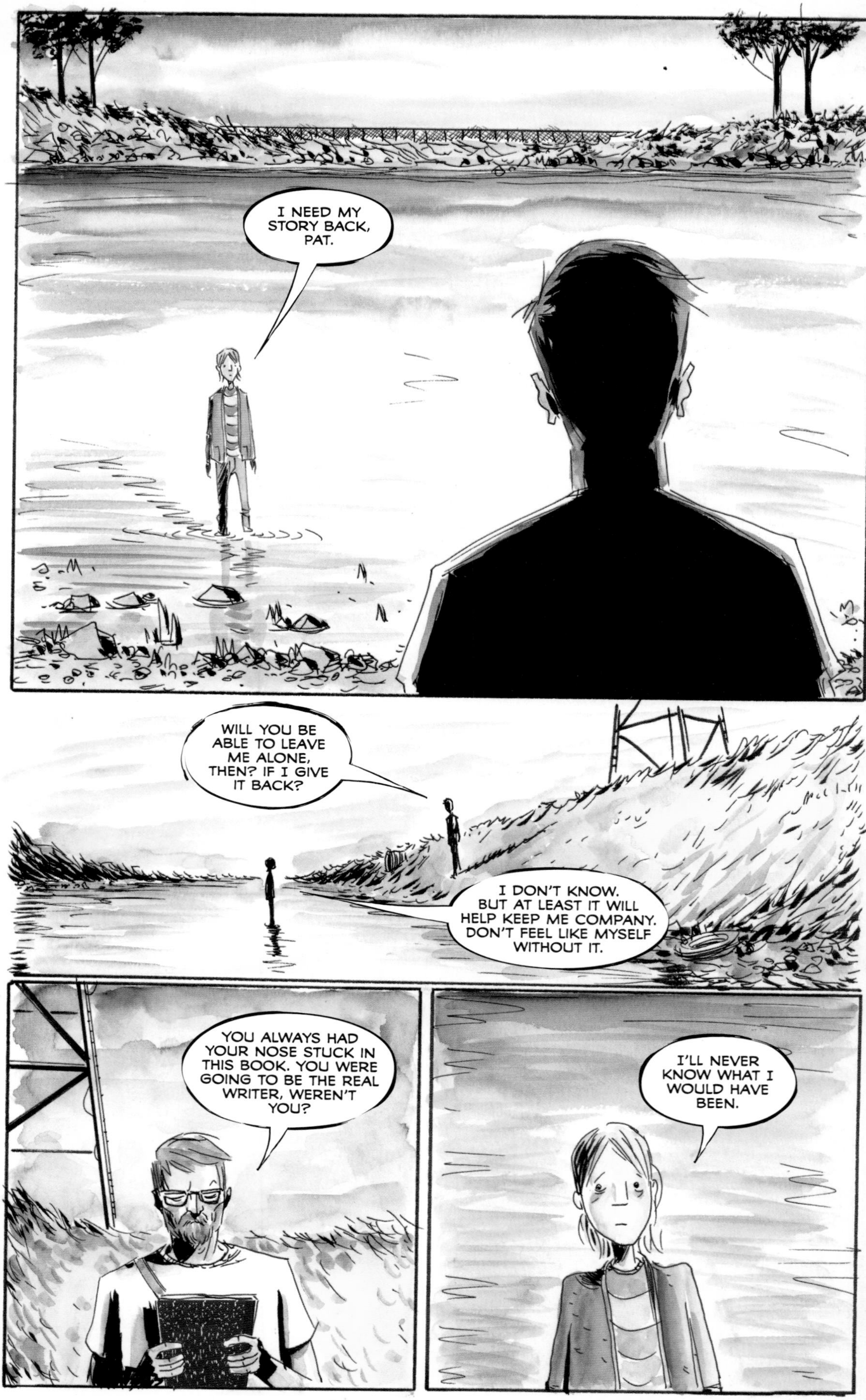
I NEED MY STORY BACK, PAT.
WILL YOU BE ABLE TO LEAVE ME ALONE, THEN? IF I GIVE IT BACK?
I DON'T KNOW. BUT AT LEAST IT WILL HELP KEEP ME COMPANY. DON'T FEEL LIKE MYSELF WITHOUT IT.
YOU ALWAYS HAD YOUR NOSE STUCK IN THIS BOOK. YOU WERE GOING TO BE THE REAL WRITER, WEREN'T YOU?
I'LL NEVER KNOW WHAT I WOULD HAVE BEEN.

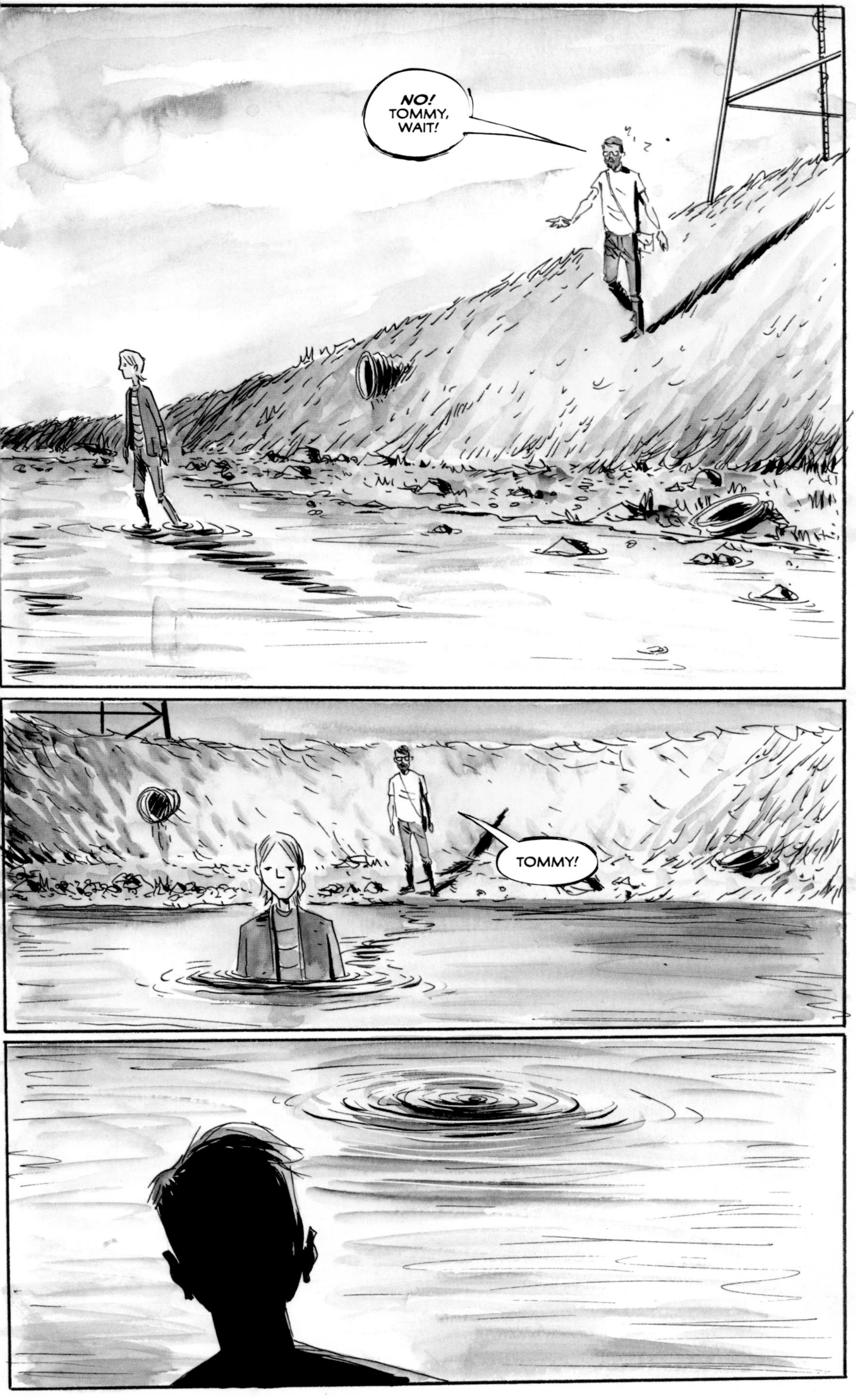
NO! TOMMY, WAIT!
TOMMY!

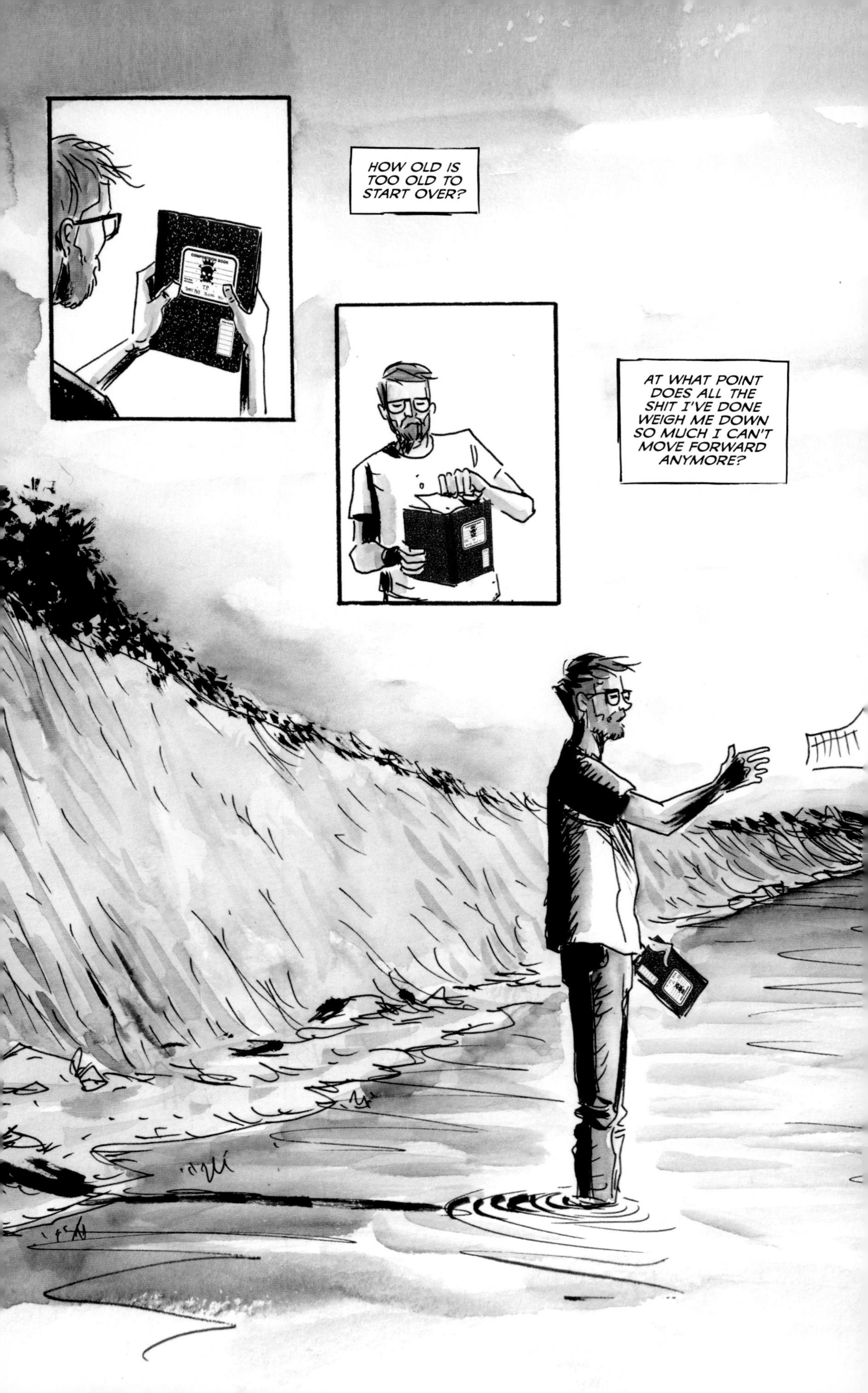
HOW OLD IS TOO OLD TO START OVER?
AT WHAT POINT DOES ALL THE SHIT I'VE DONE WEIGH ME DOWN SO MUCH I CAN'T MOVE FORWARD ANYMORE?

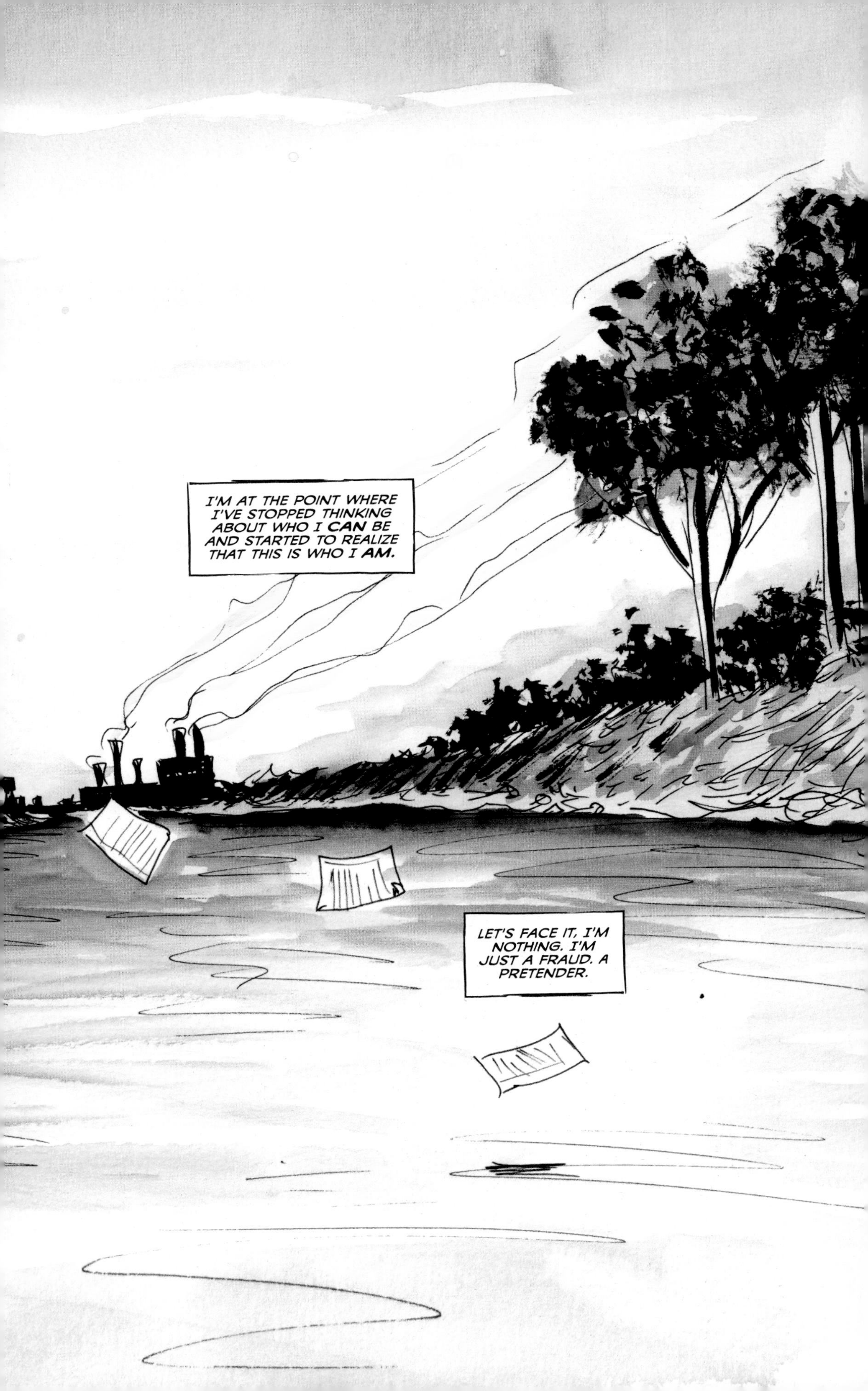
I'M AT THE POINT WHERE I'VE STOPPED THINKING ABOUT WHO I **CAN** BE AND STARTED TO REALIZE THAT THIS IS WHO I **AM.**
LET'S FACE IT, I'M NOTHING. I'M JUST A FRAUD. A PRETENDER.

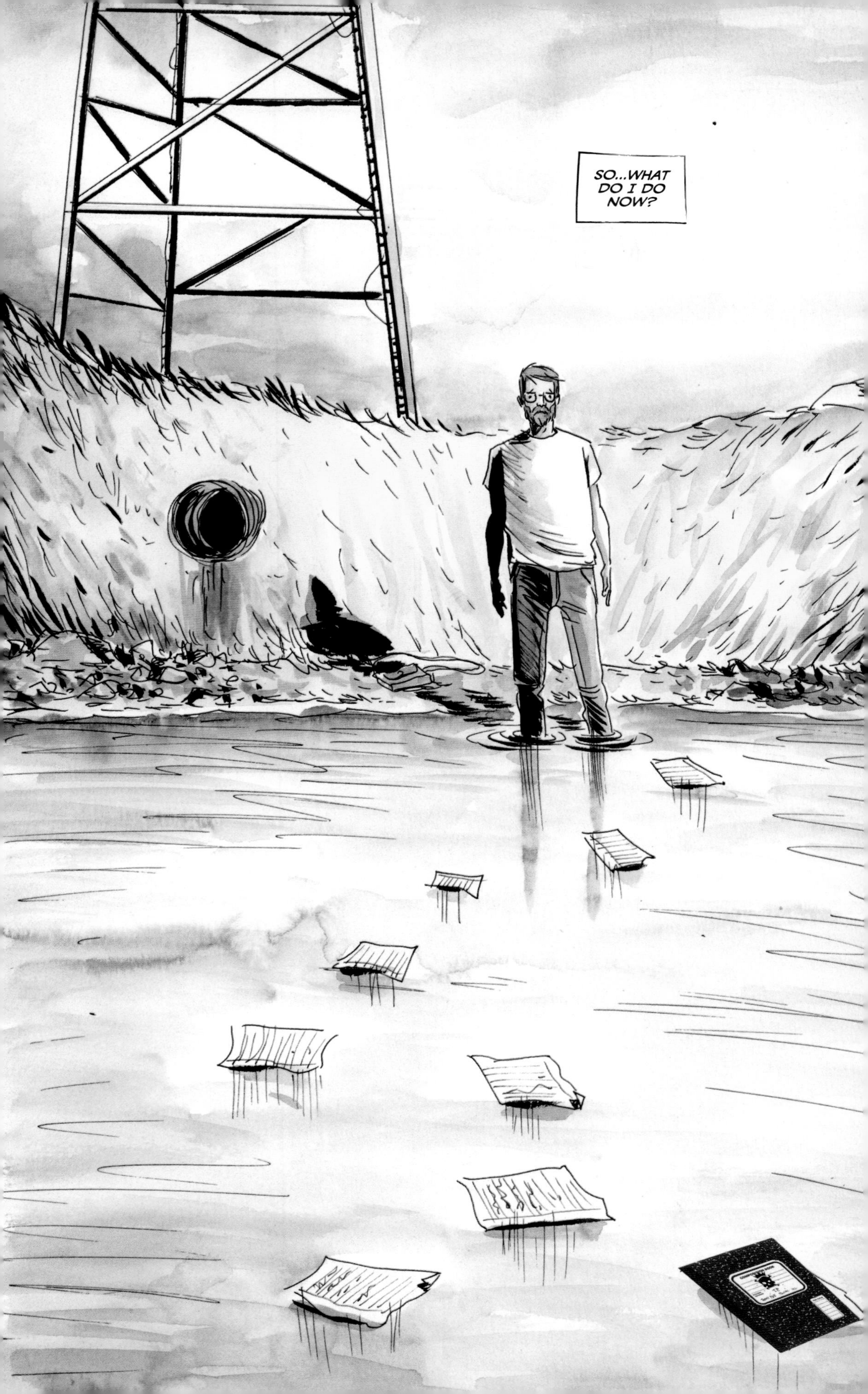
SO...WHAT DO I DO NOW?

CHAPTER FIVE

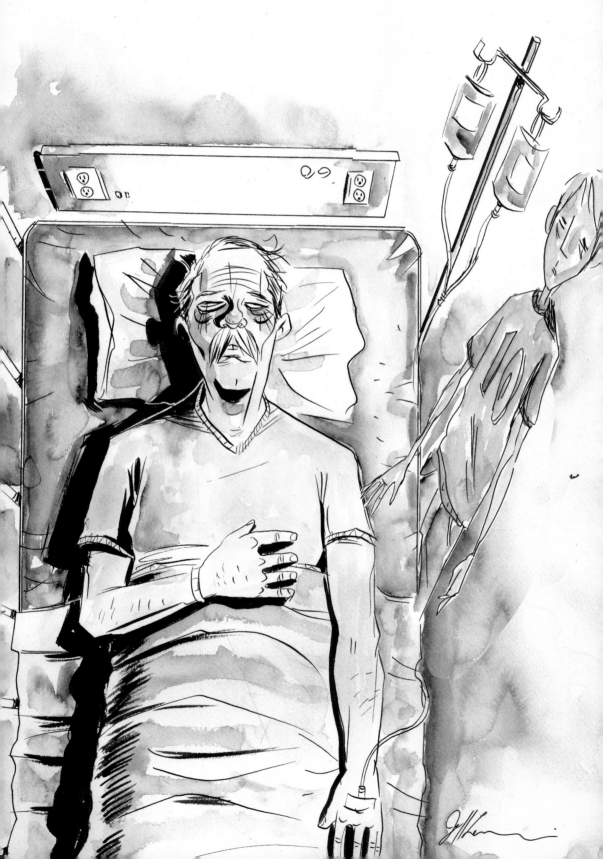

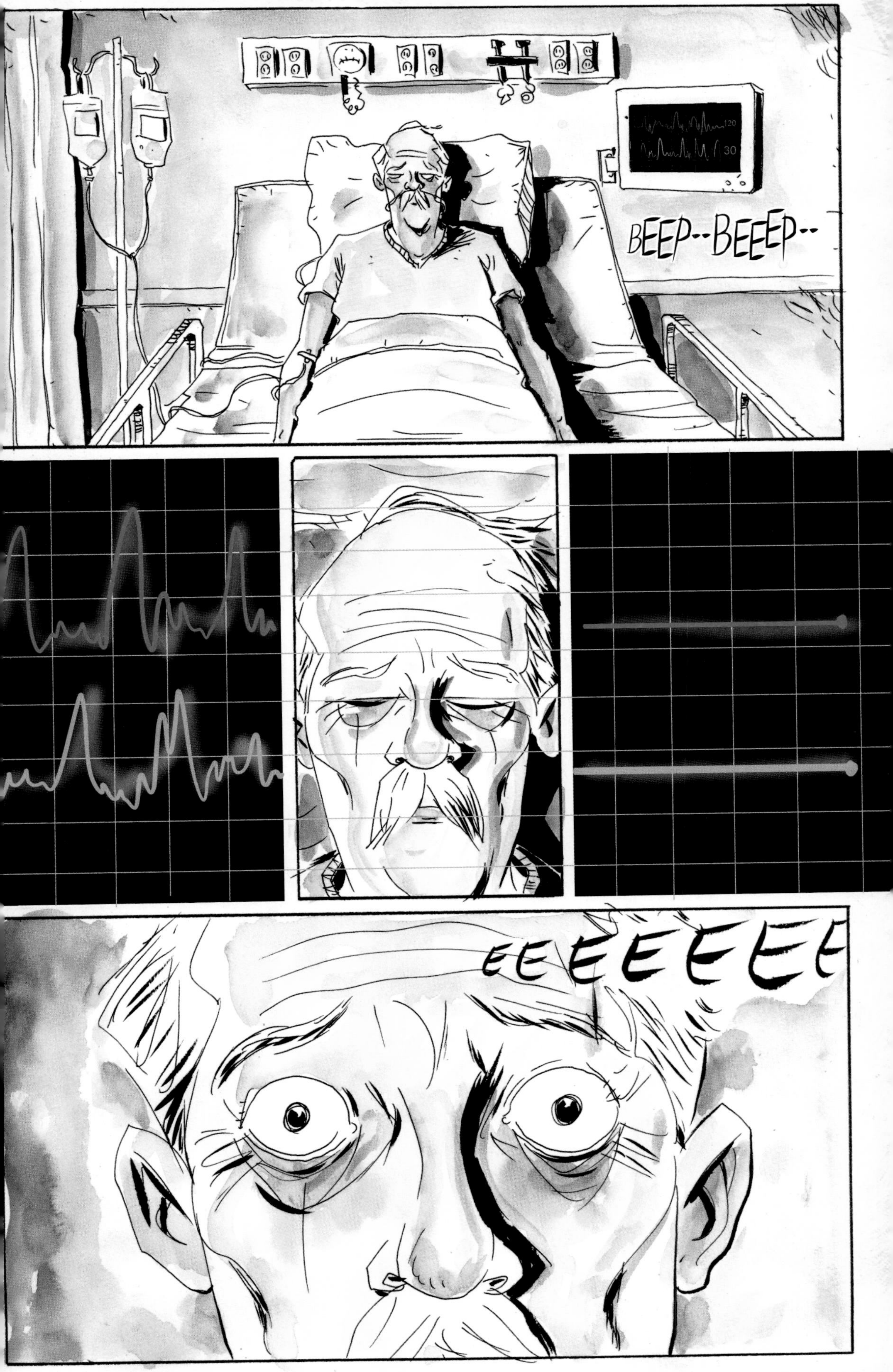

120
30
BEEP--BEEEP--
EEEEEEEE

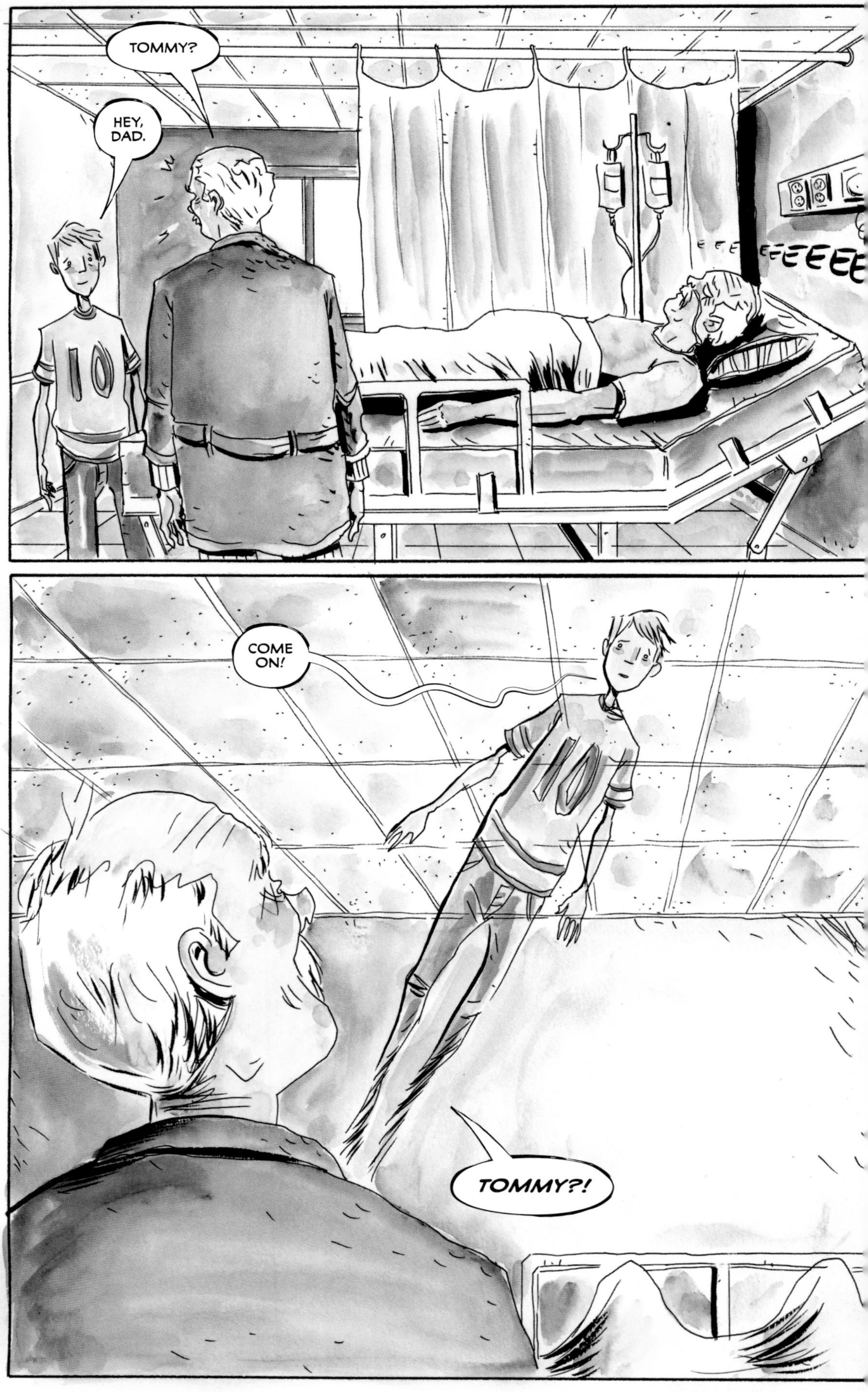
TOMMY?
HEY, DAD.
E E E EEEEEE
COME ON!
TOMMY?!

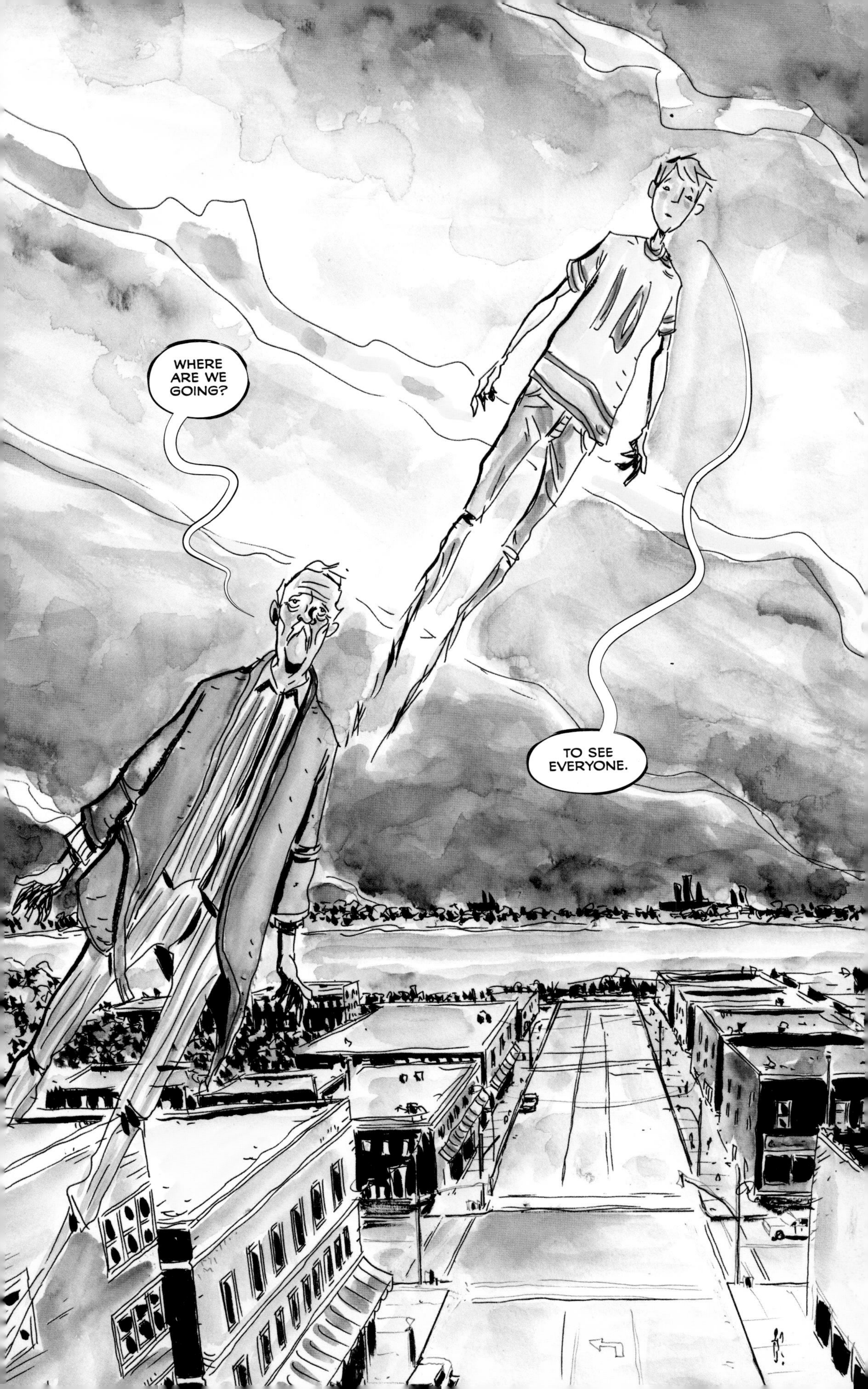
WHERE ARE WE GOING?
TO SEE EVERYONE.

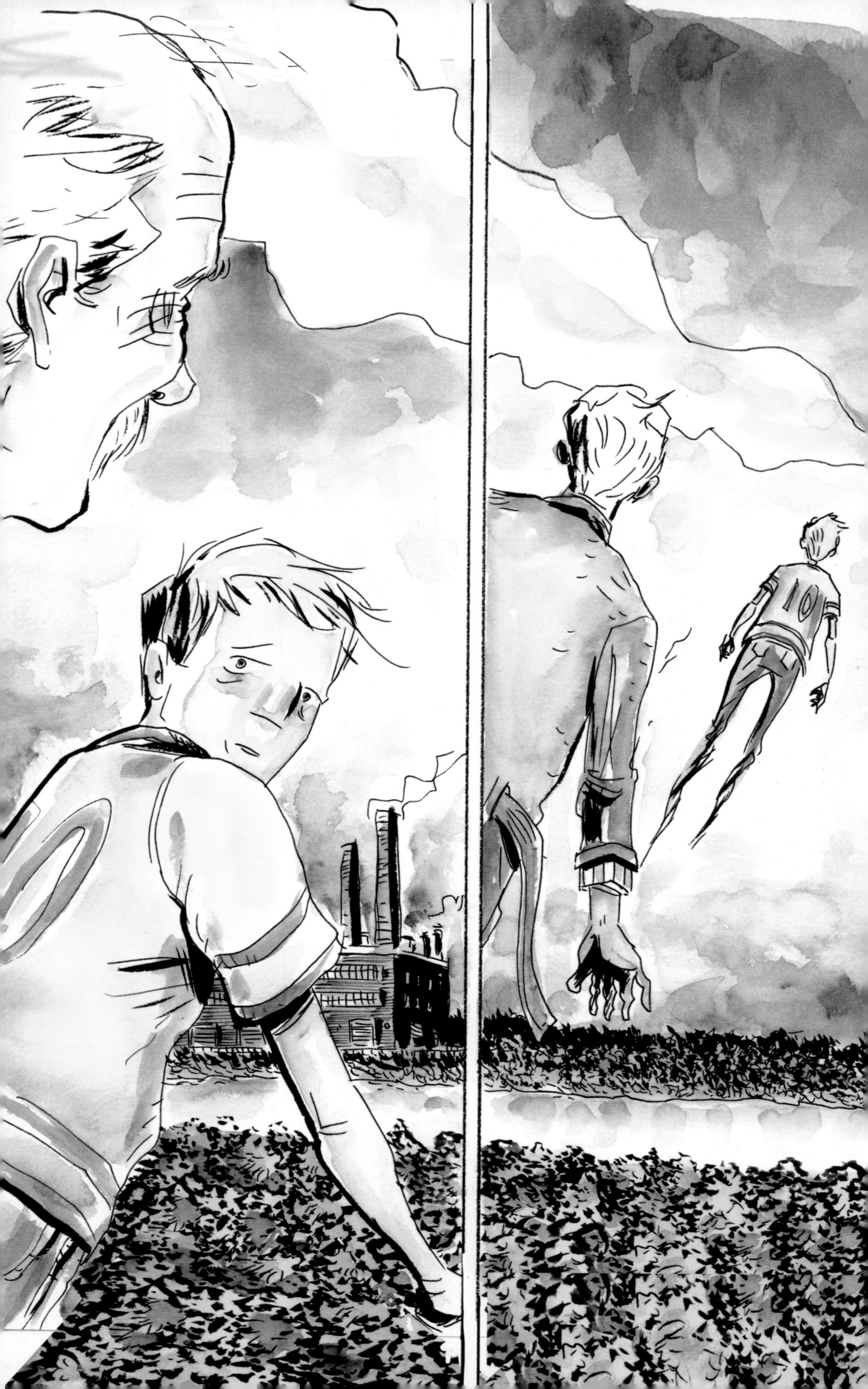

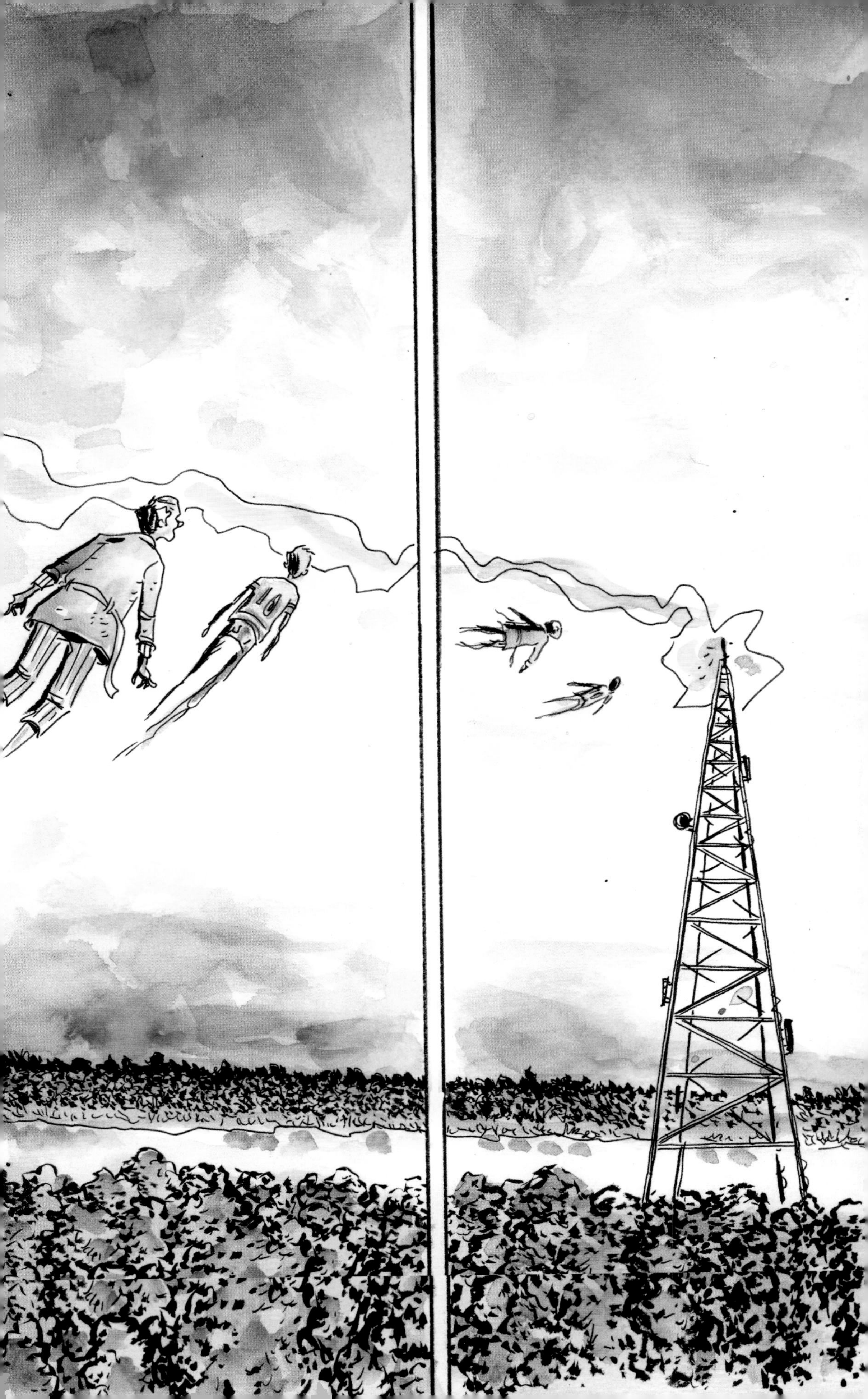

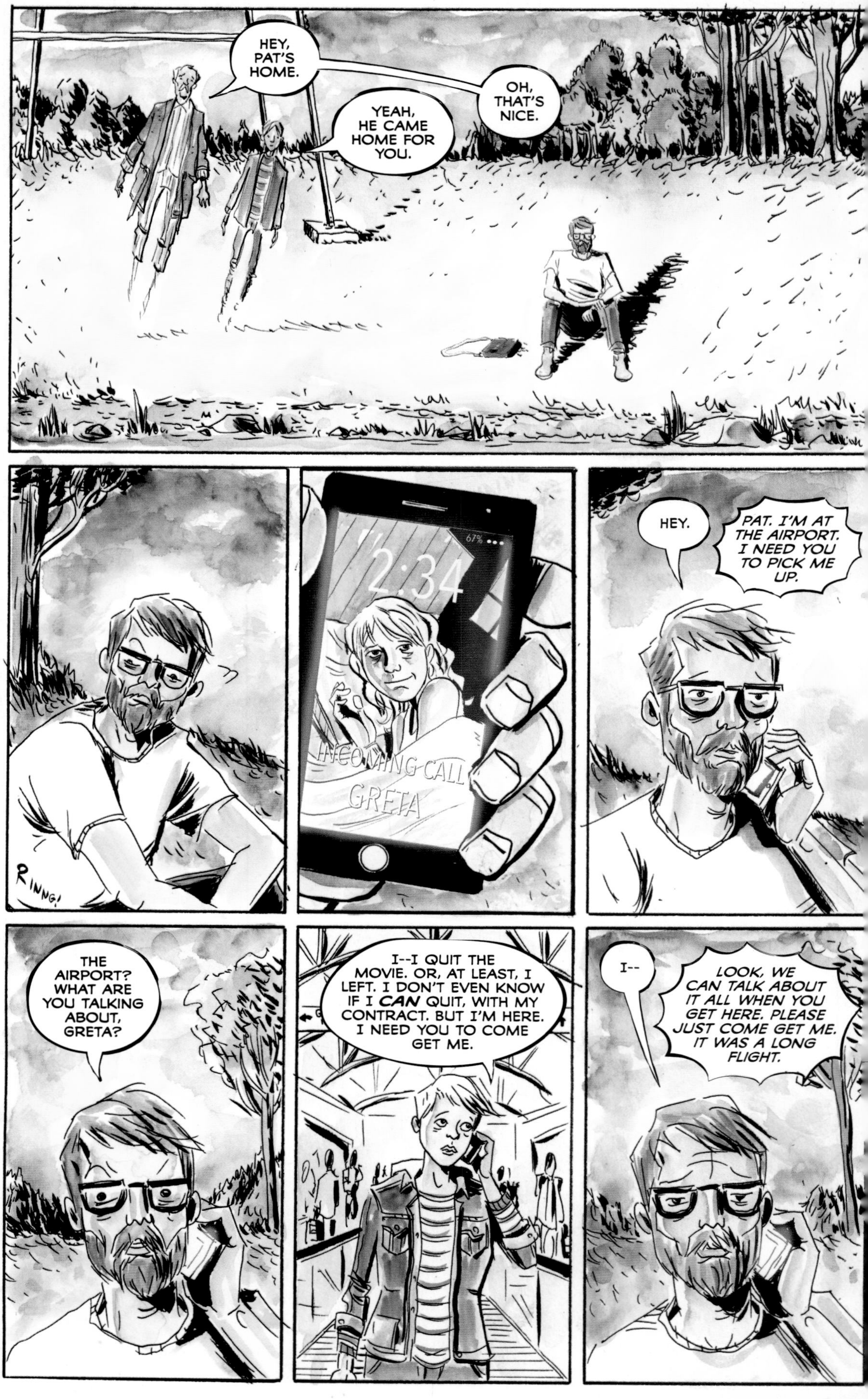
HEY, PAT'S HOME.
OH, THAT'S NICE.
YEAH, HE CAME HOME FOR YOU.
RINNG!
2:34
INCOMING CALL GRETA
HEY.
PAT. I'M AT THE AIRPORT. I NEED YOU TO PICK ME UP.
THE AIRPORT? WHAT ARE YOU TALKING ABOUT, GRETA?
I--I QUIT THE MOVIE. OR, AT LEAST, I LEFT. I DON'T EVEN KNOW IF I CAN QUIT, WITH MY CONTRACT. BUT I'M HERE. I NEED YOU TO COME GET ME.
I--
LOOK, WE CAN TALK ABOUT IT ALL WHEN YOU GET HERE. PLEASE JUST COME GET ME. IT WAS A LONG FLIGHT.

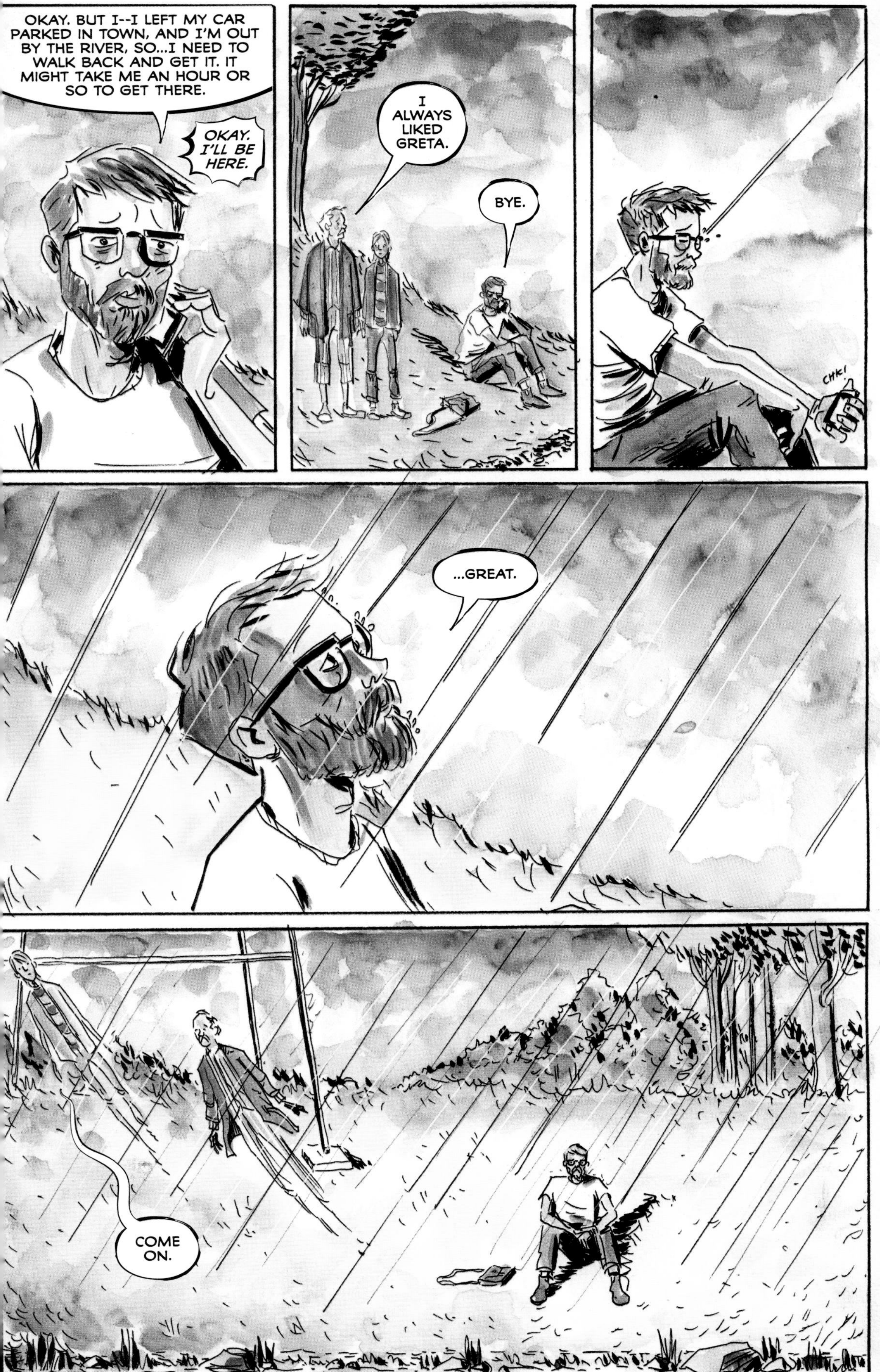
OKAY. BUT I--I LEFT MY CAR PARKED IN TOWN, AND I'M OUT BY THE RIVER, SO...I NEED TO WALK BACK AND GET IT. IT MIGHT TAKE ME AN HOUR OR SO TO GET THERE.
OKAY. I'LL BE HERE.
I ALWAYS LIKED GRETA.
BYE.
CHK!
...GREAT.
COME ON.

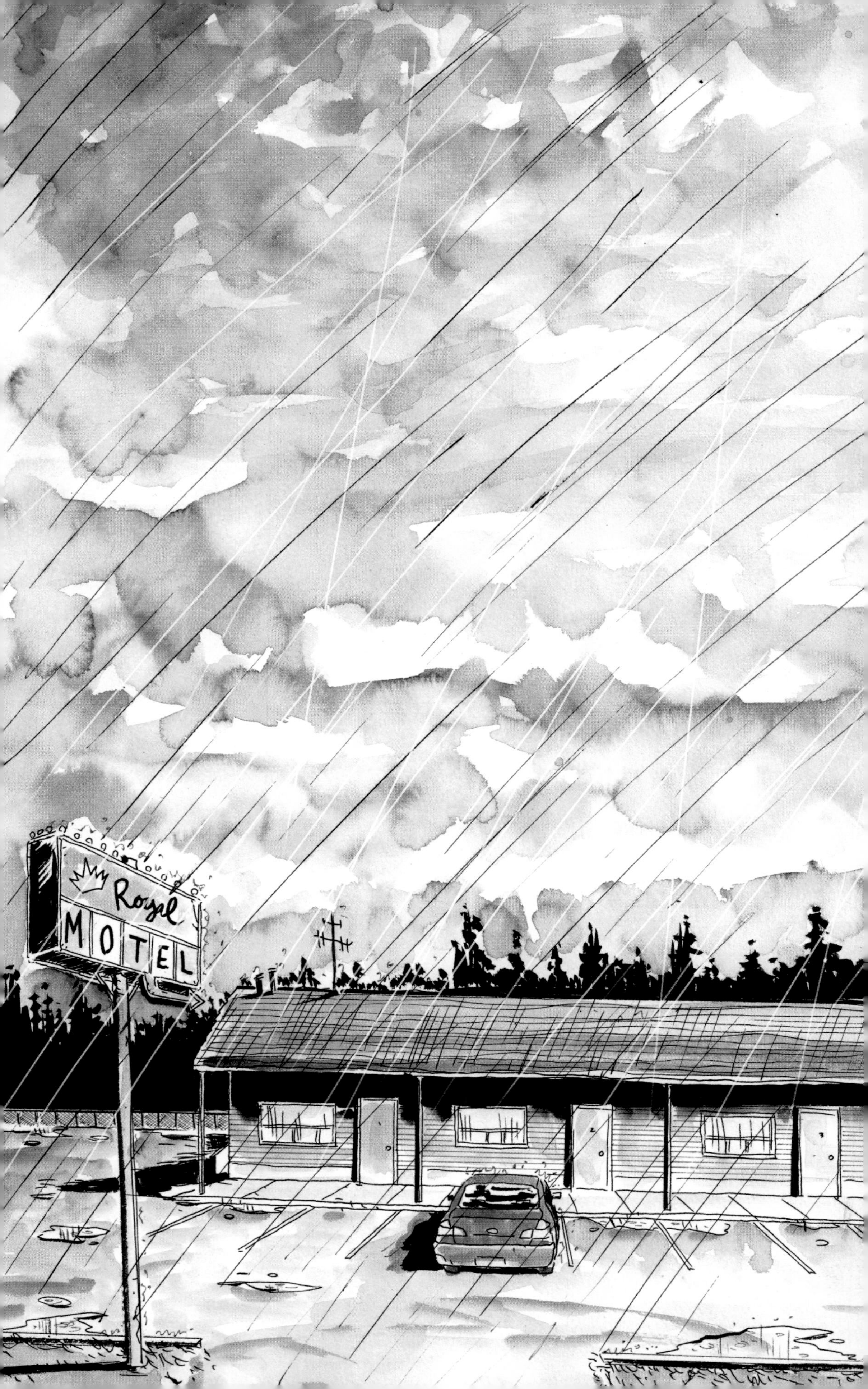
Royal
MOTEL

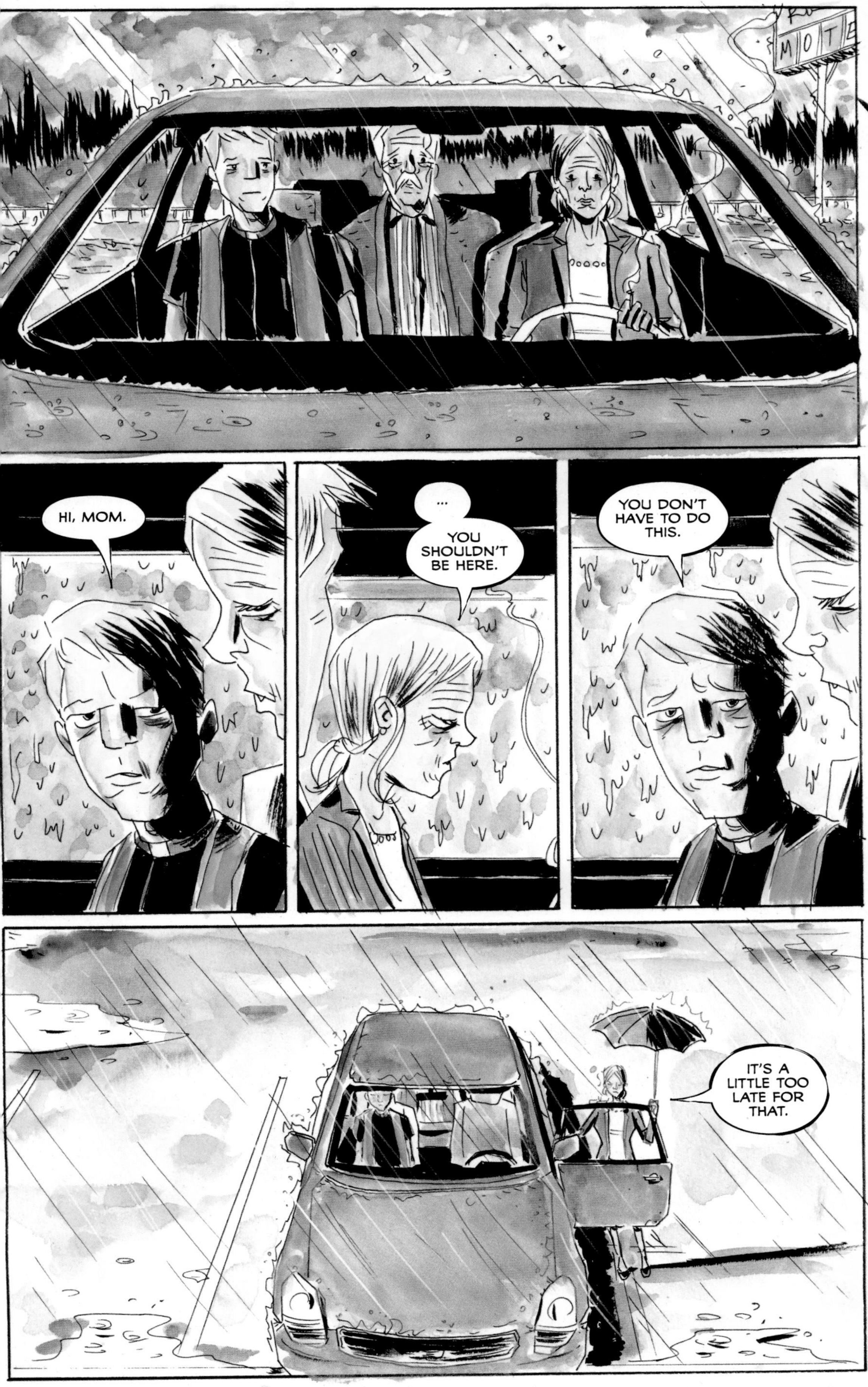
HI, MOM.
...
YOU SHOULDN'T BE HERE.
YOU DON'T HAVE TO DO THIS.
IT'S A LITTLE TOO LATE FOR THAT.

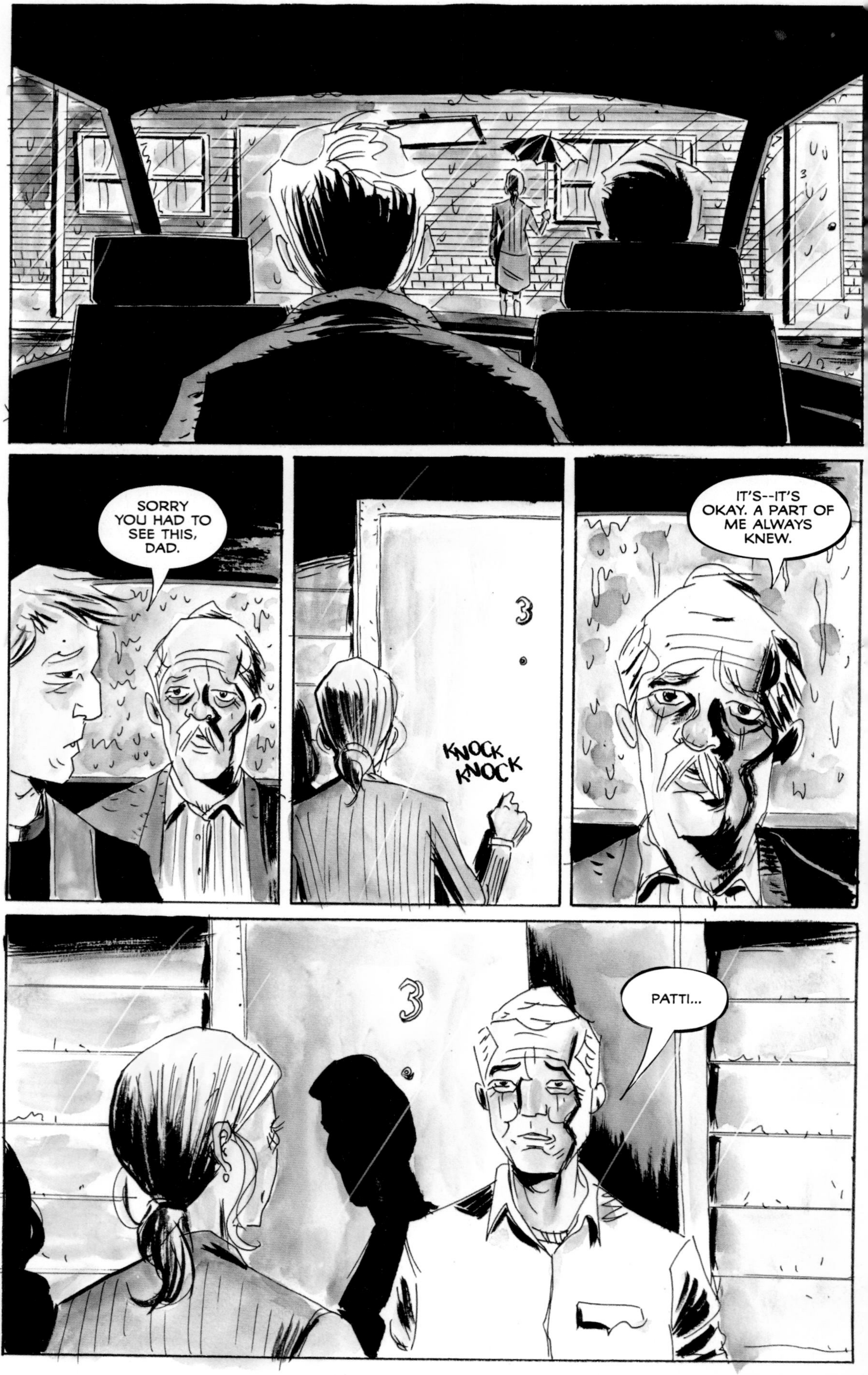

SORRY YOU HAD TO SEE THIS, DAD.
KNOCK KNOCK
IT'S--IT'S OKAY. A PART OF ME ALWAYS KNEW.
PATTI...

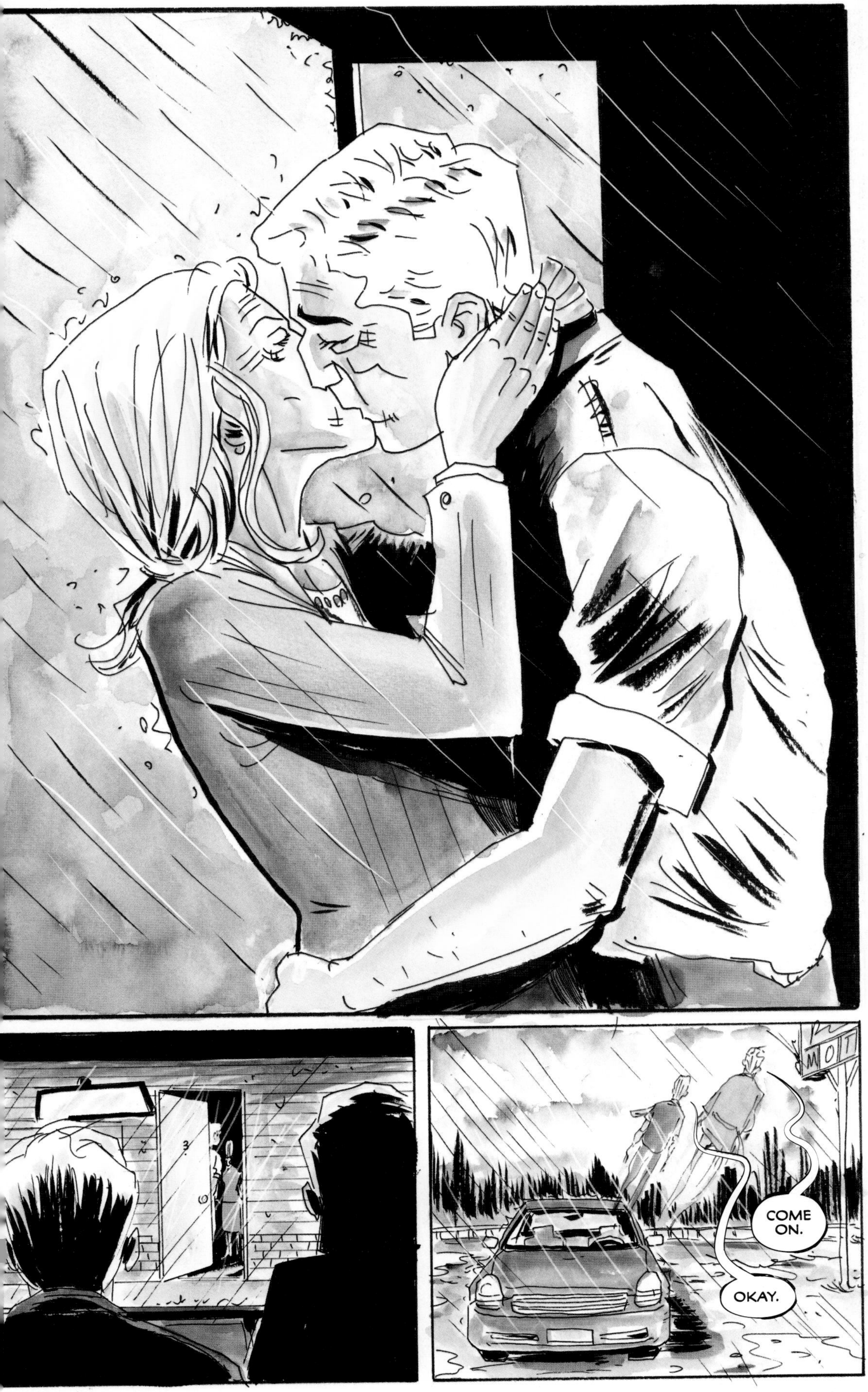
COME ON.
OKAY.

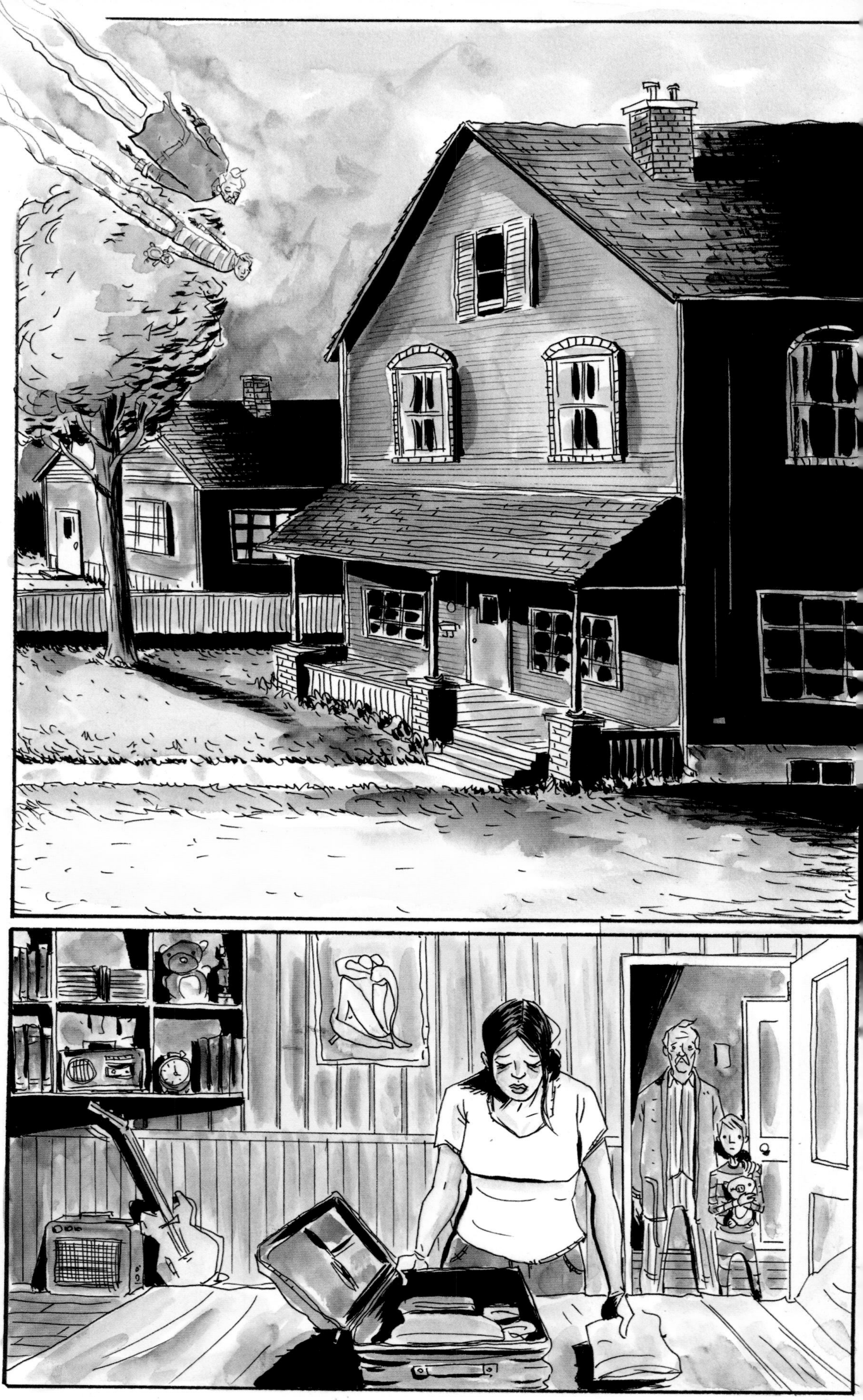

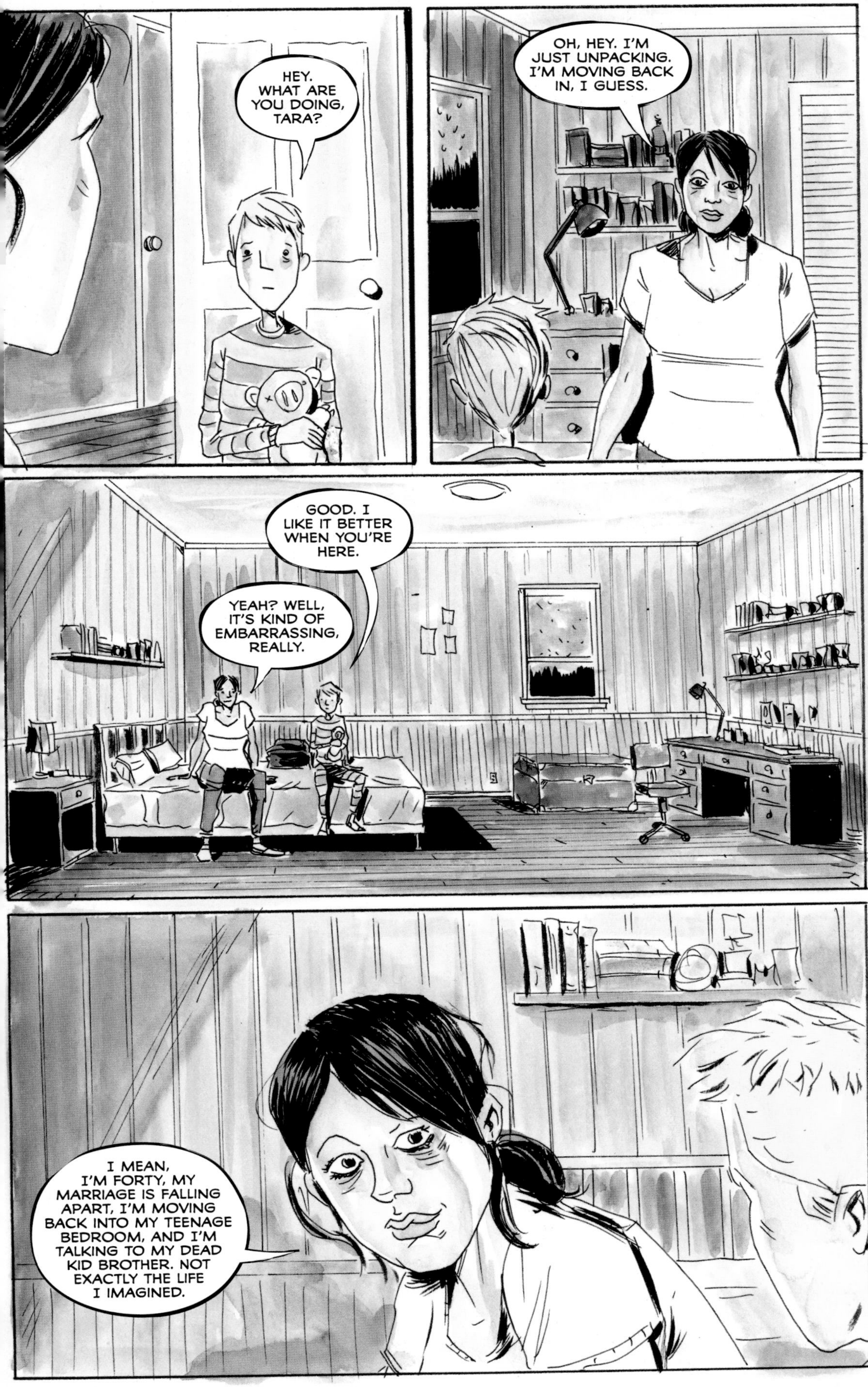

HEY. WHAT ARE YOU DOING, TARA?
OH, HEY. I'M JUST UNPACKING. I'M MOVING BACK IN, I GUESS.
GOOD. I LIKE IT BETTER WHEN YOU'RE HERE.
YEAH? WELL, IT'S KIND OF EMBARRASSING, REALLY.
I MEAN, I'M FORTY, MY MARRIAGE IS FALLING APART, I'M MOVING BACK INTO MY TEENAGE BEDROOM, AND I'M TALKING TO MY DEAD KID BROTHER. NOT EXACTLY THE LIFE I IMAGINED.

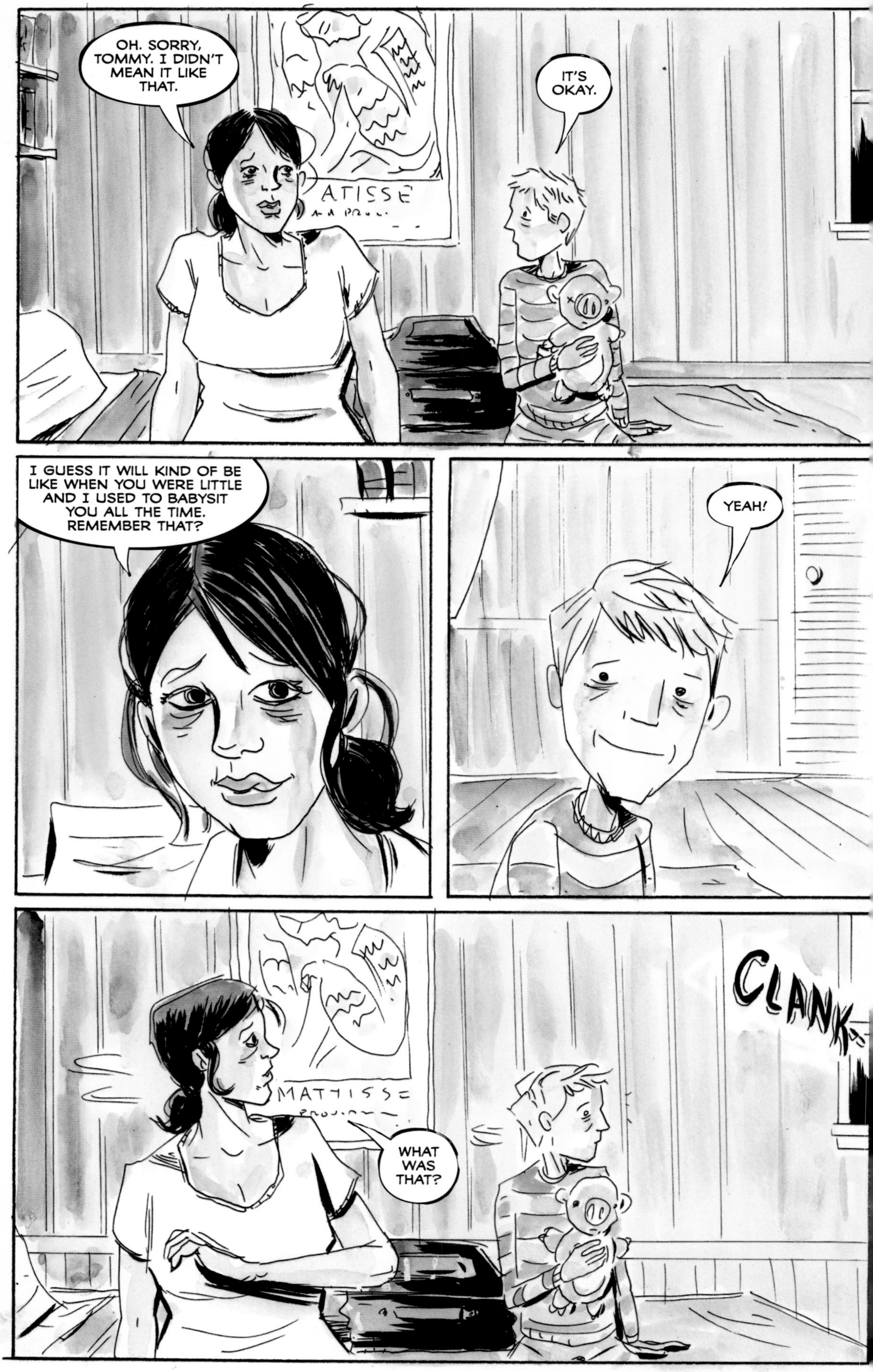
OH. SORRY, TOMMY. I DIDN'T MEAN IT LIKE THAT.
IT'S OKAY.
ATISSE
I GUESS IT WILL KIND OF BE LIKE WHEN YOU WERE LITTLE AND I USED TO BABYSIT YOU ALL THE TIME. REMEMBER THAT?
YEAH!
CLANK
MATTISSE
WHAT WAS THAT?

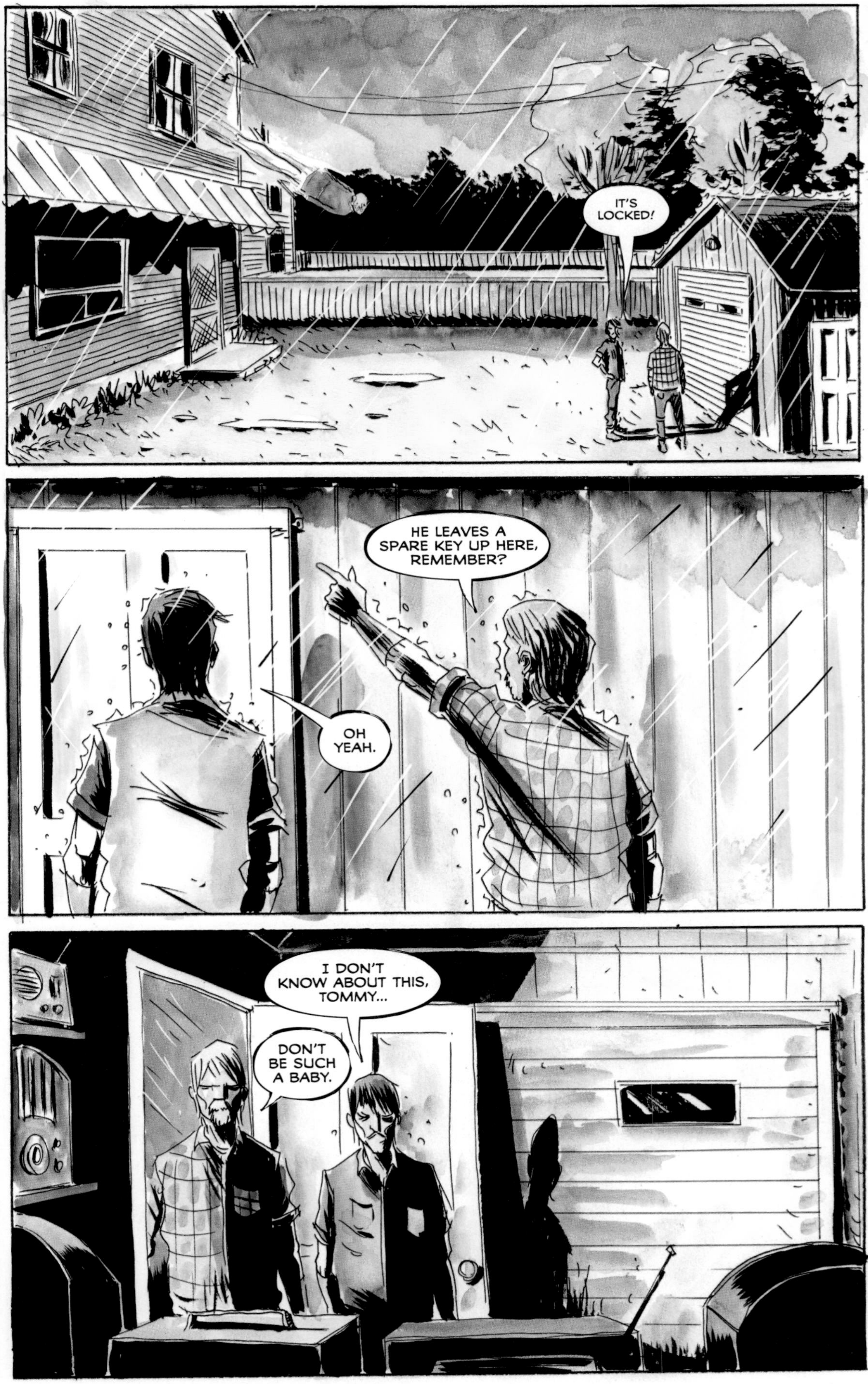
IT'S LOCKED!
HE LEAVES A SPARE KEY UP HERE, REMEMBER?
OH YEAH.
I DON'T KNOW ABOUT THIS, TOMMY...
DON'T BE SUCH A BABY.

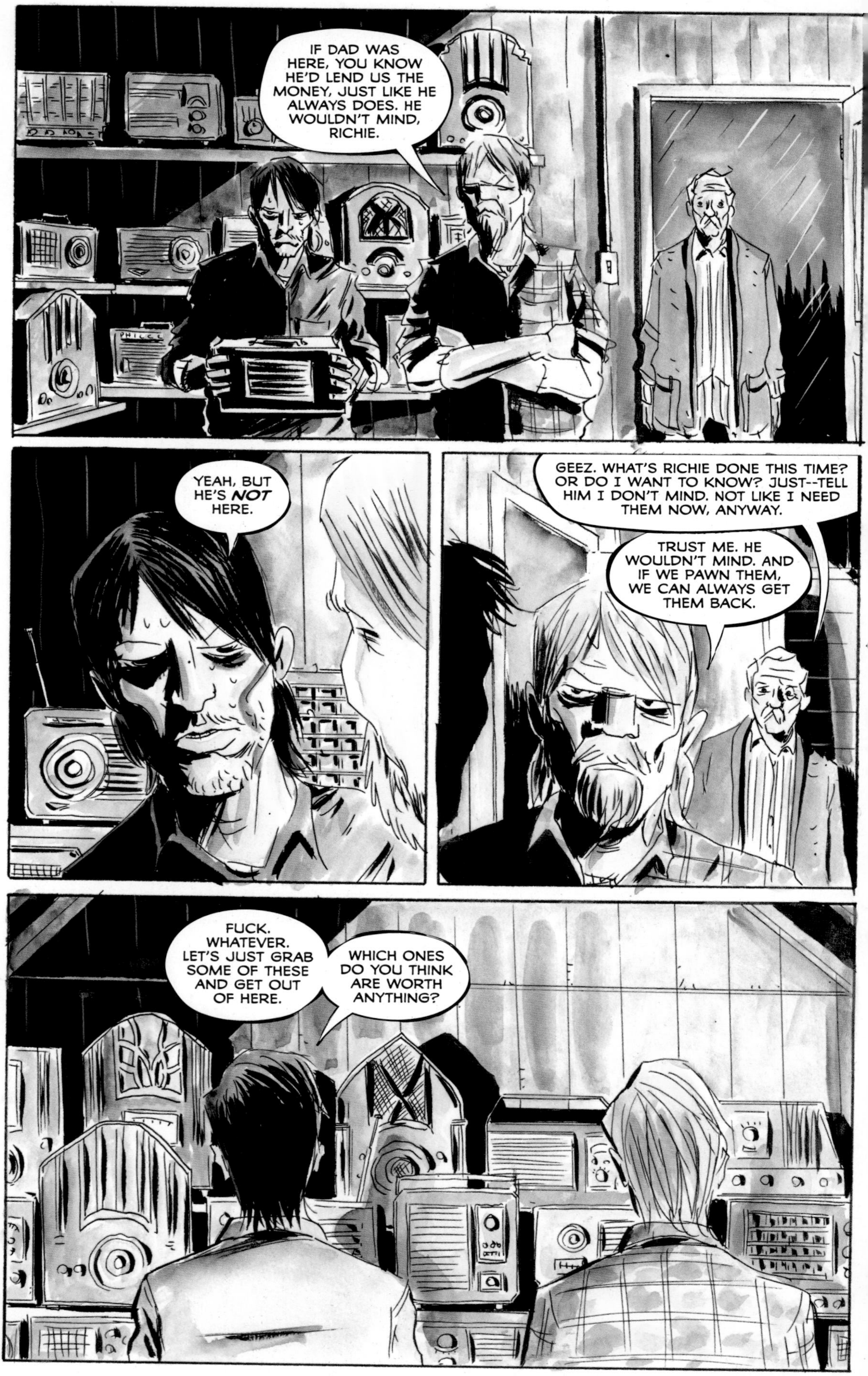
IF DAD WAS HERE, YOU KNOW HE'D LEND US THE MONEY, JUST LIKE HE ALWAYS DOES. HE WOULDN'T MIND, RICHIE.
YEAH, BUT HE'S ***NOT*** HERE.
GEEZ. WHAT'S RICHIE DONE THIS TIME? OR DO I WANT TO KNOW? JUST--TELL HIM I DON'T MIND. NOT LIKE I NEED THEM NOW, ANYWAY.
TRUST ME. HE WOULDN'T MIND. AND IF WE PAWN THEM, WE CAN ALWAYS GET THEM BACK.
FUCK. WHATEVER. LET'S JUST GRAB SOME OF THESE AND GET OUT OF HERE.
WHICH ONES DO YOU THINK ARE WORTH ANYTHING?

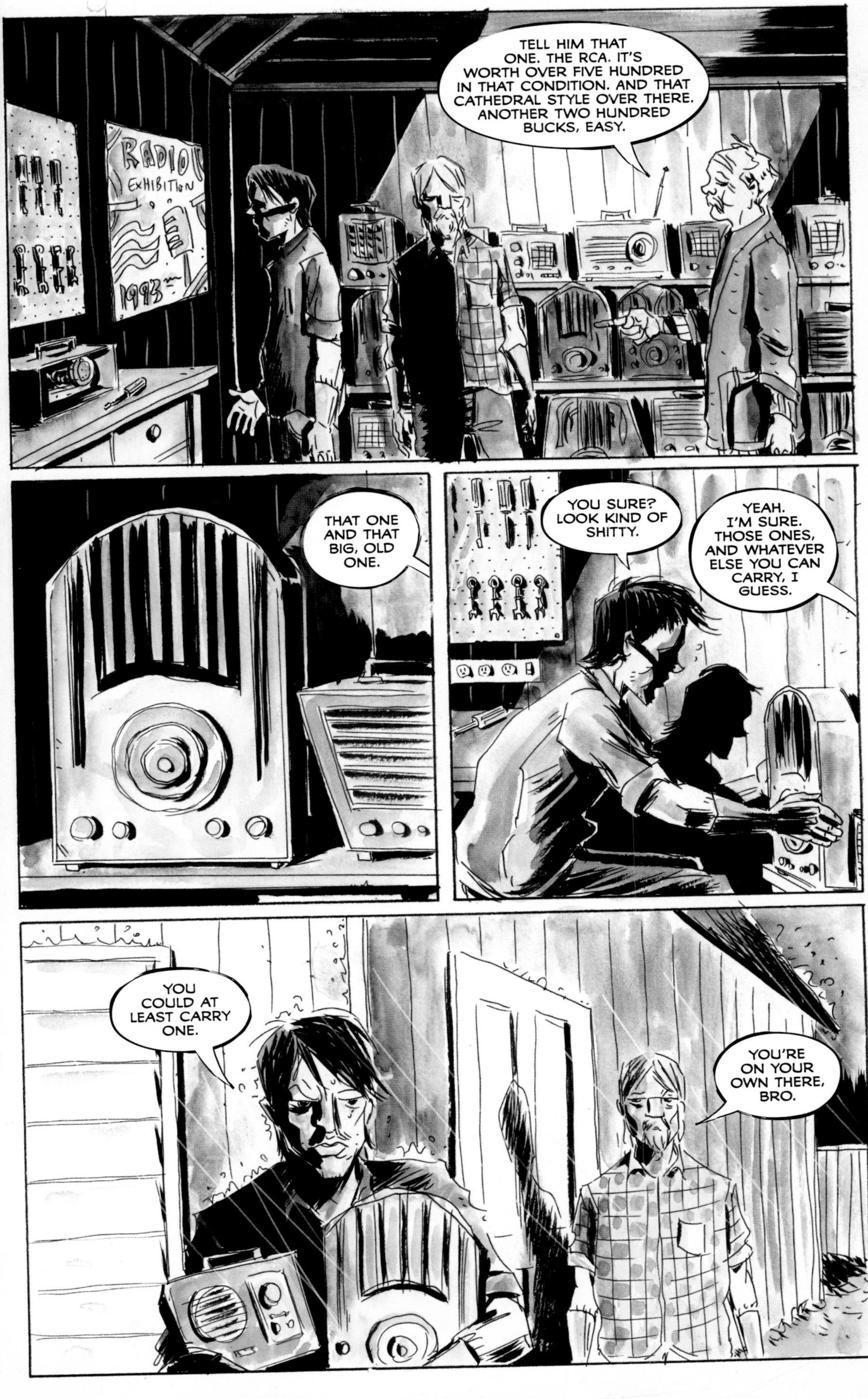

TELL HIM THAT ONE. THE RCA. IT'S WORTH OVER FIVE HUNDRED IN THAT CONDITION. AND THAT CATHEDRAL STYLE OVER THERE. ANOTHER TWO HUNDRED BUCKS, EASY.
RADIO EXHIBITION 1993
THAT ONE AND THAT BIG, OLD ONE.
YOU SURE? LOOK KIND OF SHITTY.
YEAH. I'M SURE. THOSE ONES, AND WHATEVER ELSE YOU CAN CARRY, I GUESS.
YOU COULD AT LEAST CARRY ONE.
YOU'RE ON YOUR OWN THERE, BRO.

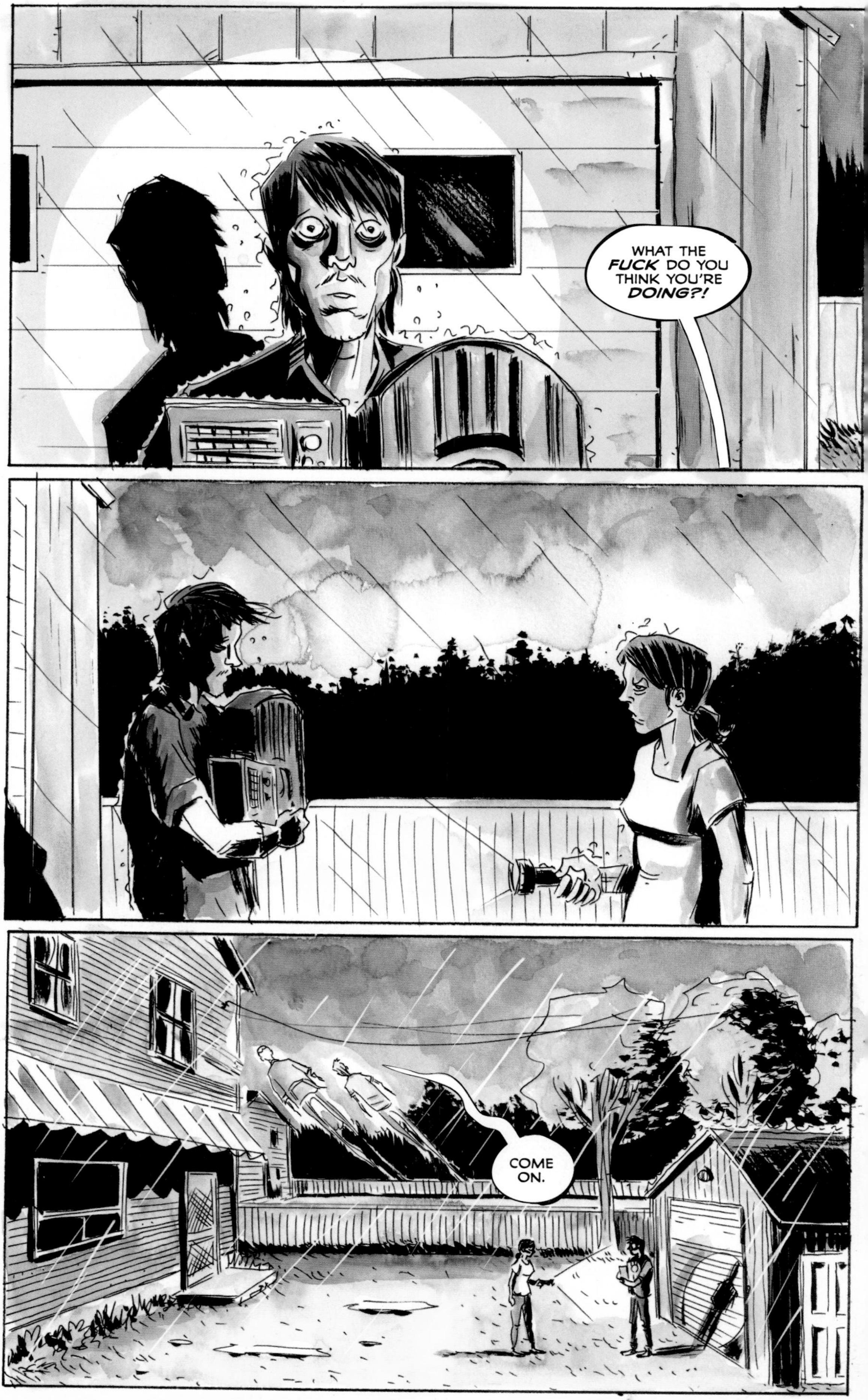
WHAT THE *FUCK* DO YOU THINK YOU'RE *DOING?!*
COME ON.

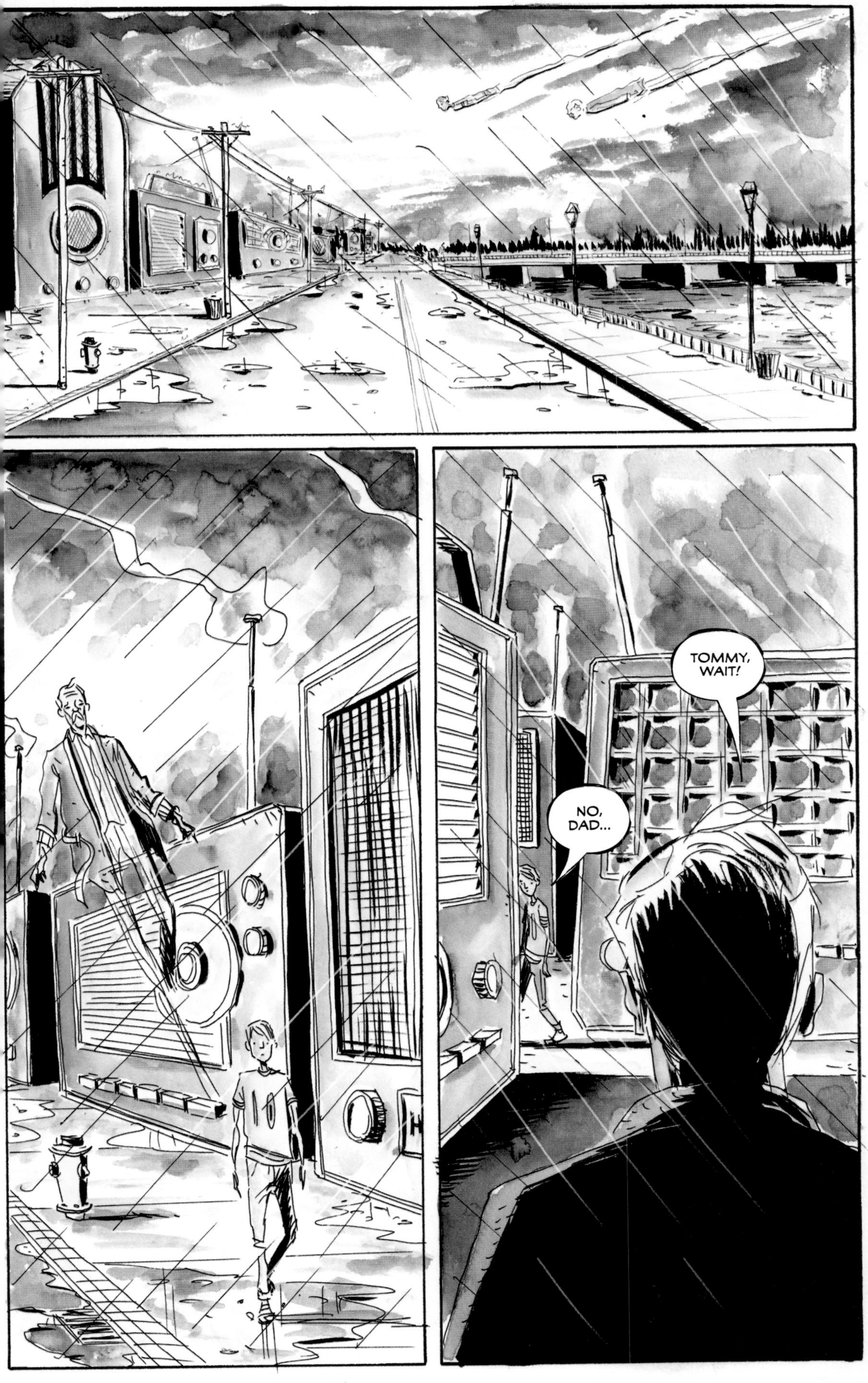
TOMMY, WAIT!
NO, DAD...

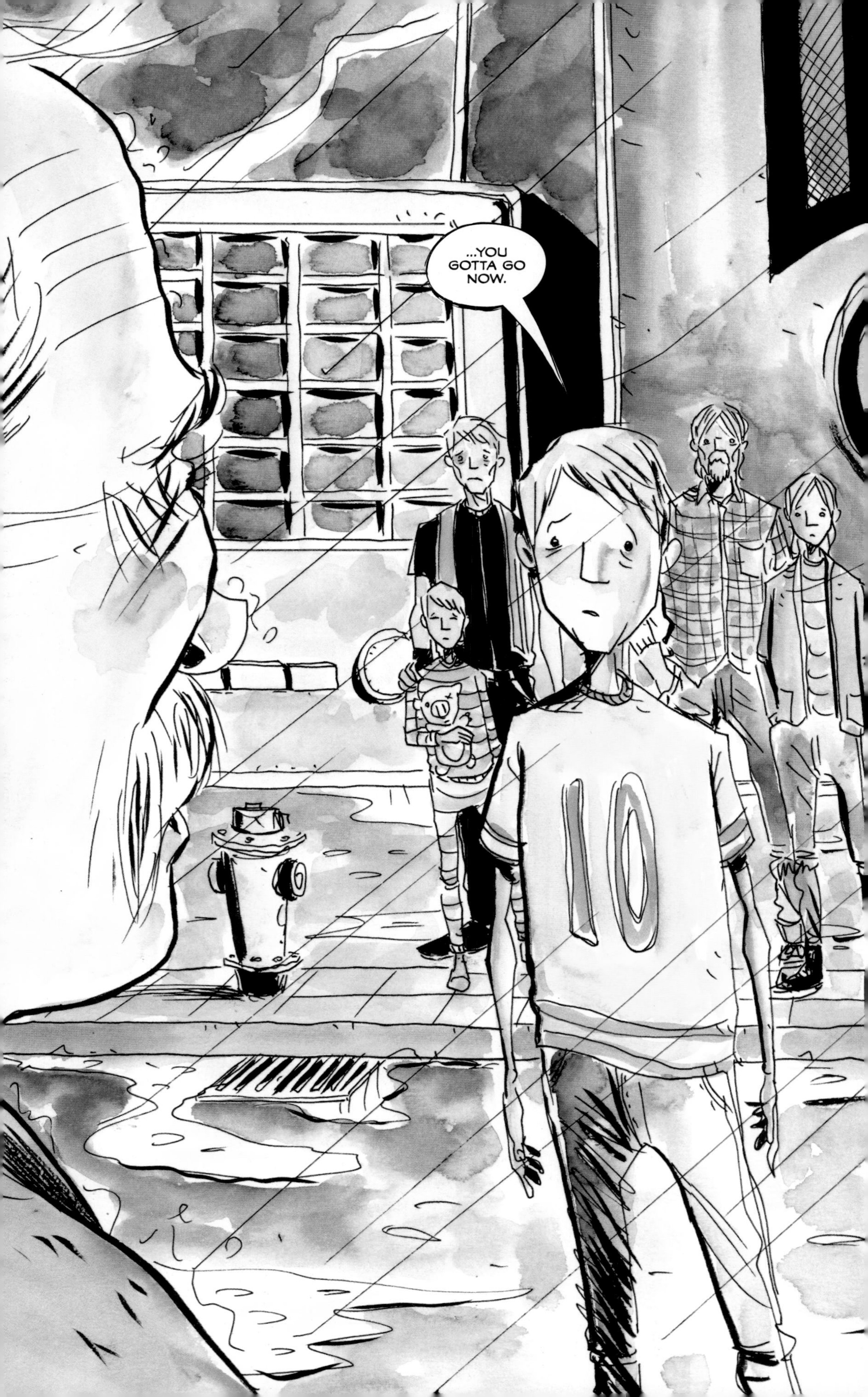
...YOU GOTTA GO NOW.

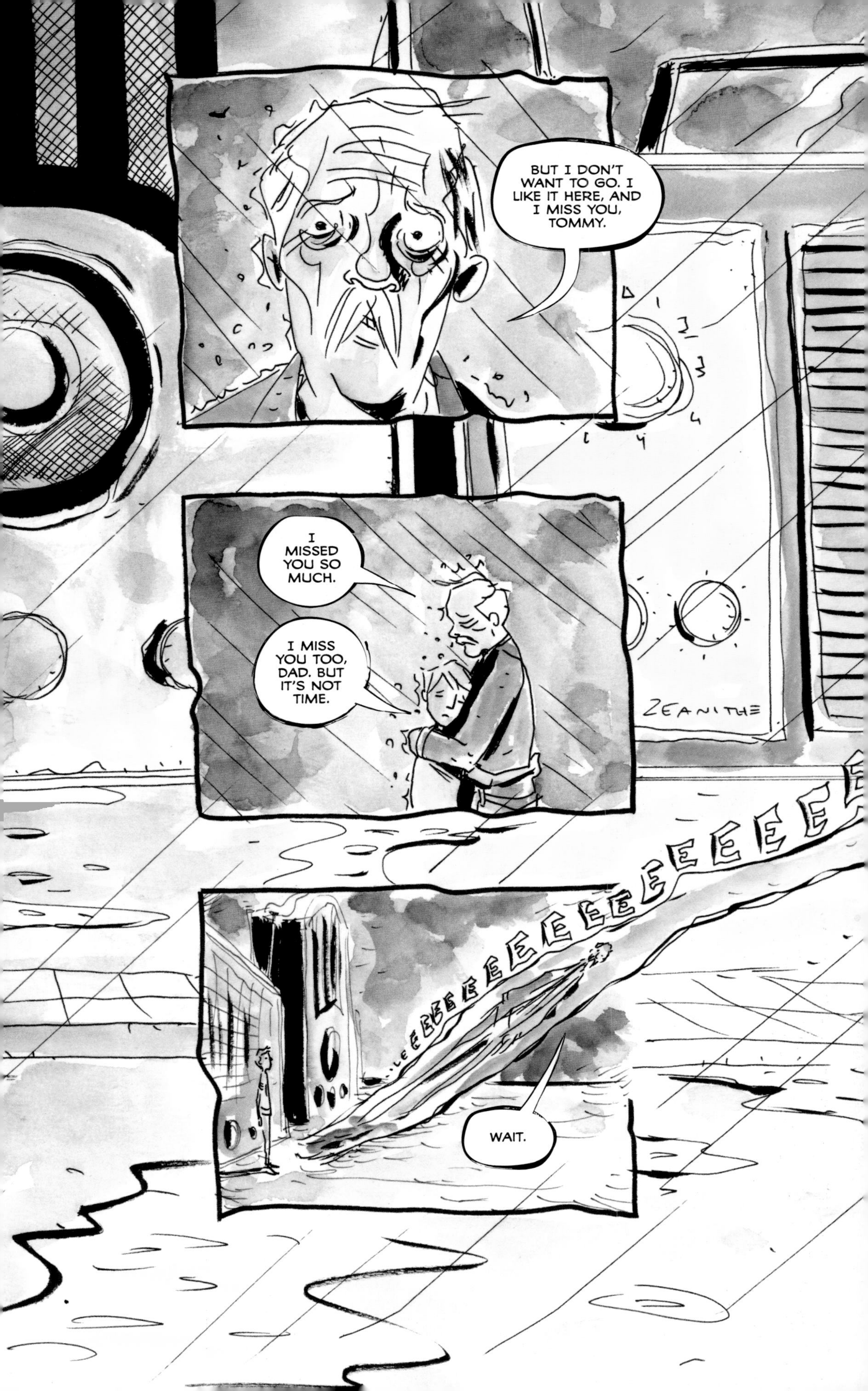

BUT I DON'T WANT TO GO. I LIKE IT HERE, AND I MISS YOU, TOMMY.
I MISSED YOU SO MUCH.
I MISS YOU TOO, DAD. BUT IT'S NOT TIME.
ZEANITHE
...EEEEEEEEEEEEEEEEEEEEEE
WAIT.

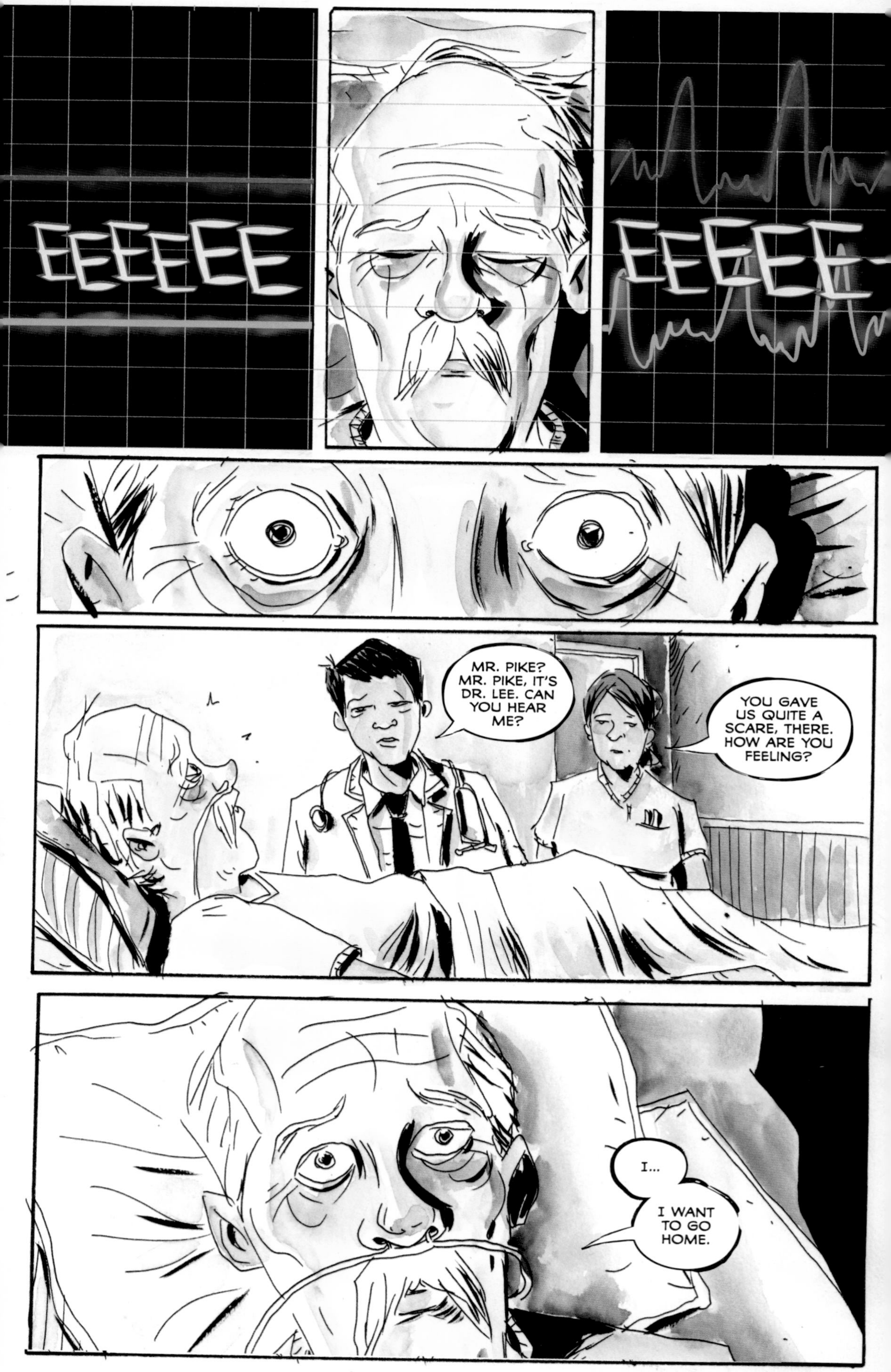
EEEEEE
EEEEE-
MR. PIKE? MR. PIKE, IT'S DR. LEE. CAN YOU HEAR ME?
YOU GAVE US QUITE A SCARE, THERE. HOW ARE YOU FEELING?
I...
I WANT TO GO HOME.

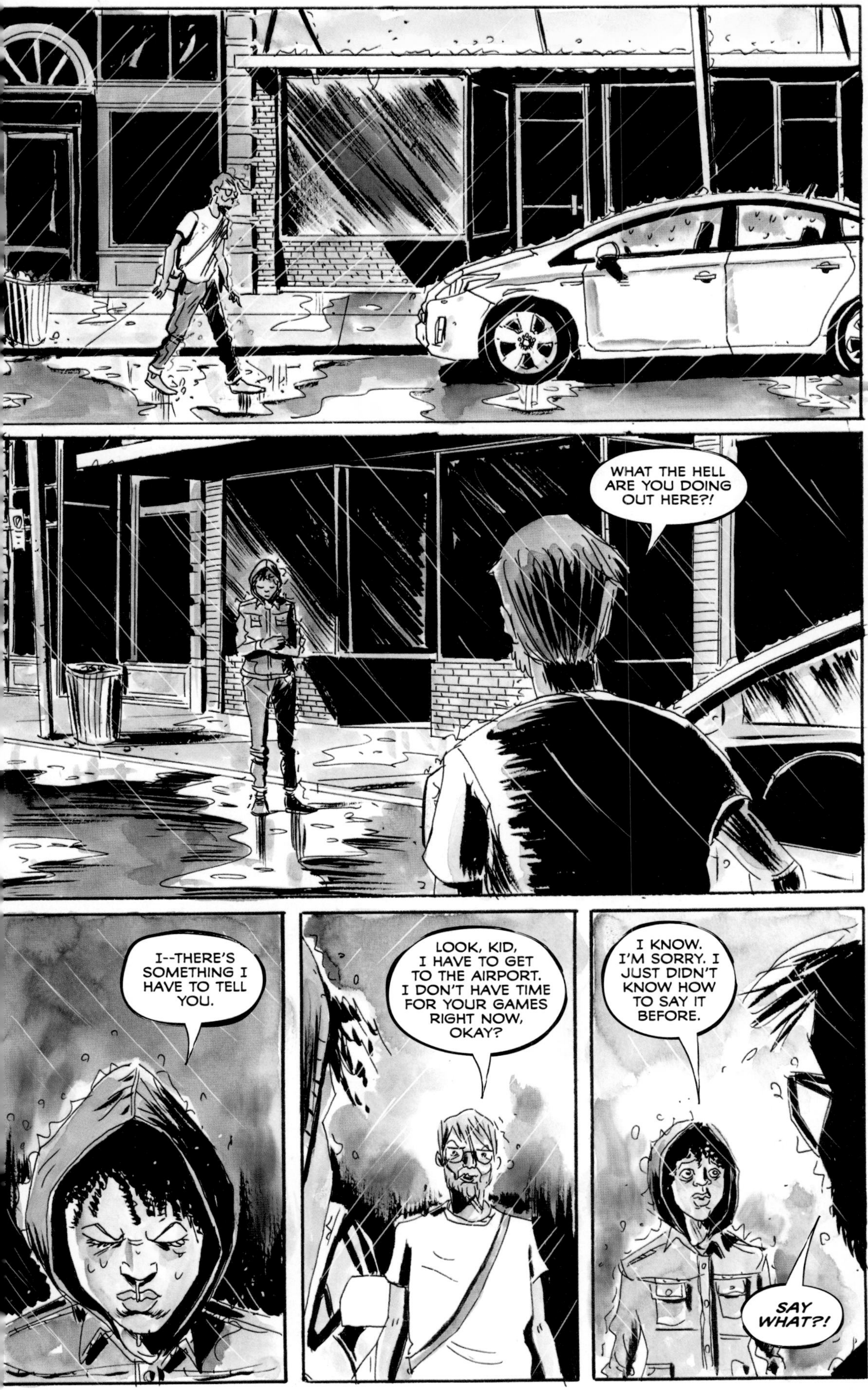
WHAT THE HELL ARE YOU DOING OUT HERE?!
I--THERE'S SOMETHING I HAVE TO TELL YOU.
LOOK, KID, I HAVE TO GET TO THE AIRPORT. I DON'T HAVE TIME FOR YOUR GAMES RIGHT NOW, OKAY?
I KNOW. I'M SORRY. I JUST DIDN'T KNOW HOW TO SAY IT BEFORE.
SAY WHAT?!

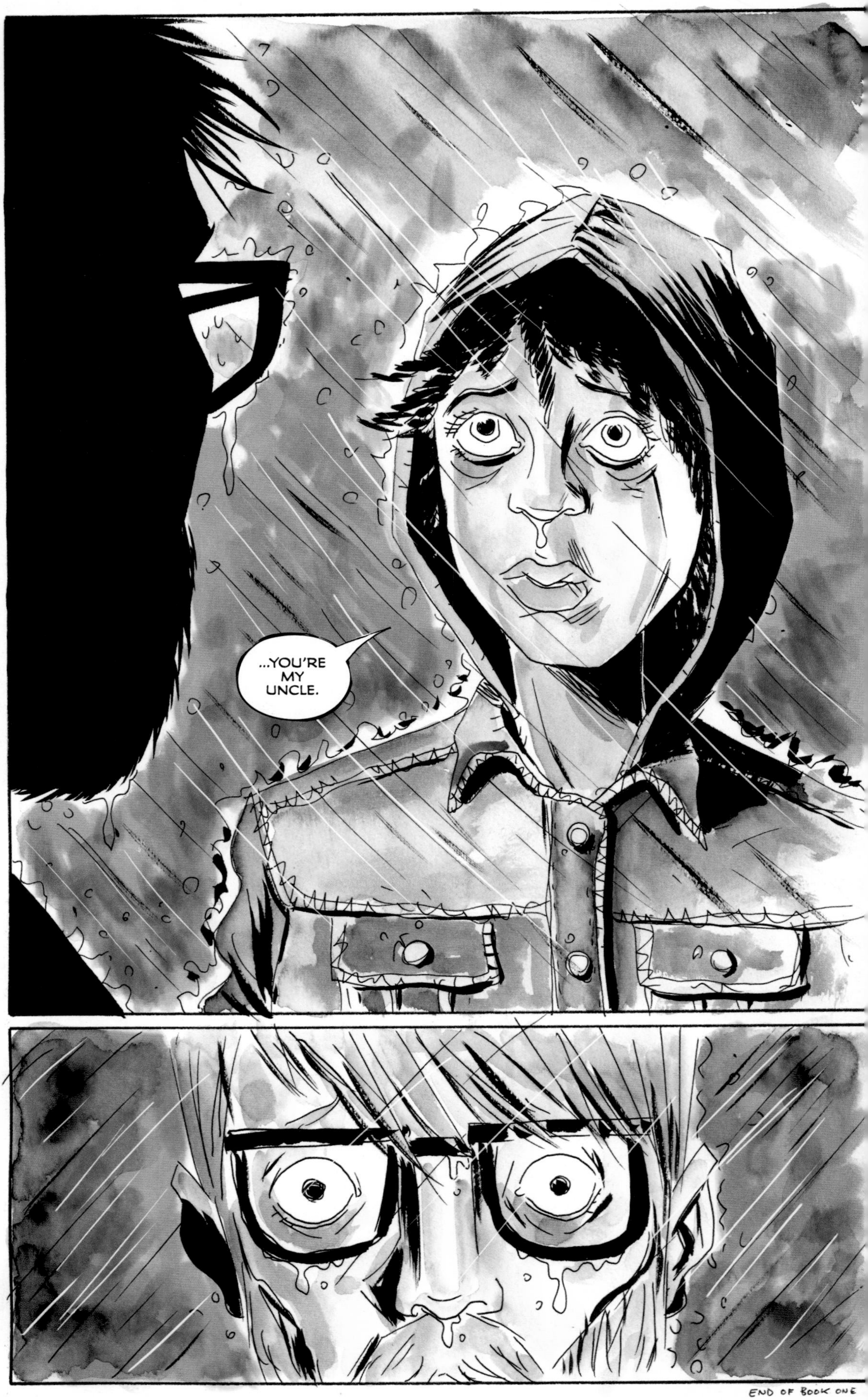
...YOU'RE MY UNCLE.

END OF BOOK ONE

BEHIND THE SCENES

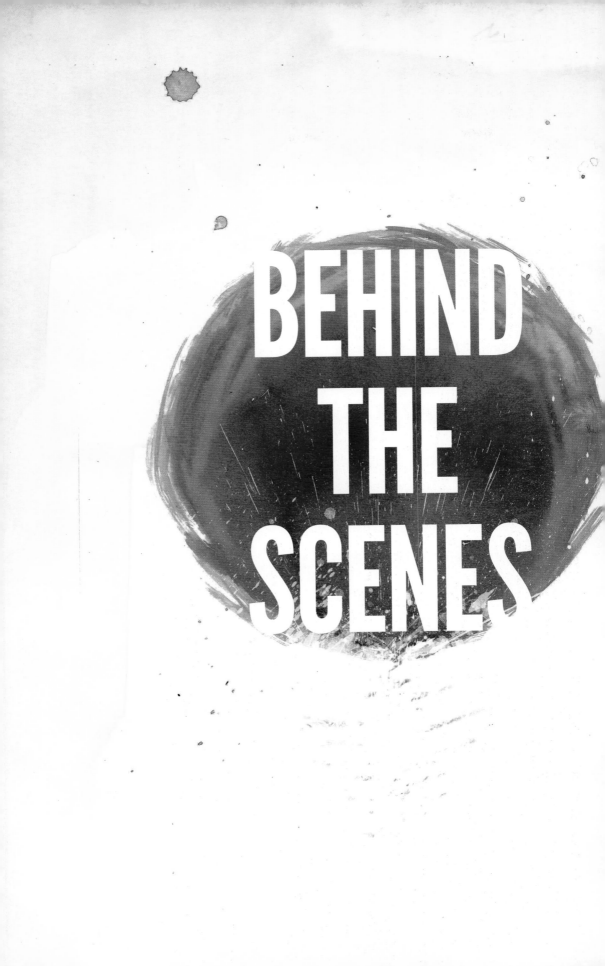

THE LOGO

I've known Chris Ross since my days with Top Shelf where he worked in production and design. In the past Chris has designed several logos for me including *Plutona* and *Descender*. So it was a no brainer to ask him to design the logo for *Royal City*.

1 ROYAL CITY

2 *Royal City*

3 *Royal City*

4 ROYAL CITY

5 ROYAL CITY

6 ROYAL CITY

7 ROYAL CITY

ROYAL CITY

I think the only direction I gave him was that I wanted it to look like a vintage restaurant sign. I love a lot of these roughs he did, but the round floating "bullet logo" stood out and I liked the design possibilities it gave me for my covers.

hese were some early attempts to capture the look and feel for *Royal City*. I intended for one of these to become the first cover or at least a promo image I ould use to promote the series.

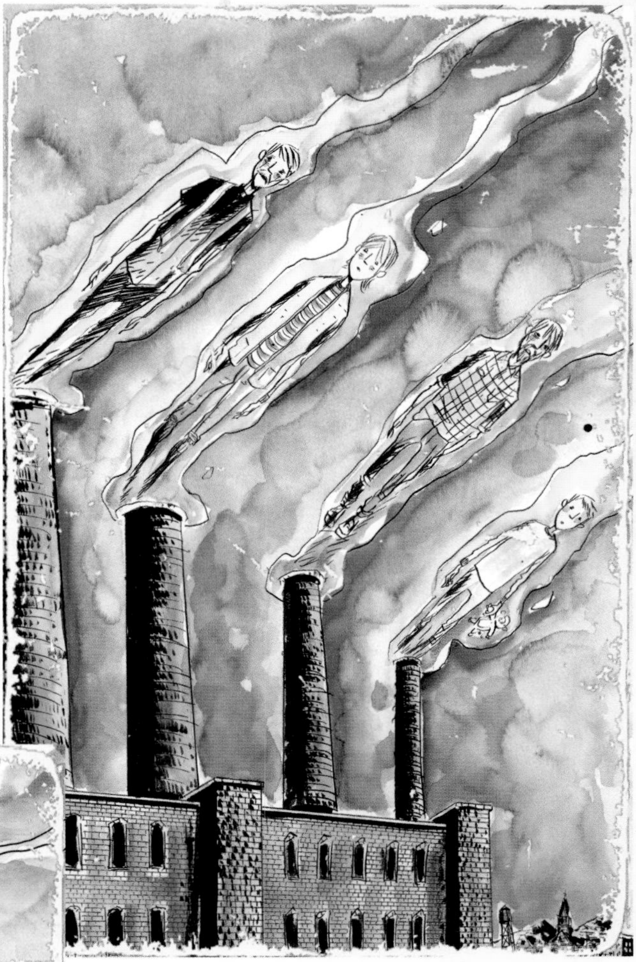

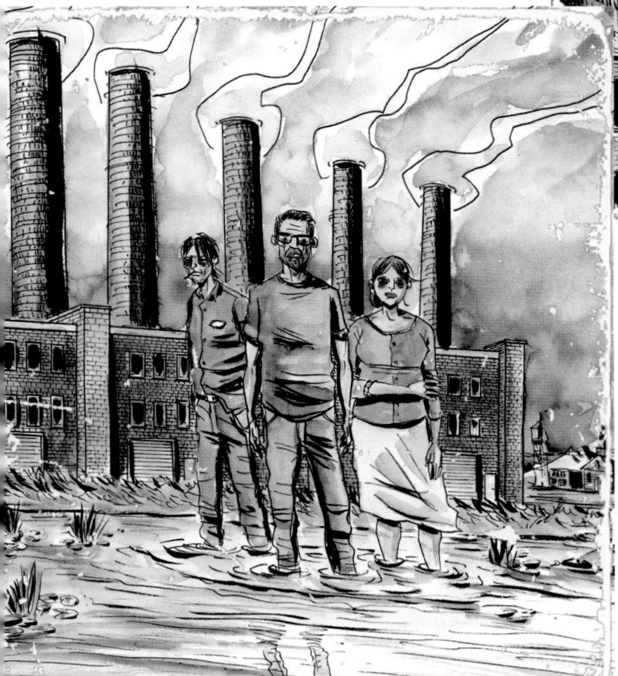

None of these really came together as I wanted, but they certainly helped to shape the look I ended up settling on.

EARLY PROMO ART

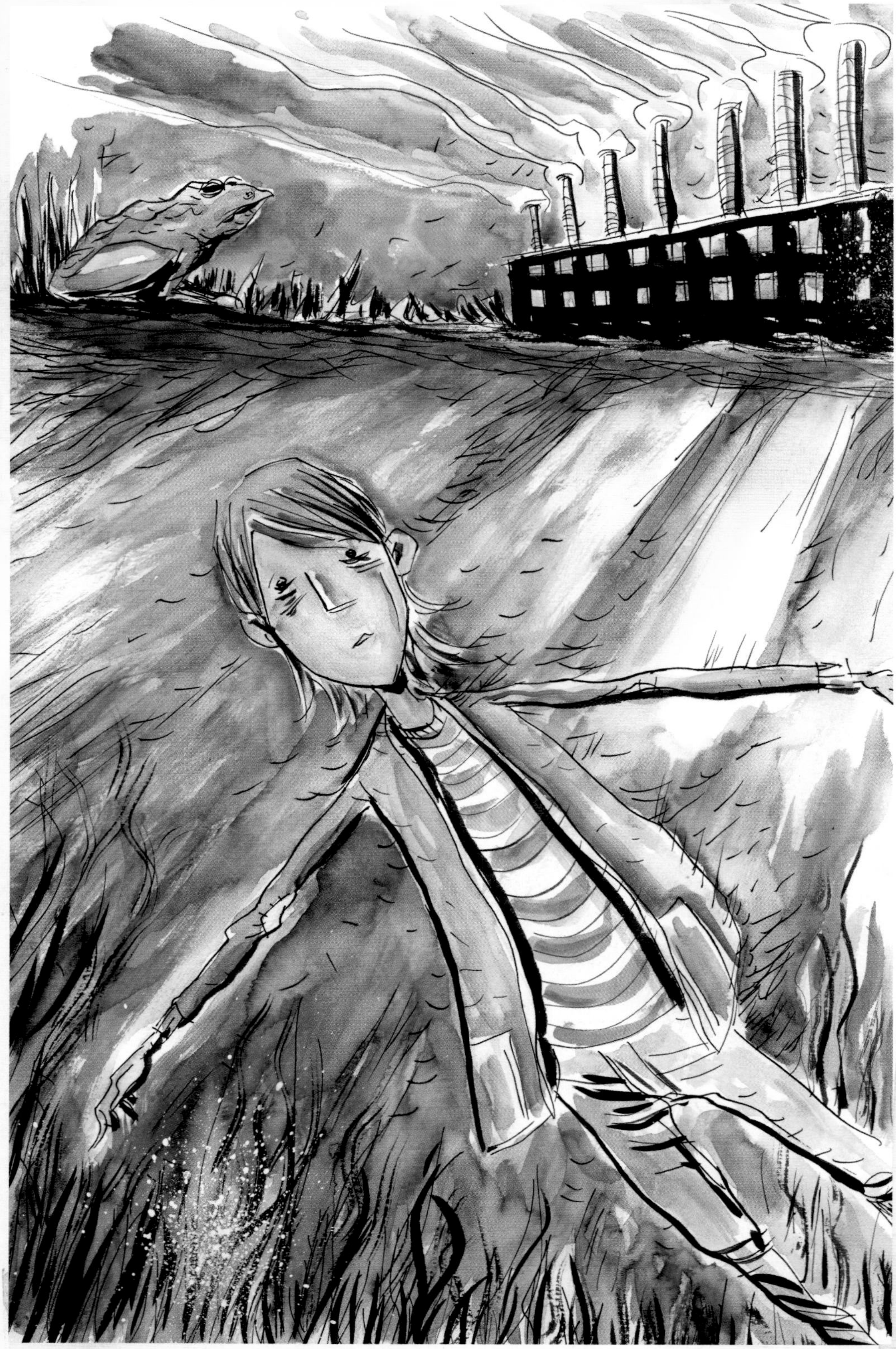

I did repurpose and redraw the image of Tommy below the water as an exclusive cover for both Emerald City Comicon and for an exclusive trade cover for Forbidden Planet and Big Bang Comics in the U.K.

his was a fun promo idea I played around with.

Instead of doing a single image, I was going to do a "comic strip" type promo image. I was getting closer to the look I ended up using for the series, but there are some big differences here. Patti looks much older than how she ended up in the final book and Tommy's ghosts look way more "spectral" here as well.

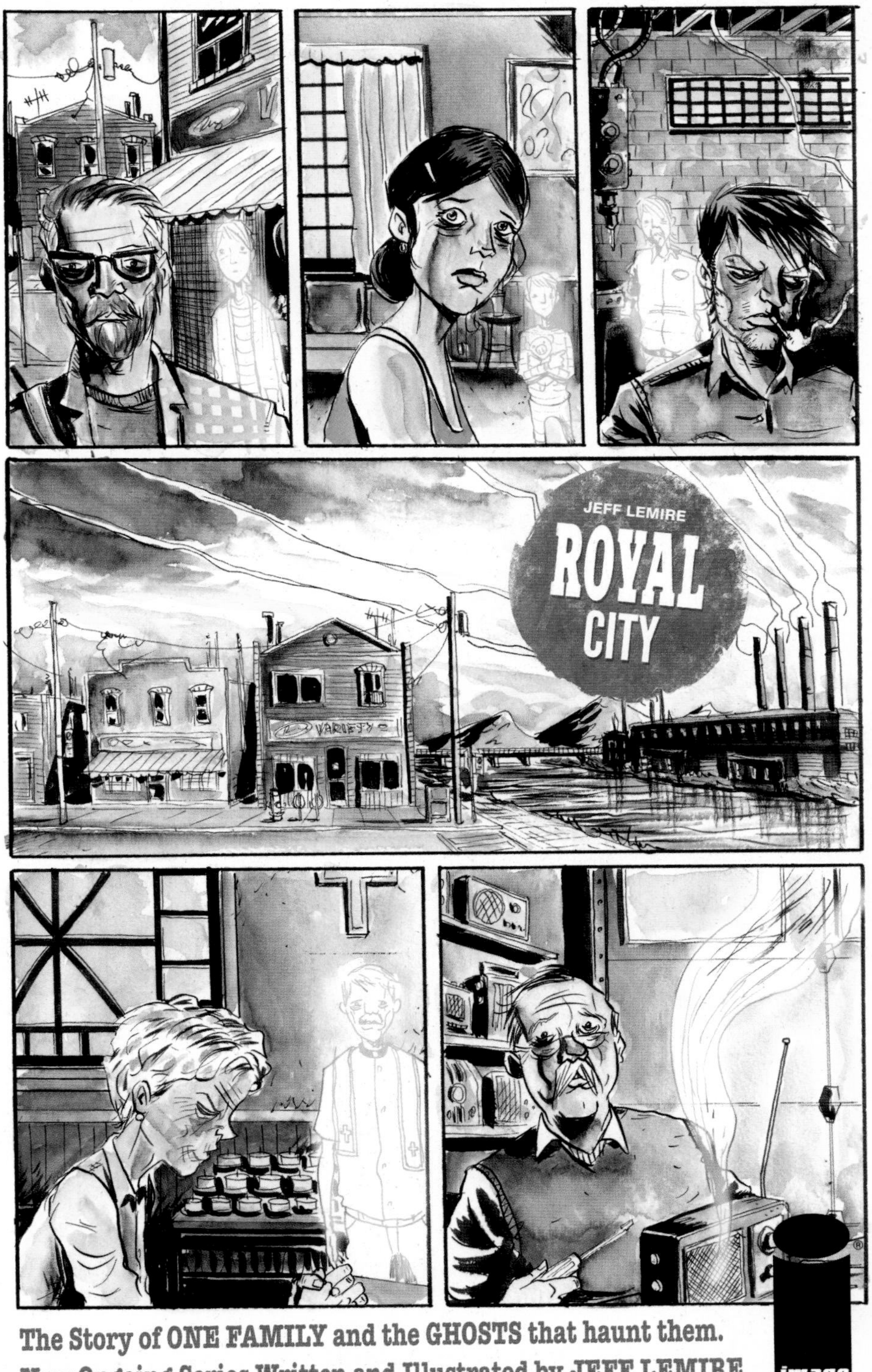

JEFF LEMIRE
ROYAL CITY
VARIETY
image
The Story of ONE FAMILY and the GHOSTS that haunt them.
New Ongoing Series Written and Illustrated by JEFF LEMIRE
FALL 2016

ABOUT THE AUTHOR

JEFF LEMIRE

Jeff Lemire is the award-winning, *New York Times* bestselling author of such graphic novels as *Essex County*, *Sweet Tooth*, *Underwater Welder*, and *Roughneck*, as well as co-creator of *Descender* with Dustin Nguyen, *Black Hammer* with Dean Ormston, *Plutona* with Emi Lenox, and *A.D.: After Death* with Scott Snyder.

He also collaborated with celebrated musician Gord Downie on the graphic novel and album *The Secret Path*, which was made into an animated film in 2016. Jeff has won numerous awards including an Eisner Award and a Juno Award in 2017. Jeff has also written extensively for both Marvel and DC Comics.

Many of his books are currently in development for film and television, including both *Descender* and *A.D.: After Death* at Sony Pictures, *Essex County* at the CBC, and *Plutona* at Waypoint Entertainment, for which Lemire is writing the screenplay.

He lives in Toronto, Canada with his wife, son, and troublesome pug, Lola.